# A
# Humanistic
# Philosophy
# of Music

# A
# Humanistic
# Philosophy
# of Music

EDWARD A. LIPPMAN

New York • New York University Press • 1977

Copyright © 1977 by New York University
Library of Congress Catalogue Card Number: 76–44573
ISBN: 0–8147–4973–9


*Library of Congress Cataloguing in Publication Data*
Lippman, Edward A.
   A humanistic philosophy of music.
   Includes index.
   1. Music--Philosophy and aesthetics. 1. Title.
ML3800.L67          780'.1          76–44573
ISBN 0–8147–4973–9


Manufactured in the United States of America

# Contents

To Vi, Bob, Marlene, Evelyn,
Richard, Cely, Lisa, Philip

# Foreword

Keats' thought that a thing of beauty is a joy forever expresses a platonic wish for something final and abstract, removed from the causal orders of the mutable world, in contemplation of which an unthreatened peace and pleasure may be found. Music, like mathematics, has always impressed the platonic imagination in just these terms, as consisting in a set of ideal, timeless structures, perfect and pure, visitors in this world but from another finer space we may glimpse into through them, and momentarily escape our chains. Contemporary philosophy of art may in part be defined in contrast with this exalted attitude, for it considers the work of art ontologically inseparable from the institutional and historical circumstances the platonist would reject as irrelevant to its formal integrity, to be appreciated timelessly. History, for the contemporary aesthetician, is not something extrinsic, of merely academic concern, but rather penetrates the essence of the work which almost has no identifiable structure in separation from the contexts of its provenance and meaning.

This modernist perception, which must of course be independently argued, receives immense support from Edward Lippman's work on music. Indeed, I cannot think of a work in which philosophical informalism has been so systematically developed in connection with a specific mode of artistic expression as in this deep study of music from a historical and cultural point of view. Lippman's book reminds me of nothing so much as Dewey's book on logic, for logic, too, is a candidate for platonic exaltation, and Dewey insisted on seeing it instead as rooted in human inquiry, of which it is the theory. Lippman has comparably sought to establish the continuities between music and conduct, as something with a natural history and a human meaning. It is a densely argued, densely illustrated study, ascending through a number of interconnected strata of musical reality, and it is a provocative and convincing piece of work, of the greatest philosophical interest and significance.

Arthur C. Danto
Department of Philosophy
Columbia University

# CHAPTER 1

# Our Field of Inquiry

The history and the philosophy of music are obviously dependent upon music for their existence, but they are not for that reason of a lesser value or importance. They are in fact intrinsic to musical experience in some measure, for it is difficult to imagine any musical activity that is totally unaccompanied by conceptual thought, or not in some way guided by theoretical, aesthetic, and historical notions, or not provocative of some kind of evaluation and criticism. But if we cannot perceive or think or act while remaining completely unaware that we are doing so, reflective thought would appear to be grounded in a central characteristic of consciousness; and as the exercise of a natural mental function, philosophy will understandably be pleasurable as well as inevitable. The pleasure it brings, however, is also due to an attendant satisfaction of our desire for knowledge and to the enhancement of our understanding.

Yet how can we justify each successive age and author in writing philosophy down instead of just engaging in it? Certainly it is only novel ideas and new values that can logically claim to be worth recording and preserving. The basis of novelty is found at once, however, in the distinctive perspective of each cultural setting and each succeeding vantage point in time, and, grounded in these, of each individual personality. It can therefore be expected that musical philosophy will produce a variety or a series of conceptions, which may be considered as the counterpart of the diverse cultural manifestations of music itself, or of the historical unfolding of its potentialities. As a particular outlook comes into being, along with corresponding kinds of music, the conceptions of other times and places will be modified or discarded in accordance with their relative compatibility to the ideas that prevail or their contradition of them.

But thought and culture build upon the past, and in so doing they should tend to produce—as they clearly have done in scientific fields—some kind of progressive insight; new perspectives should not simply succeed but also somehow amplify or incorporate older ones, becoming by that token more complete. In the case of a cultural product such as music—as opposed to an essentially constant object such as the physical world—we are dealing not only with an increase in our knowledge and understanding, but also with a change in and an enlargement of the very object of study, a change which itself often contains progressive and cumulative elements. Thus we can reasonably hope to achieve something more than the presentation of a contemporary perspective coordinate with others; our view should provide a conception of music in many respects more complete than those of the past. But we cannot expect to secure an understanding of music that will remain definitive or that will be complete in an absolute sense, any more than we can expect to narrate the whole story of culture; for the future obviously transcends both systematic analysis and history; the unpredictable novelty of human creativity is at least as evident in speculative thought as it is in patterns of behavior or in art.

Throughout most of its history, philosophic thought concerning music proceeded from encompassing metaphysical principles and overriding religious and ethical interests. The properties of music were conceived in accordance with these more general concerns. But in the course of the 19th century in Europe, increasing attention was given to perceptual properties and to the details of artistic experience. (During the same period

2

the philosophy of history underwent a parallel transformation; it ceased to consider historical phenomena in terms of pre-ordained patterns of the course of events and turned instead to the individuality of particular cultural configurations and to the distinctive characteristics of their process of succession.) The 19th-century approach to aesthetics, however, was really more scientific than humanistic; generalization was based on an arbitrary selection of a few types of music that were at hand, and the psychology employed was elementalistic.

The method we will employ in the present study, on the other hand, will rely on the unprecedented scope and depth of contemporary humanism. The discoveries of history and anthropology have enabled us increasingly to examine a wide range of artistic experience, so that the foundation of inductive aesthetics has taken on a new breadth and importance. The aesthetician and the philosopher of art can no longer content themselves with an awareness that is limited either in range or in sensitivity. A corresponding change has taken place in the area of psychology, where the search for inherent features in human perception has similarly drawn closer to musical experience. For it is now not so much the analytic laboratory experiment that arouses our interest—the investigation of elemental acoustic events by physics and physiology, or the behavioristic measurement of isolated tonal attributes and intervallic responses by psychophysics—but the study of configurational and cultural properties. Influenced by phenomenology and Gestalt psychology, our experimental procedures have turned away to some extent from the examination of abstractly defined elements and the artificiality of the laboratory task in an effort to discover the intrinsic organizing capacity of perception.

This capacity, however, is dependent in part upon society and culture. Indeed not only the configurational properties of melodic phrases but even the nature and meaning of individual sounds and tones are partly shaped by cultural forces. It is only in modern Western civilization, for example—which a century earlier had invented the analytic procedures of psychophysics—that electronically generated sound with precisely constructed wave forms could become musical material. The synthesizing power of perception, then, whether it results in the hearing of a single tone or of a melodic and harmonic configuration, is really a compound in which the inherent and cultural components cannot be separated. For the effects of cultural conditioning are essentially the same as those of native endowment. Both have a corporeal manifestation as part of the structure and function of the nervous system, and the exercise of the ability they shape jointly is in both cases accompanied by a feeling of self-evidence and naturalness. In this respect our perceptual faculty is no different from our creative capacity, which selects or devises materials for art and then combines or forms them into meaningful patterns. Thus the basic data of psychology—tones, intervals, melodic phrases—will be ultimately of the same nature as the data of history or anthropology.

Both cultural and psychological studies were strongly influenced by the philosophy of natural science, which reduced history to the isolated specimen of music and psychology to behaviorism. The musical composition was examined objectively by dissection, while perception, with equal objectivity, was studied by tabulating previously-defined responses to simple but essentially meaningless tasks. To be sure, historical tendencies were responsible for this situation: the decline of function and genre left the processes of musical evaluation and understanding without a foundation; the single composition was exposed to the advances of practitioners of "analysis" and "aesthetics."

A humanistic history and psychology, on the other hand, will not take either the musical score, the phonograph record, or the behavior of laboratory subjects as facts of a real world, but will proceed instead phenomenologically, trying to determine the nature of the objects of awareness as they are given by consciousness itself. For it is clearly always the operation of the mind, now on the inchoate matter presented by history and culture, now on that presented by nature and human nature, that produces the objects of knowledge. In psychology, of course, the auditory perceptual objects we study are generally

4

not examples of music in the full sense of the term; they tell us more about perception than about music. They point directly to transhistorical and transcultural features of music but only indirectly, therefore, to music itself. A further consideration is called for to determine the extent to which the elements and configurational properties we have examined are in fact part of musical experience or relevant to it. Although psychology and history are fundamentally akin, it can be said with some justice that the one deals more with the activity of consciousness and the other more with its objects. We must add the qualification for psychology, however, that the activity of consciousness is not only grounded in corporeal experience but also shaped by social forces; and every abstraction from the organic totality or from the whole of culture involves the danger of misunderstanding.

As far as aesthetic objects are concerned, we may consider them to be modifications of the objects of common-sense experience. Thus a fundamental way of understanding them is in terms of the processes of biological and social adjustment, in which objects—whether animate or inanimate—appear either as extensions of the self or as related and interacting instrumentalities that are variously compliant, resistant, or inimical. The process by which we construct our everyday world is motivated by basic impulses of life: by the desire for a comfortable environment, for the satisfaction of vital needs, for play and exploration; and the development of this world takes place through sensorimotor experience. The individual objects and the other persons we become familiar with and learn to deal with are both useful and interesting; often they possess aesthetic attractiveness as a prominent feature. But true aesthetic objects are those in which aesthetic properties are dominant. It is only by exception, however, that this dominance entirely suppresses either biological or social functions. An aesthetic object represents a degree of abstraction from the normal practical involvement of perception; yet it plays a role in our orientation; it has its place, and helps us to know our place, both in our immediate environment of space and time and in our world of imagination and history. And if we participate in a

5

musical performance, or attend a recital as a member of the audience, or even listen alone to a phonograph record, the experience is in every case structured by social institutions and relationships.

It is clear that objects of every type exist only as counterparts of human existence. Their properties in general, their weight, size, color, sound, and feel, and their reactions to our actions, all have meaning only in relation to the being and behavior of man. This is true also of the conceptual forms that accompany our sensorimotor experience, for these arise, just as sense experience does, from the intrinsic properties of consciousness and of our sensory apparatus. Our ability to deal with the physical and biological world in which we are placed is due to the fact that in the last analysis we have a similar nature; and even cognition would seem to rest not only on bodily mobility and sense perception but also on neurological patterns which are governed by the same physical and chemical possibilities as those found in external physical objects. Similarly, in the very different realm of historical and cultural understanding, our knowledge depends upon a basic kinship in experience with other human beings.

Thus the things we experience and know are colored and even constructed in great measure by ourselves, both by the constancies of human nature and by the idiosyncrasies of particular cultures or individuals. This is obviously the case with our knowledge of people and their creations, but it is true also of our knowledge of the physical world. In the case of our knowledge of thought itself it is tautological, although precisely in this area—in logic and mathematics—the belief has been especially strong that we know objects which are absolutely independent of human existence.

It is only art, aside from practical life and engineering, that is directed at least in a general way, toward objects perceived by the senses, and the philosophy of art cannot fail to make this characteristic a primary consideration. Yet every field of human endeavor must have some reference to such objects. History and science, for example, in spite of the obvious differences between them, are alike in being centered on objects of a conceptual or theoretical nature. Science dissolves the world into fields of forces, harmonic patterns, and equations: imaginative structures which change in step with man's creativity or with the pressures of the scientific community. In order to underpin and verify such objects we must extend our native sensory capabilities by means of a highly intricate instrumentation which nevertheless ultimately registers what it detects on charts or in numbers that are accessible to ordinary vision. History too creates theoretical patterns of consecution and relationships that differ with each historian; and it is perhaps even further from validating objects of common-sense observation, for the people whose experiences we seek to narrate are no longer having these experiences. Yet we depend again, ultimately, upon the observable clues they have left behind in the form of writing and artifacts. Anthropology is more concrete than both science and history; it provides the presentness of scientific facts without their abstraction from experience, but the theoretical objective is present as well, in the project of description and interpretation. Indeed theoretical formulations will soon occupy the same dominant position in anthropology that they do in science and history, for the simple societies that constitute its object of investigation are rapidly vanishing. Every field of study is subject to history as well as to the varying interests and concerns of culture. Even the sensory ingredient of art may take on the less immediate form of imagined experience, as it does characteristically in the case of literature; and even in music, sensational qualities at least occupy a position of lesser prominence in *The Art of the Fugue* than they do in the music of Debussy or Stravinsky.

Anthropology (and to some extent sociology also) would appear to provide the logical corrective to the fallacious assumption that aesthetic experience can be understood in isolation or by means of deductive reasoning from general metaphysical principles. This can be seen most readily in the instance of participation in a musical ceremony, when the full concreteness of sensorimotor experience and its integration into society and culture as a whole make the anthropologist a model for the philosopher of art, who must be content, however, with the description of such a situation instead of its actuality. But history and science also are relevant to the philosophy of art; indeed they are indispensable to the achievement of a humanistic view in this field. For science has developed an increasingly adequate treatment of human behavior and experience, not only in the field of psychology, as we have indicated, but in that of biology as well, where elementalistic analysis in terms of stimulus and response had similarly attempted to mechanize a total adaptive process that involves the dynamic interaction of organism and environment and demands description in terms of goals and purpose. No concatenation of separate causal pathways, no matter how complex, can provide an adequate understanding of musical perception or account for the processes of composition and performance. But through the adoption of more appropriate conceptions of organic behavior and of the process of perception, biology and psychology now provide a kind of humanism that complements the expanded study of social and cultural experience in the fields of history, anthropology, and sociology. It is in fact a fortunate circumstance, and perhaps not a merely fortuitous one, that the impressive expansion of our historical and ethnological knowledge has been accompanied by a growing insight into the nature of sensory perception and the role of consciousness in the constitution of experience; for music appears as the joint products of history and psychology; and just as history extends the range of our experience, so psychology deepens and grounds it. Thus the cultural and biological sciences are two sides of the humanist coin, or if we may further specify the image, the one group is its public face and the other is its reverse or underside. In addition, the entire mint is impressed upon a natural material that enters significantly into the determination of the qualitative possibilities of the design.

To be sure, art is much more a product of mental forces than of natural ones, and this is especially the case with music, as opposed to the spatial arts. As we widen our acquaintance with any art, we will almost always increase correspondingly our understanding of the possibilities and even the principles of mentality. Our knowledge of the potentialities and laws of

8

nature will hardly undergo a comparable expansion; for artistic objects—as we have indicated—are shaped largely by human experience, by the conjunction of culture and embodied consciousness; and each of them—unlike successive individuals of a biological realm or individual specimens of a mineral—will generally reveal to us a new facet or area of the soul. This often remains true even when we are dealing with works of art bearing a familial resemblance to one another, although not of course in the case of routine production or technological manufacture. But it is also true that the investigation of man-made objects—even of only a few samples—may in some respect yield information about the inherent properties of the natural as well as the mental forces that enter into their constitution. It follows that natural science should be capable at least to some extent of enhancing our understanding of works of art as well as of other products of culture and history.

It is an examination of the elements of art, however, rather than of whole artistic works, that would seem best able to demonstrate the value of natural science to aesthetics; for in our elementary responses, where we apparently have eliminated the influence of the relative values of culture and style, we will have isolated and will therefore be able to determine more easily and accurately the role of physical and physiological factors and processes in our experience of tones, intervals, or sounds, and possibly also then in our experience of music. These considerations also apply to the role of mathematics in music, although mathematical relationships have often been used as an explanatory principle in melodies or entire compositions as well as in isolated intervals or chords.

The study of elements is attractive because it promises an easy road to the understanding of music—to general principles and features of universal validity. But the promise is to a great extent a false one. The problem of how nature and mind combine in the creation of experience remains present in our consideration of an abstracted constituent of art, reduced in fact to an elemental form in the test tube of psychophysics, but the experience to which we are thus given access becomes an artificial product of an experimental mentality; it now appears rather to be trivial instead of fundamental, and its significance is almost totally divorced from the meaning of the work of art as a whole. The influence of even a small configuration on any of its components is os such strength as to cast doubt on the importance and even the relevance to the whole of any knowledge of the component in isolation.

In addition to this, even the simplest responses and the most elemental qualities are doubtless historical variables, for however immediate and independent of culture they may seem to be, they will in some way be shaped by the conceptions to which they are linked, by particular musical attitudes and ways of hearing and feeling. Thus we no longer can make the mistake of presuming that elementary sensations are absolute or that they preserve in isolation their qualities as parts of a whole; invariance with time becomes a problem to be investigated rather than a property that is presupposed. Yet underlying both the contextual and historical variability of tonal quality and tonal relationships, we may nevertheless hope to discover tendencies which are both universal and musically significant and which can be set aside only under the most unusual circumstances.

Further consideration will reveal the value to the philosophy of art of two large groups of studies: those dealing with the natural world, both physical and biological, from a mechanistic standpoint, and those having to do with consciousness and its setting in human behavior. As a matter of convenience, mathematics can be annexed to the first series. This "physical" series can then be taken as running from mathematics, the physics of vibration and sound, the acoustics of musical instruments, tonal systems, enclosed spaces, and electroacoustics, through the anatomy and physiology of the voice and the ear, to auditory neurology and even the study of orientation and environmental adaptation. The second or humanistic series extends from the biology of adjustive behavior (and even from comparative zoology), through the psychology of perception, learning, habit, talent, and creation and the psychology and pathology of audition and vocal expression, to all the divisions of history, linguistics, social and cultural anthropology, and sociology.

Adaptive biology is clearly in a key position, since it represents the junction of the two series. The humanistic studies, as we have seen, fall into two divisions, psychological and historical, the first of which may be considered humanistic because it emphasizes purposive biology, native configurational forces, and intentional mechanisms as opposed to a physical elementalism based on stimulus and response, on cause and effect. What this emphasis produces, however, may still be considered a type of science—one appropriate and adequate to its subject; for in contrast to the historical and social studies, which are more properly considered humanistic in their concern for personal and cultural individuality, the biological and psychological studies, even when they are phenomenologically grounded, are concerned with the regularities of behavior, just as most physical sciences deal with the regularities of events.

In any event, we cannot fail to distinguish the invariant features of adaptive behavior and consciousness from the individuality of the ways of acting and perceiving and creating that are produced by society and culture. These are what is most properly meant by humanism, and we will take them in the present investigation as the most significant aspect of music. It is more than unlikely that either biological or cultural evolution and variety will ever cease to exist, although we can project at least in imagination a society and culture that would have a uniform environment of climate and topography and that would be all-encompassing and unchanging, so that the meaning of humanism would gradually disappear. It would disappear also as a consequence of restricted, trivialized, or standardized human experience, brought about either by comprehensive social control or through evolution or biological manipulation. The possibility of the end of humanism—which is essentially equivalent to the end of man as we know him—is a corollary of the protean nature of its subject matter. But leaving this eventuality out of account, there can be no doubt that a philosophic understanding of art rests fundamentally on historical insight and knowledge. Like all historical understanding it is concerned with objects made by man, which we may logically expect to be more amenable to knowledge, or at least to permit a different

11

or additional kind of knowledge, than objects lacking this dimension of meaning and having simply a natural existence. The physical existence of art is not the central aspect of its being, as we can see readily in the case of literary works that do not call for acoustic realization and are not identical with their printed copies. Thus the scientific study of both the material and perceptual properties of art can find a place only as a contribution to a comprehensive understanding that is basically historical and cultural. Art—and perhaps life also—differs from other creations of culture only in that making and forming become reflective activities attended to for the sake of their own properties and values.

In general, then, the philosophy of art is confined neither to the humanities nor to the sciences, but spans both, applying their knowledge to its own more encompassing purposes. It is important to emphasize this point, for the identification of philosophy with the humanities may result in an extreme relativism that denies durable constituents to musical experience. This would be no better than the metaphysical prejudice that rests on a scientific or theological mentality and seeks to deny the value or reality of novelty and personal expression or of change itself. We can no longer set out to demonstrate that either change or permanence is illusory or inconsequential; our interest is rather to determine, on the basis of what we can learn through both humanistic and natural science, the interplay and relative importance of change and permanence, the types and degrees of constancy.

The understanding of music will be achieved primarily by means of history and psychology, but it can be furthered also by natural science, which examines the physical matter and processes that underlie artistic material and support human experience. We may expect these supportive processes to determine many transhistorical tendencies of music, or many "transhuman" features, but they will do so within a total humanistic context. Sound may follow certain unvarying physical principles in enclosed spaces, for example; and the general nature of indoor music, its range of properties, will be correspondingly determined in certain ways: a wide range of loudness will become available, the native persistence of auditory sensations will be extended by reverberation, and so forth. But within this framework, it is cultural and social forces that create the particular acoustic qualities of actual concert halls and music rooms as well as of the music that is heard in them. The relationship within art of the scientific and humanistic determinants must always remain the same. No matter how speculative, mathematical, or stylistically universalistic music may become, it remains at its most dehumanized an individual creation of mentality and culture. In maintaining this view we place history in some sense above science; but to be able to do so is a distinctive prerogative of a philosophic viewpoint. The question of distinguishing minerals or flowers from works of art, for example, is neither a humanistic question or a scientific one, for the entities involved belong to two different orders of being and fall within different divisions of knowledge. They can be compared only from a perspective that encompasses them both, and the same is true for the comparative study of nature and imagination in their contribution to art.

The priority of history over science can be seen even in the experience of natural objects, in the qualities and values of a lake or a forest or a range of mountains, which change in response to the outlook of the culture. Indeed even the objects of natural science, since they are in some degree theoretical, are formed in part by culturally varying prejudices and preconditions (although their nature may change very slowly or infrequently); and every expression of human intelligence, not excepting even action and behavior, reveals the cultural bias of the people and times that produce it, so that it contains truth only as the property of a particular perspective. In thus representing a culturally specific mode of formulation, science as well as history bears a fundamental resemblance to art, although our contribution to the object of our knowledge, what we bring to what we know, is relatively inconspicuous in the field of nature and science, and much more apparent in history and art, where it can hardly be overlooked or ignored. There are certainly two paths that lead to knowledge: one of universality and abstraction and the other of individuality and concreteness, the first as typified, for example, by the Enlightenment, which turned even man into an object of science, the second as embodied in the theory of historical knowledge that was elaborated by Vico and later by Dilthey. Yet scientific truth is a changing creation of man and culture, and humanistic truth has its own universal properties. The difference conceals a basic kinship and numerous affinities. Truth is in every instance a type of compatability with some larger or more fundamental body of experience, and it is always a composite of external data and human inventiveness. Neither in the sciences nor in the humanities can we speak of eternal truths or a fixed human nature, for both the external matter entering into knowledge and the contributions necessarily made by man are caught up in continuous processes of change. Thus apart from history itself and from the nature of its progressing momentary configuration, and beyond the elemental and supportive constituents furnished by contemporary scientific knowledge, we can discover in the experience of art only a deployment or realization of a priori possibilities in the various societies of the world, or a certain relationship between history and logic, as Hegel perceived; we are confined to generalizations and theories that are always subject to revision.

It is common to experience of every type, in addition, that the conceptual and the sensible are inextricably mingled, just as in our biological make-up the mental and sensory constitute a nervous continuum. Art nevertheless remains a distinct department of experience, for here alone the sensible is paramount in spite of the participation of thought, while in science and history and philosophy the goal is a theoretical structure in spite of the reference to sense. Yet even the conceptual structures arrived at by philosophy have a resemblance to aesthetic experience, for they are not compounded of thought alone, but represent a whole outlook, a disposition, a way of feeling. They are, in fact, inseparable from the language of which they are constructed, just as art is from the material it forms. Fundamentally we can only know what in some sense we are, whether the ingredient we contribute consists in reliving the experience of others or in the biological and physical facts of our nature and the intrinsically formal and mathematical constitution of intelligence; in the most abstruse and abstracted formulations of science we ultimately discover the human mind, just as in the products of history and art we find again our own experience.

Whatever the nature of art may be more specifically, whether enlisting solely or primarily sensible perception and imagination or involving more comprehensively all the varied faculties and resources of human intelligence and feeling in a characteristic relationship, it undeniably demands of philosophy a breadth that comprises both scientific and humanistic studies. But aesthetic experience is also peculiarly suited to philosophic inquiry in a more particular way, for it seems to have a certain kinship with philosophy—even to contain in itself an incipient philosophic property. This consists in the prominence of the relationship between the aesthetic object and its creator or observer. The experience of art, and especially of music, is not just one knowing or doing, of perceiving or undergoing; it includes all of these, for in a way that resembles love and religion, aesthetic experience reveals the deepest properties of the relationship between self and world, and also of the community between the self and others; it is a holding in suspension, an enjoyment, of the archetypal duality as well as the unity of existence; it is a devotion to human creativity that produces an exaltation of the reverent. But this feeling and awareness and understanding of the connection between the self and its object and of the community of existence is nothing less than the experiential basis of the central problem of metaphysics, which each philosophic perspective formulates in its own conceptual terms.

In addition, the explicit attention given to the construction of an object in art will represent externally and in the large the immanent constitutive function of consciousness and thus should bring into clearer view one of the fundamental phases of perception and knowledge. Formation for its own sake is perhaps more than a coordinate of action and reflection; it seems to involve if not incorporate in some way both our ethical and our theoretical capacities.

One of the major concerns of a humanistic method will be the idiosyncrasy that is contained in the individual artistic product. Indeed we may well deal more with this idiosyncrasy, even if it is not present in every example of art, and with the complex humanistic values that art can possess, even if they are not in evidence everywhere, than with the more obvious constant features of artistic structure or significance. To elucidate the fashion in which music is a patterning based on the attributes of tone, for example, even if we assume that this conception, properly developed, has unlimited historical validity, which is probably not the case, would not bring us very close to our object of study; for how this patterning is produced, whether by personal, social, or historical forces, how it is thought of, whether as a language or a mathematical exercise, whether of the feelings or the reason, are all so much of the essence of music that to leave such considerations out of account must be to miss almost everything of philosophic importance. But this point can be made again and again, until it would seem that only in the specific sonorous forms and conceptions and social contexts of a historic genre and ultimately of a single composition, do we grasp adequately and fully what music is. Aesthetics would seem fated to become historical aesthetics, at least as a means of achieving more penetrating and more comprehensive insight. Is not this condition, however, which confronts the process of generalization, indicative of the mode of truth that we find in art? For we cannot doubt that art deals primarily with sensuous individuality, and it may logically be expected to reveal most clearly the character of its being and its truth in the realization and fulfillment of its own nature. We may take pleasure in it as a historical spectacle of style and associated conceptual thought, but our ultimate questions, while answerable only in the light of this historical character, must be directed to its individual varieties, to the particularity of experience, the qualities of which may not be abstracted from, canceled out, or set aside in the search for what art is, for this can be found only in concrete specificity. There must then be a convergence of our sensitivity to the particular and our broader interest—a revelation in particularity of the general or essential nature of art and of artistic truth. In some sense, we know, this truth must be historical, for a historical manifestation can contain no other kind.

Our method cannot rely exclusively, then, on abstract notions of the nature of hearing and tone, which would be basically similar to the reliance on numerical abstractions in the proportional thought of antiquity and the Middle Ages. Instead it must remain sensitive, in spite of the search for generality, to the specific shapes and conceptual forms in which music manifests itself in history, and to the actuality and detail of musical experience. The result of such an approach is not history, however; our goal is not to construct a narrative, but to create and describe a map; we differ from the historian in our concern with general features and types rather than with change; in the crucial matter of the uniqueness of each musical experience, for example, we are interested in individuality as such, in its values and varieties, rather than in particular instances; and in connection with change itself, we attempt to determine its nature rather than to describe its course.

As man moves ahead in time creating ever new varieties of music, the expanse to be surveyed in the past grows continuously larger and changes its appearance. Each station point within each culture or stratum of society has its own view of the historical as well as the contemporaneous landscape, with characteristic prominences and stylistic relationships, and each perspective contains its own truth: it is only a particular view, always in various respects a partial one, but not thereby false. Whatever knowledge we are able to arrive at will thus be limited in its meaning and its relevance for the future, but the limitation is one that is intrinsic to knowledge and that cannot be removed: the contribution of the observer is as inescapable in humanistic study as it is in the natural sciences. To be sure, we can introduce considerations of artistic or humanistic value, or seek to set up an ideal of musical experience that has perhaps been approximated or approached in certain instances; we may even select, for whatever reason, particular kinds of musical manifestation upon which to focus our attention. But the more general kind of truth accessible to us would seem to depend on an inventory of the artistic possibilities uncovered by anthropology, history, and sociology, together with an examination of the nature of each type of music and its relation to the others. Doubtless features will be found that are common to all the music known to us, although their importance may turn out to be slight and their number few. Apart from this, supposedly universal truths in the philosophy of music have been the result either of quick generalization from limited experience or of an equally suspect deduction from larger metaphysical principles.

Precisely one of the characteristics of our present outlook, however, is its disinclination to account for music as the manifestation of some ideal entity, whether changeless or progressing according to a preordained scheme. Our humanism is fundamentally secular. On a different scale, there is a somewhat comparable disinclination to explain musical experience in terms of underlying physical processes. In neither case are we dealing with a confession of failure, but with a determination to find meaning and truth in the realm most immediately at hand; the past, we feel, in its concern with metaphysics and physics, has overlooked the inherent forces of life itself. An empirical approach will of course entail its own conceptions of truth and reality—in the present instance these rest on the three supporting notions of the constructive capacity of the human body-mind, the objects of common-sense experience, and the physical world of science—but the conceptions now will derive from the organization or explanation of musical perception in its own terms, which is a very different matter from a dependence on idealism that is preconceived or premature. Neither the Platonic Forms, the cosmic and psychic structures of the *Timaeus*, the logical advance of Hegel's Absolute, or the primal Will of Schopenhauer would seem capable in any event of supporting the full detail of concrete musical experience or the complexity of its historical and cultural significance; yet it is here that our interest lies and in this humanistic sphere that we desire to find the truth.

The philosophy of art must consequently use rather than ignore musical experience; it will be a systematization of historical knowledge, even though it may also provide in return a new

18

orientation. But if musical experience is to be our starting point, the question arises as to the compass of this experience, as to what it comprises and what it excludes. The problem of what we are to comprehend by music, of its definition and concept, is not only of essential importance at the outset, but has also become particularly pressing because of the large domain that has been revealed by historical and ethnological research and because of the daring explorations of the present into new territory. We find possible today for the first time an adequate grasp of the whole field of music in time and space that our historical position permits us to see; we have penetrated the mists that concealed or obscured vast areas; and in spite of the absence of notation that will always keep the details of most of the musical territory beyond the reach of accurate observation, we know something at any rate of what music has been like almost everywhere, and can even guess the general nature of its preliminary forms and origins.

The present seems to mirror prehistory in that music is made not simply of tone, but instead or in addition of nontonal sound, whether speech or noise. Thus music as an art of tone in which other kinds of sound are at most incidental would seem to develop from and return to, at least at times, an art of sound or noise, and the largest alternative that confronts us is whether our subject concerns the shaping of specifically tonal material or of sonorous material in general. Certainly sonorous duration, even when it is not tonal, is susceptible of elaborate patterning that includes simultaneity; sounds contain an untold wealth of distinctions, although to be sure, not with the prominent unidimensionality, positional precision, and serial order poseessed by tones in their property of pitch. And if nontonal sound does not possess the potentiality of tone for order, it can contain something of the continuity we find in tone; while the absence of this continuity in the case of tonal material, on the other hand—as in staccato and pizzicato pieces and in pointillistic serial music—does not in the least destroy the claim of a composition to musical status. Thus we are left merely with the serial order of pitch as the tonal criterion that will serve to define music, and it would seem advisable to consider our province more broadly to be the art of sound rather than the art of tone. In general, then, music necessarily includes or is based on or consists of the patterning of sound and silence in the dimensions of time, space, and sonorous quality. Of these dimensions, space has been the least prominent, and sonorous quality has been represented chiefly by pitch. Past preference, however, need not continue to hold for the future.

This brings us logically to a methodological problem related to that of definition and scope, namely, the possibility of dealing with only part of the territory of music rather than its totality. To be unaware of the whole panorama or of any of the various aspects it may present would certainly be unwise, since the properties of any section we examine will be more perfectly understood in comparison with what can be seen elsewhere. But with this point granted, there can be no objection to finding some areas of music more significant philosophically than others. This is indeed a corollary of the distinctiveness of our vantage point in time. Thus we might want to consider primarily the state of music at the present time, or the earliest forms of music we can discover. Or we might be interested primarily in music as an art of tone rather than sound, or in the musical work of art rather than in music that is improvised, or in abstract instrumental music rather than in dance or song or ceremonial music. The ground of such preferences cannot be provided by the evolutionary notion of the achievement of maturity, or the progressive revelation of the "true nature" of an art, as though with purely instrumental compositions, for example, music came of age; for this would be to apply to history the inappropriate biological model of the development of an individual organism. Instead the philosophical value of a given type of music, such as abstract instrumental works, must be found in the promise it holds of greater relevance to the problems of the nature and meaning of art as we conceive them than the varieties of music that are more concrete and comprehensive in expression or tied to specific occasions. If we are to understand art most fully, it might be urged, we must somewhat paradoxically approach it in its rarest and most isolated form, for this is its purest.

If we center our attention on abstract instrumental music,

however, we are confronted with peculiar difficulties of method, for the two routes that seem to provide access to our subject are indirect. They suggest themselves first of all because instrumental music has evolved from more comprehensive musical arts, and secondly, because it lacks the independence of other fields of invention and expression so that it tends to turn elsewhere for its forms and significance. Of the corresponding avenues of approach to instrumental music, the first is a route of historical explanation, the second a route of systematic comparison. The first seeks to understand music from what it has been, the second from its analogies to other fields. Together these approaches might seem to provide a comprehensive means of getting at the nature of music; but they leave out of account the elements of novelty and autonomy. The historical explanation, which will obviously provide us with the understanding of a process of development, will not necessarily provide us with the understanding of the outcome of this process; indeed it will do so only to the extent that antecedent stages are still present in the modes of conception and apprehension, in the structures and meanings, of the resultant musical species. To the extent that these earlier patterns and meanings have disappeared and been supplanted by novel features peculiar to instrumental music in its own right, the developmental explanation will fail to encompass a significant part of the matter before us, and provide only peripheral insights into music or an understanding of occasional or extrinsic traits. We may turn, then, to those other fields of expression, in particular to language and mathematics, which exerted an influence over musical form or meaning not because they were combined with music in a composite art, but by reason of their prominence in culture or their dominance over modes of thought in general. But again, an explanation that seeks to account for music in terms of analogies or parallels with such fields will fail to furnish a significant degree of insight into instrumental music to the extent that this art contains its own peculiar properties.

Now if we ask how instrumental music could come to contain these independent properties, we seem to be asking a historical

21

question (even if it is not one encompassed in the special history of the composite musical arts from which pure music descended), so that at least upon preliminary consideration, the analogical and historical approaches appear between themselves to provide a complete explanation of the nature of music. It is obviously not possible in general, however, to find antecedents or historical explanations for emergent properties, since creativity and unpredictable novelty are of the essence of biological and mental life. If we stress the indirect routes to the understanding of instrumental music, it is because these are the most easily discovered and the most readily negotiable; they cannot be stressed, however, to the exclusion of a direct examination of instrumental music in its own right. To a great extent, such a direct examination will not be historical or cultural; it will be "empirical" in the different sense of introspection, phenomenological intuition, and laboratory experiment. But as devoted to autonomous properties, it will be the more successful as we are informed in advance of what the derived properties of instrumental music are, for only then will we be able to identify what is in fact not explainable on the basis of either its origins or its outside relations.

Contemporary avant-garde music can claim special importance as a key to the understanding of music in general, for as the most recent product of musical culture and experience, it has in fact the greatest summary value with respect to the past, or at least the greatest summary potentiality, although the actual use it makes of this advantage will obviously depend upon the quality and extent of the composer's historical consciousness. Contemporary music represents a limiting case, of course, since our gaze can be directed from it only backward in time; we cannot see ahead except in imagination and by way of prediction. An older work, on the other hand, not only appears upon the scene in a musical environment that stretches backward into the past, but also has an existence that continues and extends after and beyond its time and place of origin. Both the meaning it has initially and the changes in meaning it subsequently undergoes are importantly determined by the whole historical course of the surrounding world of music. To understand any music is thus in some degree to understand all music, if not all of culture; the special advantage of contemporary music is partly illusory. It is obvious, in any event, that the preservation of music and the associated emphasis of historical considerations introduce entirely new and larger possibilities of musical understanding, although it is well to remember that our conception of the historical nature of musical experience is by no means universally applicable. To be sure, music always manifests some form of the interplay of tradition and change; but the past often remains present without question; it is not always accompanied by a freedom of choice in the utilization of older artistic means, in which elements that are recognized as superseded may again be taken up and incorporated into the current idiom. The distinction that can be made between a traditional and a historical mentality has an obvious corollary in the contrast between constancy and change, for tradition entails persistence while historical awareness, although it may choose to respect convention, may equally elect to alter or disregard it. But musical experience has not always comprised an awareness of itself as stationed in a historical progression of stylistic change, nor will it in all probability always continue to do so. In contrast to such awareness, which also includes a projection of the future course of technique and style, the experience of art can be historically naive, without concern for the course or rate of stylistic change, which may be relatively slow and unperceived, and not motivated by speculation or by the desire for personal distinctiveness. Historical awareness, on the other hand, really encompasses a number of different possible attitudes and practices, from a simple appreciation of the age and values of current styles to the most highly speculative attitude toward composition, which conceives it as an advance into unknown regions of expressive quality or formal relationships. Within this dynamic outlook, the past can be ignored entirely, felt as a dead weight obstructing progress, be used as a key to radical innovation, or turned to account by means of the selective revival of those features or intact stylistic configurations that are felt to possess some relevance to present interests.

The copresence of antecedent styles is comparable to the copresence of current styles, both those of interacting social groups and those of interacting cultures: as an end product of historical interest it seems paradoxically capable of vitiating historical qualities altogether and fostering a universal style, or at least a universal sphere of stylistic possibilities, timeless as well as worldwide. Sufficient eclecticism, at any rate, would make it increasingly difficult to preserve a sensitivity to the particular qualities of other times and places, and tend to cancel out the aesthetic and humanistic values that reside in musical history, sociology, and anthropology.

We may now logically give some attention to the relationship between history and aesthetics, for these fields often appear to engender a problematical or even irreconcilable conflict between a knowledge about art and a knowledge of it: between an understanding of artistic and general trends that is mediate and a direct sensory intuition of individual works. Yet this opposition between conceptual knowledge that disregards the properties of aesthetic experience and the actual presence of the individual work isolated from any context and known for its own sake and purely in its own terms will not withstand the test of closer examination. If the work of art were truly isolated, there could at best be a certain musical aspect of general history based on verbal and pictorial evidence and on preserved musical instruments, but strictly construed, there would be no history of music itself, since no resemblances could be found between different works and no internal artistic connections could be established. In spite of musical notation the historian would be no more able to exercise his profession than he would in connection with nonliterate musical cultures or in attempting to write a history of human behavior. But musical works of art, and individual musical performances (which now can also be recorded), are obviously not literally isolated from one another; they not only bear clear resemblances among themselves, but equally observable connections with other aspects of culture. In addition, the perception and creation of art by no means

24

exclude conceptual thought, either that intrinsically involved in the technical and aesthetic features of the art itself, or that formulated consciously and separately from the primary experience and bringing external knowledge to bear upon it. A distinction between aesthetics and history cannot be based either on a hermetically sealed-off work of art or on a total absence of conceptual thought; other types of consideration must be invoked.

When we reflect on the music of some past era or distant culture or even of some present social group of which we are not members, the experience to which we appeal will not be first-hand, and might therefore seem to be relatively uninformative to the philosopher or aesthetician. A 14th-century performance of a motet is obviously no longer possible, and the experience of musical composition and listening that surround such a performance are equally events of the past which are no longer amenable to direct inspection. Similar considerations obviously hold for the social, cultural, and conceptual contexts of such a musical work. Thus revival necessarily implies abstraction and disruption; it involves new perspectives of experience, which are characterized most fundamentally in terms of the duality of their position in history.

Yet the historical image of experience is also experience. History always involves a degree of revitalization, especially in the case of art, so that in some sense at least we really continue to appeal to our own experience rather than merely to that of the past. It cannot be denied, of course, that the potentialities of our relationship to music change when we turn from the products of our own culture to those of an earlier or distant origin. New kinds of significance make their appearance. We are able to see the whole field of forces of which an older work is the nexus, because we are able to see the future and thus the place of the work in the course of history. This larger view is therefore a consequence of the detachment of music from our own milieu and from our everyday concerns. And it is detachment, similarly, that characterizes our view of the contemporary music of another culture. But then music of distant provenance in time or space really emphasizes a characteristic feature of all artistic experience, for formulation in itself produces detachment; the material that is shaped and the experience that is embodied are of necessity lifted to some extent out of the normal course of existence. And with this fundamental detachment there is created at the same time a symbolic relation. Art has meaning because we are concerned with the experience of which it is the occasion; our apprehension of the formed material puts us in touch with a more important artistic totality. Now the reference of this larger experience to some third entity is doubtless a dispensable part of the symbolic relation, but it is certainly an enhancement of this relation; a reference to the past or to another culture deepens the meaning of artistic form by expanding the experience it signifies.

Thus what history contains of mediacy and distance is in fact strangely conformable to the special quality of detachment that distinguishes aesthetic experience. It is also conformable to the tendency of the arts toward autonomy and isolation from everyday life. The earlier or distant origin of a work does not disqualify it, but instead enhances its aesthetic qualities in their own right. Even the context of the work becomes aesthetic, for distance imparts a detachment to the whole surrounding complex of social, cultural, and conceptual factors. It may consequently be argued not that history is irrelevant or hostile to aesthetics, but that artistic apprehension is most adequately exemplified only when it is historical. In fact the very nature of works of art entails some measure of preservation and permanence, and since works of art present aesthetic properties in their most distinctive form, the central place of history in aesthetics is inescapable. Unmitigated immediacy is a liability rather than an asset in aesthetics, and it is consequently an advantage rather than a troublesome detour to reinstate modes of thought and feeling that have become obsolete and are therefore not immediately intelligible. Indeed in an older work, as we have seen, the context itself is transformed into a component of the aesthetic situation in a way impossible for contemporary art; for the current context in which a modern composition finds itself, even were we somehow enabled to see it clearly and as a whole (although the future must always be excepted), could not be regarded so dispassionately as to become part of the disinterested activity of aesthetic experience. It is thus a source of aesthetic value that we can respond to older music, or realize its potential beauty, only by adopting a corresponding sensibility removed from our own. Then every constituent—environment as well as music—will be separated from actuality and take on an ideal character. The distance may stultify life, but not the peculiar life that is art.

To make the past live, however (which more explicitly stated, means to endow a present experience with the quality of pastness), demands that we reconcile conflicting properties; and it requires a kind of artificial diligence to combine a sense of detachment with spontaneity of response; or to view the matter in reverse, it requires a special sympathy to endow with immediacy an experience we know to be of distant provenance. Either the immediacy or the detachment will tend to gain the upper hand, depending upon the actual degree of relationship to the music of our own time and cultural circle, but a properly aesthetic experience will succeed in balancing the two. This conflict of past and present is at its height in music, for sound and tone seize the attention, the flow of music irresistibly involves our consciousness, even to the point of completely falsifying the original conceptions and feelings by supplanting them with our current modes of experience. The temporal nature of music is such as to keep it vitally present, not such as to permit or sustain our awareness of the past. (It is only our personal past that music has the peculiar power to summon up by association, and even this earlier personal experience is at once endowed with extraordinary vividness.) Thus only by insisting forcibly at first upon an attitude of contemplation and upon the participation of historical knowledge can we maintain our detachment even from a musical work of the past and grasp correctly the experience it formulates. Otherwise we will be carried along by a spontaneous course of feeling that may be entirely foreign to the music we are hearing or performing. It is only on subsequent occasions that we cultivate an appropriate musical sensitivity, and that historical conceptions are somehow to a great extent absorbed into the intrinsic properties of the work. A second and cultivated immediacy comes into being, accompanying and partly replacing that important aspect of detachment which is produced by various kinds of conceptual knowledge and imagination bearing upon the original social and cultural context of the music.

The case of contemporary art is somewhat different. (We may here include composition along with performance and listening.) Contextual elements are present but we do not need to become aware of them and to incorporate them; for the most part they are a normal constituent of our experience without being brought to consciousness separately at any time; and in some form they do not cease to play a role even when music is separated in principle from practical life, to become an apparently autonomous and isolated activity. Thus immediacy is more naturally comprehensive in the art of the present than in that of the past or of other cultures. Yet various types of detachment remain characteristic, fundamentally because formulative processes are an inevitable feature of art, present even where they seem not to be—in improvisation, for example, or in states of ecstasy. As for the claim that aesthetics deals with immediacy alone, and with the specimen of art in isolation, and that this is true regardless of the provenance of the art—for historical and distant cultures as well as our present environment—it simply cannot be sustained. The experience of art would be reduced to insignificance if conceptual tendencies did not check the immediacy of emotional and volitional forces, and if conceptual constituents did not supply the context that detachment removes.

Yet it is not simple to determine the kinds of contextual and conceptual factors that are relevant to musical composition, performance, and perception; and the precise way in which such factors are related to music or affect it is often equally difficult to determine. The relevance of biographical and psychological knowledge has been as problematical as the value of a knowledge of society and culture and history. The motivation of music and the subjective reaction to it would seem to be largely fortuitous matters in respect of musical form and meaning; they have essentially a personal significance that belongs to biography rather than to art; their connection with music is explainable but apparently neither essential nor uniquely determined. The motivation is a cause of the music, the reaction an effect, but there are certainly more proximate and therefore more specific and significant causes and effects than these to claim our interest. On the other hand, it can also be maintained that pervasive or extramusical factors of the psychological makeup of the composer or performer, like external or general aspects of society and culture, enter into the essential features of musical style and the intrinsic significance that resides in musical perception. Are the varied contexts of art irrelevant or constitutive? Should they remain outside the domain of aesthetics or are they in fact transformed into specifically artistic properties? There can be little doubt of the proper outcome of this continually debated issue. Many contextual factors undeniably exert an influence upon art and thus will further aesthetic apprehension and complete our understanding; they will also on occasion enter decisively into the activity of creation and performance and into the very constitution and meaning of the artistic product. Indeed even those aspects of the psychological and cultural context of art which stand outside any causal or constitutive connection with it are not aesthetically dispensable. Even as purely conceptual factors they are legitimate and valuable parts of artistic significance—not of creation and understanding as we at first tend to define them, but of a broadened comprehension of art that will provide an enhanced and more ramified experience.

It follows from these considerations that there is little difference between a historical and an aesthetic apprehension of art. In general history, of course, works of art contribute to the end of an appreciation of a total pattern of human culture, so that their own value is subordinated; but in musical history the situation is reversed: the art is in the foreground of interest and the culture is used to enrich and complete our understanding. Now aesthetics differs from this only in its emphasis: it is systematic rather than narrative, and as a concomitant, concerned with the presentness of the past rather than with the past as seen from the perspective of the present. It abstracts the

29

manifestations and patterns produced by change from the story of the change itself, making their pastness part of an analysis that rises above time; it deals with the historical experience of art as experience rather than as historical. The nature and experience of the individual work of art are consequently an important focus of our interest and one of the main sources of our understanding; but although we are concerned to a lesser extent than the historian with tendencies and trends and with relationships between compositions, an understanding of the individual work will nevertheless rely heavily, as it must, upon the values that derive from its generic membership and its position in larger patterns of change and influence.

But conceptions of the large types of music that are peculiar to a culture or a social stratum, and within these, of musical genre, are important concerns of musical philosophy in their own right, and not only as entering into each individual experience of music. Whether such conceptual objects, the largest of which is music itself, belong to aesthetics as well as to the philosophy of art is a matter essentially of terminology: they are certainly aesthetic in the sense of implied and conceived and imaged experience if not in the more literal sense of actual perception. But as we have mentioned, there are types of narrative literature in which the sensory experience connected with an individual work—even though it belongs to a unique object—exists in imagery only rather than actuality; and we would not for this reason altogether deny such works an aesthetic status. Indeed as far as sensory experience is concerned, musical philosophy can hardly be distinguished from musical aesthetics, although it more naturally encompasses the theory and foundation of aesthetics and it also helps us escape from the traditions that overstress passive reception and avoid history.

The apparently inconsequential selection of an area of investigation, of a problem or an issue, is actually a matter of considerable importance; it conceals within itself the presuppositions of our time and outlook and it circumscribes the possible results of our undertaking; it contains at once both a conception of the whole study and a reflection of its cultural setting—of traditions of thought and of our position with respect to them. Within humanistic study itself we are faced with the alternative of historical concreteness and abstract generalization; the first of these implies in all its forms the constituent roles of change and of cultural specificity and the merely accessory role of science; while the second, which we take to be philosophic, entails the essential relevance of science and the accessory but indispensable role of concrete experience. And if the philosophical outlook of the historian governs his selection of subject matter and the whole nature and cast of the picture he paints, the historical position of the philosopher similarly influences the nature of the theories he formulates. In both cases it is best to make explicit what often remains unrealized, for this will ensure the resultant historical or philosophical constructions the fullest value they can secure. We can come to terms with the historical position of our own inquiry, then, and turn it to greatest advantage, if we attempt to assimilate traditions of thought rather than to disregard them.

The field of study known as aesthetics is obviously the product of a particular course of historical events as well as an abstract possibility of the organization of ideas, and the conception we entertain of it at any time is accordingly based on our attitude toward the specific historical complex as well as on our systematic evaluation of the field as a defined area of thought. In the whole progress of experience and speculation that bears on the formation of aesthetics, the development and nature of the arts themselves are of primary importance, since it is with art that aesthetics is chiefly concerned. During the 18th and 19th centuries, the period in which aesthetics itself flourished, opera and instrumental music were without doubt the most important manifestations of the art of music, and they consequently became the major areas of interest and speculation in musical aesthetics.

In the name it adopted from ancient Greek, the field of aesthetics represented sensory perception to be its major concern. But it took up also whatever older traditions of thought seemed to come within its province, regardless of their original ideological environment and significance. Thus ideas connected with art as this was understood in antiquity and the

Middle Ages, ideas of beauty and expression, of divine inspiration, nature, imitation, sublimity, and taste—all these were collected from widely varied sources that ranged from cosmology and ethics to rhetoric. The confluence of this remarkable diversity with new efforts to define a philosophic field of inquiry resulted in considerable confusion. The varied conceptions comprised by aesthetics—originating in different periods and in different contexts of thought—produced a large ideological range and a lack of unity that obstructed a single clear definition. The complexity was increased in the case of music by the composite and changing character of the art itself, and the 20th century witnessed an increasing uncertainty as to what the field of aesthetics represented and a tendency to reject it altogether. This was a corollary, to a great extent, of an interest in structure rather than in beauty of appearance, external form, and emotional effect.

One of the oldest aesthetic strata is made up of notions of beauty descended from Platonic and Neoplatonic cosmology and connected chiefly with vision and with organic form. Accompanying this in music is a similarly ancient group of conceptions connected with medical, moral, and social influence . Both of these spheres of thought took on new importance in the Renaissance, when the conception of beauty—although it remained largely visual and organic—became as fundamental a value of art as it was of nature, and the conception of musical influence became more one of arousing feeling than of molding moral character. In the sphere of music especially, expression began to compete with and supplant beauty as the central artistic value. If beauty represents the Classical ideal in aesthetics, expressiveness can be connected with the long tradition of Christian art. But this tradition does more than reinforce a second standard of value within aesthetics; it encompasses values that are in conflict with aesthetics altogether: the value of significance as opposed to form, of plainness as opposed to stylization, and of intensity of feeling as opposed to beauty.

Starting in the Renaissance also, and completed in the 18th century, a series of changes in the arts and in the conceptions attached to them led to the idea of fine art as comprising a specific group of more or less coordinate members. An important bond uniting the group was the appeal, based on expressive impact, to a wider middle-class audience; for while the appreciation of compositional technique demands a sophistication that is specific to each art, sensible and emotional effect is not only more superficially apparent but also a feature common in some measure to all the arts. But it is obviously a precondition of the kinship of the fine arts that painting, sculpture, and musical composition secure a status equivalent to that of architecture and poetry. A decisive factor in the case of Renaissance music was the use of notation in working out and preserving unified polyphonic works and the concomitant development of a science of composition; while at the same time painting and sculpture were freed from the opprobrium attached in antiquity to manual work (for this was not consonant with Renaissance secularism and empiricism), and they also found a scientific basis—in perspective and anatomy. Another unifying factor was at hand in the ancient notion of imitation, which had an additional influence in connecting art with ethics and epistemology. Finally the idea of freedom from practical interests—which was descended from the ancient aristocratic motivation of the liberal arts and the conception of pursuits that were appropriate to leisure time—was also to become an important constituent of aesthetics, and had further effects somewhat complementary to those of imitation in connecting art with contemplative and purely theoretical interests.

During the 18th century two opposed forces took on decisive catalytic importance, one of taste and criticism, which was concerned with the moral value of art and was basically social and contemporaneous in origin, and the other of the cognitive character of perception, which took account of the predominant position of sensory experience but was deeply rooted in older traditions of the beauty and the epistemological value of art. Modern aesthetics arose out of the contest and reconciliation of these two principles, the one by nature spontaneous in its action, grounded in the individuality of the perceiver, and addressed also to the idiosyncrasy of the work of art, the other accounting for beauty in more general terms as the sensible perception of perfection—a peculiar and subordinate type of knowledge that stopped short of concepts. Within this framework, fixed by Kant in the notion of judgment and in the quality but not the fact of purpose, aesthetics secured its autonomy and its definition with respect to morality and knowledge. The interest in nature persisted tenaciously, however, doubtless because the field dealt primarily with perception and apprehension rather than creation.

But the development of instrumental music presented peculiar and difficult problems, and musical aesthetics was concerned largely with the feelings attached to this new species of art, especially because of its apparent freedom from imtation and concepts, and with the question of these feelings as seen in the light of the composite musical arts. Musical aesthetics clearly represented a field of thought in its own right. Indeed the place of performance and participation in music in itself ensures the special nature of the art, for behavior and morality here become intrinsically involved in music, and the sphere of practice joins those of forming and contemplation, which elsewhere divide art and aesthetics between them. Thus music cannot easily be done justice by general aesthetic theories, and 20th-century interests have further revealed this difficulty, for symbolic, phenomenological, and linguistic conceptions are all, each in its own way, of quite a special nature in their application to music, just as the areas of psychological and historical study have been, or the notion of feeling. In addition, very much like Hanslick, we have experienced a reaction against the inevitable prominence and continual repetition of ideas of feeling in musical thought, just as we have against expressiveness in music itself; we have become more interested in ideas that are specific to music in detail, to musical form and to purely musical meaning. Apart from the general growth of mass culture and the striking revision of basic conceptions in philosophy and in all the sciences, the radical changes that music in particular has undergone in the 20th century, together with the new social and historical perspectives that have illuminated it, would have expanded the range of musical thought and called the traditional notion of "aesthetics" into question.

Much of the restrictive implication of the conception of aesthetics is connected with the heritage of the word as designating sensory experience and sensible qualities. If the Platonic tradition had placed little value on the truth or the knowledge given by the senses or even on the beauty they presented, 18th-century German thought established a substantially different tradition of its own. Schiller and Kant, for example, while quite aware of the broader enlistment of human capacities and sensitivities that may be unexpectedly entailed by sensory experience and the richness of significance that often lies in it unsuspected, emphasized respectively the notions of *Schein*, or pure appearance, and of the resemblance of art to nature. But we now find both appearance and naturalness to be limited as characterizations of art. Certainly the idea of appearance directs attention to the importance of specifically sensory values and to the related property of the detachment of art from everyday experience. These are properties bound up in the creation of artistic fiction and in the special character of artistic truth. And the criterion of naturalness provides a basis for the conformity of part to whole, whether as an enhancement of beauty or as a reinforcement of some specialized variety of expression. But appearance and naturalness, on the other hand, also have a connection with concealment and aesthetic surface, and it is this connection that the temper of our time finds restrictive and therefore seeks to avoid, for these are characteristics of art that arise from an aristocratic class and are connected predominantly with contemplation and enjoyment, with an external or superficial understanding. Aesthetics bears the marks of the time in which it was born; it transmits a rococo heritage that confines the quality of art to the province of beauty and pleasure and insists that stronger expressive qualities must not destroy sensory charm, for this would be to destroy art by exceeding its bounds.

Although the forces of social revolution posed a threat to these values, the prevailing bourgeois sphere of 19th-century art for the most part adapted them and provided for their continuance. It is only after an interregnum of Expressionism and primitivism—both openly destructive of aesthetic values—that an alternative idea becomes dominant in the Neoclassic objectivity of the 1920s and in the music of Webern and Stravinsky. Constructivism and the craft of composition replace an art that conceals art and that is at times beyond conscious control. As a technical corollary, contrapuntal and rhythmic interest displaces harmonic sonority and harmonic form. Here we may say that the notion of structure is set against that of form; craft and technique, the artistic intelligence that enters form in the process of formation, replace finished form, which is more addressed to sense. Structure is thus form that is perceptible in its full detail and that is conceived typically in its own right, without reference to significance. Characteristically its internal relationships are established according to rule, by the application of fixed principles of transformation or elaboration to basic patterns. The result is therefore hierarchical, at least by implication, and rationally coherent. But the separation of structure from significance—however useful it may be in general as an analytic procedure capable of providing insight into fundamental properties of art and language—is a relatively limited and unproductive method of study in the field of music, where form and meaning are so intimately fused. And it is of course unthinkable, for the same reason, as a method of composition. These considerations, however, do not diminish the new importance of structural thought or change the fact that a rejection of the values connected with aesthetics accompanied the development of 20th-century musical style. Aesthetics took on the particular negative connotation of aestheticism; it began to be replaced by history and anthropology, and by novel kinds of technical and philosophical thought, as part of the general and deep-seated changes that were transforming every aspect of life and knowledge.

Perhaps the most symptomatic manifestation of the shift in musical values can be found in the replacement of large orchestras by small ensembles, of fused sound by clearly audible detail. There is a transformation of treatment even within a single medium (Mahler's dissection of the orchestra,

36

particularly in his Ninth Symphony, is a striking example), but it is evident that each sonorous medium has its own propensity; there is an inescapable difference in structural implication between the ensemble song of Webern and the lied of the 19th century; and in the string quartet, to take another instance, it is extremely difficult to hide any of the tonal constituents or to mask the individuality of any by the unexplained novelty of their joint and overall effect. In the face of changes such as these in music and in the conception of music, including in particular the broadening of our social and cultural comprehension, it is obvious that many of the historically particular features of the field of aesthetics would appear in an unfavorable light and make the adoption of a new designation for our study more desirable than the alteration of a traditional one. Aesthetics now has its logical place in the backwash of Romanticism that feeds our pseudoculture. The same negative position need not be taken, however, with respect to the use of the word "aesthetic" in general, although its diversified heritage of meaning will make it heavily dependent for its significance in each case on the surrounding context of thought.

Conceptions and terminology have a historical nature just like the more tangible products of human creativity. Not only is the work of art itself a historical manifestation, as we have indicated, but in addition, our conception of it is part of its history. As its autonomy and distinctiveness increased in fact, so did the conviction grow that an understanding of art was properly concerned with the qualities of the individual work alone. This position involved the contradiction that a thoroughly unique entity is unintelligible, but it was a position that could be sustained and in a sense justified, although only very imperfectly, by the appeal to an absolute, classical—and therefore again nonhistorical—canon of beauty, which could serve as a basis of evaluation and understanding. Indeed aesthetics had initially taken up such an absolute conception of art and beauty as one of its most ancient and important constituents. Another basis of evaluation could be found in the individual work itself, the general character of which—if we adopt a principle of consistency—could be taken as a standard for the details. But no basis of understanding or judgment would exist in an artistic tradition and an encompassing community of other works, or in society and culture in general.

It is no coincidence, then, in view of the absolute nature of its object, that aesthetics should develop as a study to which history was irrelevant, or that its characteristic criteria of appearance and naturalness—although they in no way exclude the possibility that volition and knowledge are involved in artistic perception—should fail to reflect the formative role of society and history and culture. Similarly, the changing significance of the field of aesthetics is doubtless connected with changes in the work of art or with its decline. Indeed the arts themselves are subject to history and culture in their number and nature and relationships; the group of fine arts on which aesthetics was based was related in some ways to the earlier cycle of liberal arts but overlooked many of these as well as many crafts and highly elaborated arts of the past and the contemporaneous world. In the 20th century, the influence of technological factors, which has always been of overriding importance, was the leading cause of an expansion and thus partial destruction of the traditional group of fine arts, and the resultant diversity calls for a new introduction of systematic principles.

Our thesis that the significance of the individual musical composition is in essence social and cultural is thus a logical counterpart of our view of aesthetics as necessarily concerned with social and cultural properties, or what is the same thing, of our replacement of it with a humanistic philosophy. Yet it would be an exaggeration to deny altogether the validity of a study of the internal structural principles and unified patterns of interrelationships that are peculiar to a single composition, or the validity of the close connection of these formal properties with the fundamental structural features of the musical system. To the extent that the values of a composition are felt to reside in unity and autonomy, and in the natural representation in its form of general musical principles of relationship, the study of the internal economy of a work in isolation will have its measure of justification. Yet even here only a limited understanding is possible; generic musical traditions and contextual factors are never really absent; they can be set aside with impunity only if their presence is assumed and somehow taken into account.

The notion of philosophy rather than aesthetics will finally not suggest at the outset the similarity of music to other arts, which is a matter to be investigated rather than assumed. For although music is without question intrinsically social and cultural, it is by no means equally obvious that it is related to other fields of human expression in the same society; what connections may exist will be dependent on the degree of social complexity and specialization and on the particular configuration of the culture; and it is clearly important to examine music in its own right before considering its kinship with other activities or its membership in a group of arts. This issue does not exist as such in simple societies, where music is integrated so closely into the social and cultural whole that it cannot be removed and still be understood, let alone compared with other similarly excised activities. Comparison here must be between different aspects of the totality rather than between separate fields. With this qualification, then, we will follow the principle of examining music itself before investigating its relationships to other aspects of culture or to other specialized activities. Certainly representational significance, for example, which is central in verbal art and painting and sculpture, has no counterpart in instrumental music. Much futile effort has been expended on this question and others as a result of the assumption that the resemblance of the various arts is necessarily comprehensive. Indeed it is difficult enough to determine the scope and limits of music itself, an undertaking which is logically prior to connecting it as a whole or even in part with other areas of expression. Doubtless more than the spatial arts, and somewhat like language, music has a compass that exceeds the bounds of what we generally conceive of as art, although not what we may describe as formativity. It is coextensive with human life and culture, and its manifestations include innumerable varieties in which the values of formativity and perception are subordinated and even submerged by expression or function—in the scarcely formalized wailing attendant at times upon death and burial, for example, or in the recitation of traditional and sacred texts. Thus we can hardly do justice to the breadth of our field unless we think of it in terms of musical philosophy; the question of art, whatever its importance, will take its place in this more comprehensive setting.

It has become obvious that there are many possible varieties of musical philosophy. Music can be conceived as the forming of material, which is a view applicable to improvisation as well as to composition, although it suggests the resemblance of musical activity to the manual shaping and constructive processes of spatial art. Or the fundamental notions involved may be those of apprehension rather than production, of the contemplation and judgment of an object, in which case music will be conceived as similar both to visual art and to nature in representing an objective form of beauty, a type of expressiveness, or a kind of symbolism. Then form will almost inevitably be understood to have a content, or to embody an idea, and the epistemological value of imitation may play a role, which in turn entails properties of truth and morality. Primarily, however, theories of contemplation are aesthetic in the original sense of the word; they are concerned with perceptual values in their own right and for their own sake. Linguistic theories provide an alternative that encompasses both formulation and contemplation; they suggest communication from the composer or performer to the audience—an expression of feelings that produces an effect and a response; but they will be framed in terms of a meaning that is specific or autonomous rather than a content that is separately conceivable. The humanistic theory with which we are presently concerned takes formulation to be the distinguishing feature of art, but it is a formulation that is specific to personality and culture and that is dedicated primarily to the values that may reside in perception, although also to those of formativity itself—to the properties of the finished object that testify to skillful constructive technique and to an understanding of the possibilities of the material that is formed. The central place of formativity can be seen even in the notion of the "work of art," which does not connect the finished object with perception and contemplation, as we might expect, but keeps alive the conception of the activity by which this object was produced. The idea of meaning, and the associated notion of value, will also play a prominent part in our considerations, not in the sense of language and communication, or in that of representation, but as a characterization of the comprehensive and peculiar import of artistic form.

As opposed to the "aesthetics of music," then, which is charged with meanings that have accumulated during the two centuries of its history as well as with those taken over from antiquity and the Middle Ages and the Renaissance, we may adopt the term *philosophy of music*, for this represents a relatively fresh and unobstructed perspective; it also implies the widest possible view and context of its subject, and does not tend to exclude fundamental considerations of any type, whether ethical, social, epistemological, or ontological. Within this field, a humanistic approach will insist on the central place of cultural and phenomenological factors. Although we cannot lose sight of the fact that man is an animal, we are concerned more with the fact that he is an intelligent animal, and especially with the fact that he is also a social one.

# CHAPTER 2

# Material

In seeking to understand and define the nature of music, we have first considered the character and range of our evidence, and can now proceed by examining various aspects of music in turn. A route that leads from elemental auditory consitituents to the large complex of culture and the activity of music as a whole, or a reverse path that runs from whole to part, both confront us with a problem that seems inherent to the construction of a complete view by successive steps. Individual features cannot be grasped correctly without a knowledge of the whole from which they have been abstracted, while the whole cannot be understood at the outset because of its various unexplained constituents. A solution to this dilemma can be achieved by discarding or subordinating the scheme of part and whole in favor of a principle of aspects. With this as a guide, we can keep the whole present throughout and conduct our investigation by illluminating successively various facets. The nature of music will then become increasingly concrete in the course of our study, but even at the beginning it will not be disregarded or seriously misrepresented.

Music reveals itself in a number of fundamental aspects: in the character of its objectivity, in the nature of its temporal and spatial constitution, in its style, and in the varied conceptions that are ingredient in it or that bear on it. These determine a field of possibilities within which musical experience is given; but the experience is conditioned also by a variety of activities: by composition, improvisation, performance, bodily participation, and listening, and by what we hear and feel and think music to be. The different relationships of music to those who experience and perceive it are possibly its most striking characteristic. Music is a changing and diversified shaping of objectivity, an activity taking place in a field peculiarly receptive to interrelated types of objective form. It is a play with objectivity, with the interconnection of subject and object, with their fusion and separation. The range from participation to detachment, from the molding of subjectivity to contemplation, is correlated with a range of types of experience that extends from an awareness of the immediate course of motion to the synthesis of temporal wholes, or from dynamic involvement to overall perception, and it also defines a parallel range of types of music. If represented objects are dispensable in music, along with the truth that resides in the fidelity or profundity of representation, a truth of human experience is intrinsic and constitutes the special virtue of the art; but it is a truth that can be viewed only through the humanity of the observer, of which it also becomes an expression. Because of the complexity of our subject, the selection of a comprehensive group of characteristics that are amenable to successive description is peculiarly difficult; many constituent features must be subsumed under a few, and these must be sufficiently prominent and comprehensive to qualify as natural and complementary divisions of thought.

The path from material to the work of art is not traversed in a single step; particularly in the case of music it represents a complicated process that involves a series of stages very different from one another in nature. Material itself is not simply matter, but the result of a purposeful selection from the possibilities provided by the natural world and the physiological endowment of man; it may be more accurately described as an alteration or a fabrication than a selection; in either event creativity is brought to bear with its concomitant purposes of expression or meaning, and like all creativity, the invention of musical material is controlled or guided by a social framework which establishes musical functions and dictates or delimits the interests and the range of conceivable expressive intentions of the individual. Sonority itself is thus in great measure a social product. Even the sounds of nature are more than matter; in becoming actual they have necessarily acquired a certain natural form. But musical form makes use not of natural sounds, but of the potentialities of nature for sound, which become a formative factor that acts together with the artistic processes of formulation—as a framework that precedes and delimits them.

But between nature and the work of art there intervene not only sonority and the instruments that produce it, but also various kinds of public formulations of this material. There is a stock of traditional patterns of sounds—simultaneous arrangements, more or less well defined melodic phrases, cadential figures, outlines of types of melody and. even complete melodies. These are to be either assembled or elaborated or both in accordance with still other public structures of an abstract kind—the generic forms of music and of ceremony—that define the overall arrangements of the sonorous patterns, along with the ritual and social functions. Further but differently abstract structures exist in the shape of tonal scales and systems, formative if not artistic products again of culture and history acting through a succession of individuals; mode, scale, and system may arise through abstraction from concrete forms, along with theoretical elaboration based on purely rational considerations, but they then also become preliminary forms that enter into and shape succeeding compositional and perceptual experience as types of initial structuring of the musical material. Finally individual musical performance and creation may either rest solely on defined genre and preformed material or else introduce still additional precompositional formulations such as motifs and themes, or series and matrices of pitch or duration, before arriving at the last stage of musical creation that is represented by the improvisation or work of art; in some cases these novel formulations of theme or thematic matrix may proceed directly from the musical system or scale, skipping over the public patterns of mode and melody and the schemes of genre.

It follows from the variety and complexity of the process of artistic creation that it will not be conveyed adequately by the schematic rubrics "material" and "form" unless these are qualified and additionally defined in their meaning. The activity of forming material is intrinsic to art; it is present in music even where it does not seem to play a role: in the adoption of arbitrary procedures, for example, in the participation of chance factors, or in the operation of subconscious forces. But it is manifested in remarkable diversity—now socially, now individually—from the very creation of material out of matter to the production of the finished work of art. The distinction between material and form is relative rather than absolute.

Thus the tone of a violin is musical material, but so is the major scale, a cadential progression of chords, the rhythm of the waltz, or a melody taken for variations. Often we speak of "borrowed material," when the point of departure for constructive activity is already the result of a formative process. But all instances of material, tone itself not excepted, are forms as well, the outcome of some manifestation of human creativeness and intention; indeed the tone of a Stradivarius violin is the product, through the agency of its instrument and the skill of a fine performer, of the most refined artistic sensitivities. In however elemental a state we conceive the material of music, it is always to some degree already formed. Even sonority in its setting of silence can be what it is only by virtue of the fact that it is not totally devoid of form, and musical material can always be described as the combination of a realm of natural possibilities and a form imposed by man. The resultant entity similarly can be experienced and known only as a composite of its objectivity and the forms intrinsic to experience and knowledge. Purely as a phenomenal object immanent to perception, it is both distinct from our awareness and also formulated by it. The external shaping and apprehension of a violin tone in the material world are in fact dependent upon the inherent processes of consciousness that constitute the inner counterpart of this tone as an immanent object of hearing, just as this immanent object in turn is dependent upon the basic sensory data supplied by a physical chain of events. Now these objects of the physical sciences are certainly not the material of music, but neither are the external intersensory objects of everyday perception. Instead it is the inner sounds that are the essential material. Musical instruments and our own voice or bodily motions of per- formance and participation can enter music only in conjunction with the intrinsically auditory sonority they provoke, while we can at least project images of music that is composed of immanent sonority alone.

Yet a comprehensive view of the nature of musical material must include two conceptions of sonority: both sound as an object immanent to auditory perception and sound as an external manifestation, with all the associative features and spontaneous outer reference that audition normally possesses, including the corporeal existence of our own activity as singers or performers. In effect, the distinction is only between a purely auditory consciousness and a multisensory consciousness of external objects and events; for many objects of hearing alone— even of binaural hearing—tend spontaneously to be perceived as immanent rather than external, while multisensory objects are normally perceived as external, and special effort is required to apprehend them as immanent. It is a peculiar and fund- amental feature of sound, then, and of music in particular, that this distinction between outer and inner can be made easily, and indeed that music often tends of itself to be apprehended as immanent to audition rather than as inextricably involved with external perception in the fashion of visual and tactile objects. Hearing is satisfied with its own objects, and has no need to relate them to further objects and events of the outside world. This is especially evident in the case of tone and tonal configura- tions, which are thus peculiarly appropriate objects for phen- omenological investigation. The essential nature of sound, however, is not all that constitutes musical experience, and to do justice to our subject, we must add an empirical perspective to the purely phenomenological one. Indeed music in general is a composite of external and immanent perception, of biologically grounded objectivity and perception occurring wholly within audition. The relative weight of the two components will depend on society and culture, although it is also controlled with surprising ease by the individual. Music abstracted entirely from the environment belongs in the company of mind without body, or the absolute work of art, or the subject purely as an imprint of what is perceived; it is a manifestation characteristic of Western civilization, and more specifically, a creation of the 19th century.

If we consider music as a product of the interaction between physical processes and consciousness, we find on the one hand that there are material stimuli to which consciousness responds, and on the other, that we come to know such a state of affairs only by an intrinsic constitutive activity that starts with the creation of immanent objects and proceeds to the construction of an external world that can further take on a conceptual and scientific character. Our final scientific "reality" is highly theoretical in comparison with the phenomenal starting point of our knowledge and it reflects the nature of our ability to know as much as the nature of what is known. But this compound character is found to some degree in every experienced or known object and it calls for a corresponding compound explanation. If we explain our experience solely as a response to physical stimuli, we overlook the process through which our knowledge of the stimuli came into being. If we explain it solely as a creation of mind, we leave unaccounted for the matter on which mind does its work. The scientific description is constructed from an external point of view and after the fact, the phenomenological one is constructed from the vantage point of consciousness itself and is genetic. But just as we cannot conceive of an external reality that exists apart from the way it is known, so we cannot examine the constituting power of consciousness without taking into account the phenomenal objects of our awareness. The causal and the constitutive processes are opposite in nature and opposite in their direction of action; and they must meet if perception is to take place. But constitution has a certain dominion over cause, for once perception has occurred, imagination and recollection become possible, and these experiences rest on intentionality alone; the external causal process is no longer actually present. Yet outer and inner are ultimately inseparable; each new perception further defines and elaborates the world, but its reflection in the self produces the same additional concreteness there as well. The attempt to describe the empirical physical world purely in its own terms reduces it to a set of equations and causes its perceptible qualities to disappear; while the attempt to examine consciousness purely in its own right correspondingly reduces it to a moving power of objectification and causes the self to disappear. Both the scientific and phenomenological reductions lead to the destruction of experience, and we must accordingly accept the fact that reality is relative to our observation of it, and that the world and we ourselves will vanish if experience is not treated as absolute and nonreducible.

Human experience can only be described adequately, then, in terms of a double process: an outwardly directed constructive activity and an inward flow of physical events. But even these processes are abstractions from the underlying interaction of organism and environment; the constructive activity belongs originally to the purposeful process of adaptation and bodily orientation which often is responsible in turn for the effectiveness if not also the possibility of the inwardly progressing physical succession. But the physical world and consciousness are abstractions that arise quite differently and are very different in nature, and their interrelation takes on the aspect of correlation rather than of obvious fact. The various types of object that are found in experience are dependent respectively on the various types of experience to which they belong—that is, ultimately upon human purpose and adjustment. There is no automatic or regular correspondence between the physical series and the psychological one. Many physical and physiological dimensions and events will have no counterpart in perception, while other stages of the physical process may account for corresponding properties of experience or objects of knowledge. On the other hand, we also come upon objects that are purely intentional or purely conceptual, some without any connection to an actual chain of physical stimuli or without any reference to sensory experience at all. Thus the outside world (which may be taken to include our body) furnishes data, the inside world of our mind constructs objects; but a correspondence between the objects and the outside is only a possibility. An alternative and sounder duality arises if we take our body as belonging to both worlds (although in different senses: as external and as an immanent organ of constitution). Then the activity that constructs and experiences objects will deploy our full being rather than mind alone. These general considerations represent the most fundamental reason that music involves a play or interplay of types of object, or what is very much the same thing, that it involves types of detachment and types of context.

Our present introductory purpose will be complete if we take note of a purely ideal conception of musical material. For just as the musical work of art is really a nonaudible entity that exists only as an object of intention and not even as the retracing or conception or projection of any particular experience of music past, present, or future, so the "sounds" and "sonorities" of this work are distinct from the perceived actuality connected with performance and from the primary presentations that belong to audition—distinct from both the phenomenal and empirical objects of hearing and also from images and concepts of these objects.

An oppositely directed extension of these terms—their application to the physical vibrations that underlie the existence of musical material—should not be endorsed. These various kinds of vibration are also constituted by a corresponding intentionality, but they are not manifest concretely, to the senses of touch, vibration, and vision, the way a musical instrument is. Of course the scientific picture of both a clarinet and its tone is a wholly intangible construct described by means of highly elaborate conceptions and theories. But the clarinet can be seen and handled while the tone can only be heard; it has no sensible existence except as an auditory object. As for the vibrations themselves, they really make up a whole series of physical events—external and physiological—which are entirely imperceptible to the senses, or at best only superficially perceptible.

Leaving electronic transmission out of account, then, there are the activating corporeal movements of the performer together with their physiological requirements such as nervous control and circulatory support (all of which has its impalpable origin in volition and intention). Then there is the mechanical vibration of a source (which often consists of two associated vibrating systems that are mutually supportive), a conversion of the vibration to vibratory compressional waves in air, the complex effects of an enclosure on these and their further conversion into mechanical vibrations in the ear, and finally a transformation of these into nerve impulses which gradually change their character and pattern as they are transmitted to the higher nervous centers. If we consider vibratory sensations to be a type of musical material, there will also be vibrations transmitted through the ground or the floor as well as the air, and a vibratory excitation in various parts of the body. But this complex of physical events nowhere contains the perceived quality and quantity of sonority; it merely supports the audible character of the sound, the physical basis of which can hardly be confused with its phenomenal existence, whether immanent or external. The physical objects of scientific thought are the substratum of musical material, not the material itself; they are the possibility of sound, not its actuality.

Sonority in its more specific sense is an immanent auditory object that possesses quality, sensory intensity, spatiality, and temporality. Its ontological status is clearly that of an object peculiar to hearing; it can not be located at all in environmental space; and it can be identified only as the objective counterpart of the auditory awareness of consciousness. These considerations characterize its ontological nature. Yet to extricate it entirely from the external sonority in which it is embedded is never really possible; if immanent sonority serves in the genesis of the outside world in epistemological theory or even in the developmental history of the individual, it has conversely evolved biologically and socioculturally from the larger environmental whole, with which it remains bound up in essentially all our experience and which it cannot fail to suggest constantly. Thus the quality, intensity, spatiality, and temporality of sound have a double aspect, and in addition to this they are not entirely separable from each other.

The quality of sonority in its immanent sense is remarkably diversified. Sound is euphonious or harsh, sustained or abrupt, reverberant, diffuse, vague, compact, thin, intrusive, clear, bright, sharp, or dull. As we can see, it is not simple to separate its spatiality and temporality from its quality. Many of its properties are also intersensory or heterosensory. Brightness, for example, like extensiveness or duration, is a property that resembles its counterpart in other sensory modalities even though it is specifically auditory; we may even say that in two or more of the modal manifestations of such an intersensory property there is a component which remains identical. Other immanent qualities of sound are heterosensory, and resemble in particular the qualities of touch. Sonorous roughness and sharpness, for example, seem to show that the ear has retained certain characteristics of its tactile precursors. Whatever the physical or biological explanations may be, it is obvious that even the specifically qualitative properties of sound are so various that they elude systematic classification and at once both challenge and defy the formative interests of art.

Of all the qualities of sonority, the special smoothness and defined pitch that belong to tone are probably the most distinctive and attractive; they have certainly been the most important for musical form and meaning. The significance of sustained tone contains the fundamental musical polarity of stimulating and soothing, either perfectly united, or—depending upon tone color and loudness—with the one or the other predominating. Pitch is connected with the periodicity of vibration of sources of sound, and thus to some extent with obvious physical characteristics such as the rigidity of self-sonorous materials, the slackness of strings, and regularity of shape in general, especially that of straight objects such as tubes and strings. Thus while quality in general contains a referential tendency as a key to the nature of the substance that produces it—whether wood or metal, for example—pitch in particular is a clue to length. This connection with measurement and with mathematics furnishes one of the reasons for the prominence of pitch in musical form and meaning; and it is a basis as well for many of the relationships of music to other fields of expression.

Comparable in importance to pitch are the consonant intervals and chords that are built on this property, which are forcibly called to attention by both the physical world and native human response. Whether rational intervals are adopted, approximated, or avoided, their distinctive quality almost inevitably gives them a fundamental role in music, and this is true even in a purely melodic vocal art, where musical instruments are of no influence and tonal fusion is essentially absent. The bewildering variety of sound is reduced to a manageable and largely rational complexity in the realm of pure and complex tones, which are amenable to systematic arrangement and detailed analysis into a number of defined attributes. But as more precisely controlled and graduated properties, these aspects of sound are more appropriately considered in connection with form rather than material.

Pitch is often found not as a dominant aspect of quality, or as one of its manifestations, but less independently and less con-spicuously, as a subordinate constituent of a more comprehensive whole. Then we would say that the quality of a sound had a certain pitch, not that its pitch was of a certain quality. In impulsive and percussive sounds, and generally in those of complex or irregular vibratory character, pitch can be reduced to a minimal ingredient, to bare perceptibility, so that its very presence is equivocal, or our feeling of definition can give way to a vague, diffuse, or approximate impression. Xylophones, *claves*, bells, gongs, cymbals, triangles, and drums produce sounds of this kind, in which pitch is only a minor or incidental feature of quality, and the same tendency can be observed in all sounds that have an extremely low or high pitch. The jew's-harp and bull-roarer, not to mention glissandos on the piano or harp, many singing styles, and speech in general, add still another type of indefiniteness in the form of pitch that is not constant, but often rapidly and unpredictably changing. Between noise and precise pitch there is a whole range of sound that gives the general impression of pitch.

In a large sense, loudness or auditory intensity is a special type of quality somewhat as pitch is; but it may be defined alternatively in its own right as a separate property of sound. It has, in fact, a close kinship with spatiality as well as with quality. Clearly the properties of sound may be defined according to various conceptual schemes; but the categories of quality, sensory intensity, spatiality, and duration have much to recommend them, especially as their generality permits us to establish equivalences between the senses.

Quantity is the most prominent aspect of the immanent spatiality of sound. A voluminous property seems to belong to sound in itself, but more accurately, this property, like every characteristic of sonority, is heard against a background of silence. The auditory musical field is always either filled or empty, completely and continuously overflowing with material, traversed by lines of sound, or flecked by occasional wisps or points. The experienced quantity of sonorous material is really relative to the size of its field or ground, and this framework in turn is established by the full deployment of the performing forces at the highest level of loudness that is utilized. Thus a solo voice has a smaller volume in a choral oratorio than it does in a madrigal because of the different sizes of the auditory fields established in the two cases. It is interesting that the voluminous property of sound is determined by time as well as by frequency constitution and intensity. A high-pitched tone or one of low intensity has a very small volume, but so does a tone of short duration. Similarly, frequencies that are widely spaced and low in loudness will produce an effect of emptiness and transparency, but so will short tones and prolonged silences. In pointlike serialism we often seem to see through the sounds to the silences upon which they are projected, an effect foreshadowed in Beethoven's late quartets by an open and fragmented style and by an extreme separation of registers. Extended passages for solo wind instrument, typically in a slow and continuous melodic style of narrow range, can also suggest large reaches of space and vast distances; the program music and opera of the 19th century is particularly favorable to this impression, since the large performing forces provide a setting of voluminous sonorities, and the representational content—an empty landscape, let us say, with a single shepherd—will reinforce the purely musical feeling. Sonorous volume clearly contains a referential tendency; it is closely allied to the volume of environmental sound accompanying it and to the size of the sources that produce both. The distinction in sound between castanets and a bass drum, for example, unmistakably combines the external difference in the volume of the instruments with the voluminous difference immanent to audition.

The immanent spatiality of sound includes also a property of position, which is manifested in pitch. By virtue of this characteristic, sounds, and particularly tones, appear at different positions in the auditory field and are designated as variously high and low. Pitch is therefore a spatial as well as a qualitative property. Unlike volume, however, which is intrinsically connected with environmental spatiality, the immanent position presented by pitch has only a suggestive tendency toward external reference, but almost no inherent connection with environmental location. High-pitched instruments are easily held up in the air like other small objects, while low-pitched ones, because of their size and weight, generally extend to the floor or must be rested on it; but tones are called high and low for a number of reasons, some of which have nothing to do with external location. External tones are in fact not variously high and low in environmental space to any significant extent. Probably the most important connections of pitch to environmental position are those of corporeal localization: of the sound and vibration of our own voice, and of the vibratory sensations accompanying the music we listen to, especially those communicated through the floor by low-pitched instruments.

A final rather elusive spatial property is a tendency toward motion, an intrusive or recessive character that certain sounds possess. Just as the color red seems to advance toward the observer and blue to withdraw, so the tone of an oboe seems to penetrate toward the listener and the tone of a flute or a French horn to recede. The property of approaching or receding is not simply qualitative; it has a dynamic nature; it is an incipient motion. But it is not motion in the full sense, for motion requires change, and thus the active role of temporality along with spatiality.

Change exists, of course, in the domain of immanent sonority, and it should be included in a complete description of musical material. Perceptibly discontinuous change will not give the impression of a single sound, but of two or several sounds, and while motion may be produced in this case also, as it is especially by discrete changes in the property of pitch, such motion will not be a primary type of manifestation, but one somewhat similar to the apparent visual motion that is produced by the successive images of the motion picture or by two alternating lights which conform to certain conditions in their spacing and their frequency of alternation. Continuous or periodic variation of the properties of sound will often play a considerable role in music—in the vibrato, for example, or in gliding vocal ornaments—but unless change is spatial it does not constitute motion. Thus motion will arise from changes in volume, pitch, or motional tendency. Changes in loudness can produce the impression of motion also, since they affect these spatial properties. Indeed the immanent qualitative and spatial properties of sound are so interconnected that qualitative change is often spatial and motion is always in some measure a qualitative change as well. Sound expands or shrinks, swoops and strides upward or downward, comes closer or departs. Needless to say, however, all the inherent spatial properties of sound are to be distinguished as belonging to immanent auditory objects from the spatial properties perceived in the external world, which are multisensory even when they are presented by hearing alone. The one may refer to the other, but for the most part, the autonomy of sound is striking. In the case of tone, it stands in sharp contrast to the normal external reference of the immanent presentations of vision and even to that of nontonal sound, although entoptic visual objects provide a parallel.

A similar distinction must be made with respect to temporality, although here, as in connection with quality, it is not made so easily. Sound is intrinsically temporal; it does not merely depend for its existence on the temporal continuity of consciousness the way stationary visual objects or concepts do, or even feelings and desires, but contains temporality as an inherent property—one that is constituted directly by the flow of consciousness and that consequently stands in the most intimate relation to it, being at once its product and the tangible image of its nature. Just as the spatiality of sound, however, in spite of its relationship to the multisensory or the scientific space of the external world, need not be embedded in or refer to this space, so the temporality of sound need not be set into connection with the everyday durational experience of outer events or with scientific time. Indeed the intrinsic spatial and temporal properties of sonority, as belonging to an immanent object of hearing, can be separated in principle and in fact even from the extensity and durational course of inner biological processes, and even from the corresponding properties of sensations of vibration, which are so intimately associated with sound.

As an external phenomenon, sound has the ontological nature of an auditory attribute of a multisensory object; this object (or event) is located in environmental or bodily space or both, and it has an origin outside our mind, either in corporeal activity or in some environmental source. Alternatively, external sound may appear as an object or event in its own right, with its own place of origin and pattern of location; but in this case, apart from associated vibratory and tactile sensations that are inconspicuous and at times altogether absent, it will be an essentially pure auditory object rather than a multisensory one. The two modes of externality are not easy to distinguish, but if we compare the sound of a bell to the sound of thunder, for example, even though both modes are present in both instances, the distinction between sound as an attribute of a multisensory object and sound as an object in its own right will become evident. Still we may speak with equal propriety of hearing a bell and of hearing the sound of a bell, and this is true in every case of external sound.

The immanent properties of quality, intensity, spatiality, and temporality remain those of external sound also, but added to them are new and literally spatial properties of location, size, and motion in environmental or bodily space. Within this second spatiality it is often difficult, as we have seen, to separate the source from the sound. Indeed the location of environmental sound is often identified with that of its source in spite of the great spatial differences between the two. But the source can generally be localized exactly, and its size and motion can be determined with equivalent accuracy. The spatial properties of the sound itself, however, can be described only vaguely at best, for its spatial characteristics are in fact extremely indefinite and at the same time we cannot benefit from the participation of vision. An external sound is not altogether shapeless, however, for in spite of its diffuseness, we hear it as having a more or less distinct place of origin. It is generally not possible to ignore this prominence that is perceived in the midst of its nebulous volume; we are really forced to attend to it in the case of a single, visible, and relatively nearby musical instrument that is situated in the open or in nonreverberant surroundings and that directs its sound largely toward the listener. Under these circumstances it becomes particularly difficult to separate our perception of the sound from that of the instrument. For through the diffuseness of the sound, the intense spot that is more distant than the rest now dominates our hearing almost exclusively. But this is obviously the spot at which hearing and the sense of vibration as well as vision will also localize the source of the sound, so that the simultaneous perception of both sound and source is almost unavoidable and clearly is a characteristic of many musical styles, especially in connection with virtuosity, vocal music, and opera.

Indeed although sound as an immanent auditory object is the primary material of music, voices and instruments are certainly a second kind of material, and they are incomparably more important than external sound in itself. This is true literally: not of audible qualities as the expression of personalities or as aspects or natural properties of external objects, but of singers and instruments themselves, as environmental objects apprehended through multisensory perception in general. In a sense, the performing media are often the most fundamental kind of musical material, taking precedence even over sound as an immanent object of audition, which remains primary only from a specifically aesthetic point of view that excludes contextual significance. Decisive evidence for this view of material exists in the selection of musical instruments for reasons other than those of sonorous quality. They may be chosen, of course, for expressive values that do not reside in the sound they produce, notably to amplify or disguise the voice, or to extend or accentuate bodily activity; clappers and stamping tubes, for example, will reinforce and thus enhance kinesthetic and rhythmic expression. But these are sources of meaning rather than instances of a distinct type of musical material. In contrast, it is evidence of the independent importance of instruments that a drum head, for example, may be made of the skin of a sacred animal, or a rattle of seeds that are connected with fertility. The shell trumpet similarly becomes an instrument, or the human bone a flute, because of what it is as a material object. In a comparable way, the shaman is suited to his vocation not because of the sonorous quality of his voice, but because of his superior intelligence and his power to communicate with spirits.

The importance of musical instruments as objects is particularly obvious in connection with ritual and ceremonial function. In nonliterate societies drums may be housed in special enclosures and carefully tended or propitiated according to prescribed procedures, while in higher cultures, religious and ceremonial instruments such as horns or trumpets are reverently wrapped and stored in a way that is again prescribed and symbolic. This concern with the instrument as an object, however, and with the material of which it is made, by no means excludes a concern with its sound as well; indeed the two act in natural conjunction, although we must remember that the value of sound is not to be sought in any abstractly conceived aesthetic standard of beauty. Still more, the sound given forth by a material is often felt to possess a peculiar affinity with the nature of the material that goes far beyond the significance of its visual and tactile qualities. This is a factor that is particularly important in bells or gongs or other sonorous objects, where the instrument vibrates essentially as a whole and its material is not under tension. The interest in material can be expressed in the classification of instruments, as it was very systematically in ancient China, for example, or has been to a certain extent in the West, where we speak, with some imprecision, of woodwinds and brass and strings.

It is an extension of the interest in instruments as such that because of a symbolic intention they are at times given particular colors or shapes which have a significance in themselves. Decorative carving or painting can play a similar role, although at times it is intended purely as visual ornamentation. String instruments may be shaped to resemble boats or funeral, barges, or their peg boxes may be turned into carved heads. Drum heads frequently bear elaborate designs. The bull-roarer may be painted red or carved to resemble a fish. Sexual connotations are particulary frequent: the gourd rattle suggests the womb, the flute will have phallic significance, slit drums and mortars with their sticks and pestles are connected with the vulva and the penis, and their playing action with sexual intercourse. Instrumental symbolism is certainly suggested by the form an instrument assumes as a natural consequence of function; it may even be suggested by the character of the tone or sound; but it testifies in any event to a concern with instruments that clearly goes beyond functional serviceability and sonorous quality.

The significance of musical instruments is culturally determined, and it is based on the availability of natural materials, on the general value and meaning of these materials, and on the meaning of particular shapes or colors. Even if an instrument is adopted by a society or a social class as the result of external influence, the significance it assumes will be an outcome of culture—in this case a product of the interaction of two groups. Generally also it is the ritual significance of a natural material or a natural object as such, even if this significance is in its turn produced or partially produced by its sonorous capacities, that is responsible along with sonority, or even apart from sonority, for its musical use. But the significance that acts as a cause need not be ritual in every case, it can equally well be cultural in some other sense—as symbolic of an admired practice of a foreign society, for example, or of a privileged class.

59

Musical utility and artistic purpose may play a role also; but it is only when a more specifically aesthetic interest begins to replace ceremonial and social motivation that sonority itself comes to outweigh the meaning of the instrument as such. Yet it would be a mistake, except perhaps in the case of electronic equipment or loudspeakers, to discount the visual and tactile values of instruments in musical experience of every kind, especially as far as the performer is concerned. It is a natural tendency to dwell on the sensuous shape of curved surfaces or purflings, or the sheen and finish of metal and wood, and to take delight in these properties especially when they are so closely associated with responsiveness and beauty of sound. The interest in ornamentation—in carving or marquetry or the painting of designs or depictions on keyboard instruments, for example—has in part the same motivation. Thus for a great variety of causes, musical instruments as such, and their sensory appeal apart from sonority, are often an important part of music, both as a kind of immediate context of the tones they produce and even more intrinsically, as a fundamental kind of musical material.

With singers and instruments as musical material, environmental location also becomes a factor in music, although to be sure not in the practical sense of the position of external objects that may serve or hinder us in our everyday pursuits, but only because location is now a feature of the special world of artistic formulation, even though the spatial aspect of musical form may at the same time remain a literal manifestation of social patterns of relationship. Thus the choreographic patterns of a group dance or stylized drama may factually embody social distinctions or functions, but they are simultaneously part of artistic formativity, which is what serves to mark them off from the positional relationships between human beings and environmental objects in general. As far as form is concerned, the arrangement and interplay of instruments has played an important role even in the more autonomous music of the West, in respect of both the varied character of their sounds and their contrasted physical positions. There are styles such as those of the Baroque concerto, the opera buffa ensemble, or the early

Neoclassicism of Stravinsky, in which the composer conceives his music and the listener hears it as consisting to a surprising extent of a juxtaposition and interplay of performers and instruments. These are heard as distinct physical entities with distinct locations relative to one another and to the listener. To be sure, there are other styles, such as we find in Impressionism, for example, in which the instruments as multisensory objects play very little part in the conception and apprehension of the music, and in which even the instrumental tone colors are not heard as the qualities of sounding objects in the external world. In any event, the material of music clearly comprises sound as an immanent object as well as sound producers; instruments easily become instrumentalities; they are manipulated not in their own right, but to yield sounds that are arranged on the basis of their intrinsic auditory properties. Indeed the typically musical properties of the resultant configurations have no environmental counterpart at all, but can be accounted for only as the immanent product of the constructive activities of consciousness. An awareness of instruments is nevertheless part of the musical conception and perception of their sound, and even when our attention is given to musical configurations, the awareness of instruments does not disappear, but instead is extended to include a consciousness of the motions of performance and the mechanical manipulation by which these configurations are produced. There is in fact a potential conflict between the two aspects of material; they are in general found together, but to some extent they tend to exclude or inhibit one another. Many people are so concerned with performance that they have no adequate perception of the music itself.

The features of environmental sound are found essentially unchanged in sound we produce ourselves—by speaking, singing, whistling, clapping, or playing a musical instrument. Even in the case of our own voice, or of whistling, we are able to localize the source of sound quite well without the aid of vision, and to form some idea of its size and of whatever motion it may have. Within the body itself, various resonances give the sound its own greater extension and diversity of location, and these are

61

perceived through vibratory sensations as well as auditory ones; in fact environmental sounds also set up similiar kinds of diversified locational patterns within the body. In sound we produce ourselves, we are again able to separate from the source, however vaguely, a spatial pattern set up by the projection of the sound that spreads out, first within the body and then outside it, to various extents in various directions. This pattern is controlled to some degree by our intentions and by the nature of the enclosed or open space in which we find ourselves. Yet sound we produce ourselves is not really equivalent to environmental sound; it involves us even at this stage of our inquiry in the nature of musical objectivity and calls into question the whole notion of the formation of material as a fundamental conception of musical philosophy. For it is restrictive to regard sound of this type simply as material that is formed. Instead we are confronted with the larger issues of performance and participation, with music as a social activity rather than an object that presents itself to consciousness or sustains itself independently. Still more importantly, music contains something of this quality of activity in its very nature, as perceived or projected, even apart from actual performance and participation. How, then, are we able to regard sound as material to be formed, as we would in the case of paint or clay or stone or wood? Is not such a view fundamentally inapplicable to music? Or at any rate applicable only to the special variety of music found in recent Western history and manifested as works of art? Perhaps we are proceeding on the basis of an equation between music and visual art that has limited cultural validity.

There can be no denying the force of these objections. Yet they can be met by an extension and a qualification of the concepts of material and form and meaning, which will be an intrinsic part of our effort in what follows. The material we form as participants in music, for example, is our own activity of performance and bodily motion; the productive process is thus comparable not simply to the shaping of sonority, but to formative endeavor in the composite musical arts such as dance or song, although the nature of the resultant form and objectivity remains to be specified. It may be said in addition, that no other conceptual scheme represents a satisfactory alternative to the procedure of modifying and redefining the meaning of the artistic categories we have chosen; material, form, and meaning, properly understood, appear to provide a framework for the most fundamental comprehension we can secure of the nature of music.

The three different modes of existence that we have defined for sound—as immanent, as an aspect of an external object or event, and as an external object in its own right—are obviously closely interrelated in many ways. They are really all present simultaneously in an actual musical performance, and they are present in imaged form in an imagined performance or in the conception of the musical work of art. One or the other may predominate, depending on whether the experience in question is actual or imagined, on the type of instruments or mode of vocal production that is employed, and on the cultural context of the music and the kind of meaning it has. Yet we may describe certain tendencies or constant features of the interrelationship. It is evident above all that music is fundamentally and essentially an immanent object. But this basic characteristic is grounded in an inherent tendency of musical material itself. Tone in particular is largely independent of the perception of its source, and musical form and meaning clearly reinforce this independence by adding to it a new level of interest. Music brings into being a higher world of experience, and we can in general distinguish artistic structure and meaning from the elemental form and character of sonority that they are built upon.

On the other hand, we must characterize hearing biologically as a distance sense. Sounds are representative of our environment and an instrument of our adaptation. If the nature of tone becomes the first step in freeing them from this function, the relatively poor powers of unaided hearing in respect of localization and the determination of size and shape continue the process of detachment. Yet what happens to the capacity of binaural hearing as a medium of external perception? Where are the cues to the location and spatial properties of environmental objects? To the temporal persistence of their activity? To their very nature and constitution? These cues must be neglected by the special interests of artistic perception; they are subordinated or set aside in the new and different purposes of music. But it is obvious that they are in some form still present; the properties of immanent auditory objects must reflect in some way the properties of external ones; the immanent character of sonority must derive at least in part from the larger external whole in which the acoustic agitation has its setting.

Noise especially, as opposed to tone, is perceived as representative of an external source and its activity. To some degree the external basis of sonorous character is purely associative; the thinness of a violin tone, for example, is due to a slight extent to the thinness of the string that produces it, but only by association rather than as a result. The volume of a low tone, on the other hand, is a true perceptual index of the large size of a bass instrument. And in the case of noise, we tend altogether to hear a sounding object rather than immanent sound itself, so that the character of the noise becomes a part or a representation of the character of the object or occurrence. To be sure, we also know at once that an oboe is the source of the tone it produces, but musical sounds, as we have emphasized, are quite susceptible of being heard in themselves. both externally as well as immanently; their sources have a tendency to recede in perception. This is one of the peculiar problems involved in using noise as musical material, for the source possesses a prominence that works against the detachment of art. Noise that is electronically synthesized or transformed is a still more problematic material, for we are confronted visually with a loudspeaker or with no actual or conformable source at all to be identified or located; an automatic expectation is provoked but disappointed.

Sounds between noise and tone with respect to the tendency toward periodicity of their vibrations and the relative simplicity of this periodicity (with sinusoidal form taken as the basis of simplicity) would seem to be correspondingly intermediate also in their tendency toward externality or immanence. This is a matter, however, that is doubtless less dependent upon the type of source than upon the whole nature of music as determined by the culture, which comprises also the conception of sound itself. Yet the interrelationship of types of objectivity remains a rule rather than an exception, and must be considered an intrinsically conspicuous feature of hearing and music. Thus a sound that is voluminous, for example, has simultaneously an immanent property of size, an extensiveness in external space (to some extent corporeal as well as environmental), and a representative function in respect of its large source. Indeed to these three kinds of objectivity we must add a characteristic fusion of spatiality with temporality and quality, for extensiveness demands a certain minimal duration (which can be taken to characterize all three objective modes) and it is certainly a qualitative property (at least in its immanent aspect) as well as a spatial one. Similarly the aggressive or recessive tendency of certain sounds is a property that is not only simultaneously external and immanent with regard to spatiality, but also simultaneously spatial and qualitative; we cannot say that the tone of an oboe is penetrating simply because it advanced into us or simply because it has a particular quality that is best described in these terms; rather both characterizations are equally accurate, just as the recessive and spreading diffuseness of the sound of a French horn is both a specifically spatial property (in an external as well as an immanent sense) and a purely qualitative one. Other properties of sound reveal the same complex constitution. Compactness or density is a characteristic example: it is both qualitative and spatial, both immanent and external, a property of both external sound and its source. Indeed as an acoustic property of an idiophonic instrument it is a valuable guide to the nature of the physical material from which the instrument is made.

The significance of the quality of sound as a determinant of its externality is extended by the realm of intersensory and heterosensory qualities. A sound that is bright, for example, will have a stronger tendency toward external reference because of the suggested association with vision. One that is rough will similarly suggest the cooperation of our sense of touch. Now multisensory objects are peculiarly involved with an external world, for the joint action of the senses, and the concordance of their separate immanent objects, is more clearly explained as a

65

result of an external situation and our adjustment to it than as the means by which we constitute this situation. To be sure, it is still the operation of consciousness that gives us our external world, but this projective process is not so readily isolated for inspection as it is within a single sense modality. The intersensory and heterosensory properties of sonorjty consequently tend to point to the external world of common-sense experience rather than only to the immanent, specifically musical world of purely auditory qualities; they point to the objects of body-mind rather than to those of mind alone. But this is no more than a tendency. The visual ideas connected with the tone of a trumpet are present by association in any event; the intermodal attribute of brightness may reinforce them; in the case of full synesthesia it may produce the visual image of a shining trumpet; but neither the ideas or the image will bear necessarily on an actual trumpet in environmental space that is producing the tone we hear; indeed they may equally well be ideas or impressions of bright light or colors with no reference to environmental objects of any kind. The heteromodal properties of hearing are equally indecisive in the establishment of externality. There is a sense in which the auditory properties of roughness or sharpness may be explained by the fact that the evolutionary ancestors of the ear were tactile organs; but there can be little doubt that they are now properly auditory qualities and that whatever activity of our tactual sensitivity they may suggest will by no means necessarily serve to set up an external object responsible for the sound we hear. The ear is also capable of actual tactile sensations, but in the feeling of vibration or pain it conveys in response to intense sounds it no longer acts as a distance sense; the sensations are in the ear itself and obviously can have no relevance to our awareness of a distant source of sound.

Much more significant for the establishment of externality is the fact that sound is generally accompanied by sensations of vibration; these are not often separated from sonority in perception or distinguished from it as a component of musical material. The vibratory sense is not only a local sense acting within and on the surface of the body, but a distance sense also, so that it can cooperate with hearing in the constitution of an external source of sound. But here we are dealing in fact with multisensory experience, and indeed, with such experience as a normal feature of what seems to be purely auditory perception. This is true also, of course, of the kinesthesis connected with head movements, and it directs our attention to the subtle nature of multisensory perception.

A purely auditory perception of external objects is more an abstraction than an actuality; even when we seek to provide the artificial conditions that are prerequisite, it remains multisensory at least by implication and imagery. But we have already seen, in any event, that the external sounds of instruments and performers can become musical material along with immanent auditory objects. They are after all not the sounds of everyday experience, and they are obviously amenable to assuming patterns which add to the dimensions of immanent sound the additional ones of location and visual qualities. Furthermore they are always accompanied by, and rest on, the objects immanent to each separate sensory modality, and they can themselves be regarded as phenomenal rather than empirical objects. In fact, the detachment from everyday experience that is a precondition of artistic material consists not only in the use and significance of the material but essentially in viewing it as constituted by consciousness rather than as as independent reality. The conventions and restrictions and dimensions of form are a by-product of this perspective. Now it is precisely external multisensory objects that act as the material for the compound varieties of music: song, dance, dance-song, and opera. And a reliance on external material is not only equally possible for purely instrumental music but in fact the rule rather than the exception.

But externality, even as phenomenal rather than independently real, is a feature more of artistic material than of artistic formations. With the creation of form and then again with the creation of works of art a fundamental kind of change takes place: a shift toward immanence, which is caused by the appearance of novel and radically different types of object—we may perhaps speak of second- and third-order objects; for the artistic object, whether literally aesthetic or aesthetic only in imagery or conception, is composed most essentially of properties that exist only by virtue of the intentionality of the creator or perceiver, however much they may appear to have an independent external existence. Yet in music, and particularly in sonorous material itself, there remains a marked distinction between external and immanent objectivity. The various types of sound tend toward the one or the other, and this is true even of sound that is merely imagined, for the subordination of externality is not an automatic concomitant of the absence of a physical source. We have mentioned that different attitudes are the chief determinant of whether the experience of sonority is directed more strongly outward or inward; they may even produce a complete obliviousness of the one or the other constituent tendency, although both phases are usually present in varying amounts. These attitudes are dependent upon personality and momentary disposition and are more generally encouraged by certain styles and cultures. But within this, the dimension that is defined by the polarity of noise and tone may very well be the most·significant one. An external or immanent tendency here is founded upon the adaptive value of sound, for irregularity and complex constitution provide us with more information about the properties and location of environmental objects than do perfect periodicity and sinusoidal variation. The biological importance of localization would imply that reverberation is also a relevant factor, for our ability to locate objects by hearing decreases markedly in reverberant surroundings (and quite in step with this, it would seem, we are safer indoors than out from such dangers as wild animals and automobiles). Thus even though reverberant sounds provide a certain kind of environmental information, they should tend on the whole toward immanence. The opposite is true in the case of echoes, which create pseudo-sources, or of standing waves, which create external points of concentrated intensity that are perceptible if we move about (although the "externality" of such points seems to be as much inside our head as outside). Apart from reverberation, noise tends toward externality and tone toward immanence, and this difference is reflected on a smaller scale in the contrast between complex and pure tone. It follows from this that the tone of an instrument will shift noticeably toward immanence if its transient components are absent (an effect that can be observed if only the periodic components of a tone are assembled electronically). Noises of articulation or bowing, for example, not only help locate a source of sound, but also are vital in identifying the nature of the source. It may be true, in addition, that tones of richer quality—the low register of the oboe as contrasted with the high register of the flute—have a stronger tendency toward externality; certainly a varied splay of frequencies greatly assists localization.

We can adduce other factors—again largely with their basis in localization—that are more obvious in their effect than either reverberation or complexities of constitution. A single source, somewhat paradoxically, will tend more toward externality than a group sounding simultaneously, for a single source can be located more easily and more accurately than a group. On the other hand, we tend to hear electronically reproduced sound as immanent, especially in monophonic reproduction, and the same is true of invisible or imagined sources; for the elimination of vision deprives localization and identification of most of their precision and reliability. It is in fact the relatively poor capacity of the ear to locate sources of sound, even if it is aided by head movements and vibration, that is partly responsible for the peculiar prominence of immanent auditory objects, which have no location in environmental space and no really conformable counterpart in empirical experience or physical science.

The remarkable control we may exercise in the determination of the mode of existence of sound can be experienced when we listen to a choral group singing in unison. Immanent and external perception will coexist in some established condition of relative prominence. But we have only to fix our attention on a particular singer by looking at him intently and trying to hear him individually, and as though magically his voice will suddenly emerge from the sound of the group and stand forth distinctly audible in itself. At the same time, it will assume a pronounced externality. It is not only vision but also imperceptible head movements that take part in the localization process. But in any event, the localization carries with it in a striking and instructive way an increase in the perceived intensity of the sound—indeed it creates a type of existence for the individual voice that it did not possess initially. The experience—which could be duplicated with a group of instruments in place of singers—illustrates vividly the difference between perception that is purely or essentially auditory and a more biological activity that involves intersensory cooperation.

In the light of our general considerations, then, we can say that the solo voice has a pronounced externality, especially in speaking rather than singing. Speech involves impulsive and nonperiodic sounds to a great extent, and it is specifically representative of the definite individuality and extreme otherness of a human being distinct from ourselves. These factors recede somewhat in the case of song, and they are contradicted by the peculiarly aesthetic values of defined pitch, but an individual singer remains an object that insists on an external status. Choral music tends much more toward immanence, for the sound of a chorus is much more generalized: it does not have a specific location and it lacks the defined otherness of a single performer. Our own voice, or the sound of a chorus in which we participate, both are heard more readily than we might expect as external rather than immanent objects, but their externality now is that of sound as a separate object rather than as a manifestation of performers or their vocal endowment.

A single instrument is heard or imagined very much as the voice of an individual. The degree of externality will of course vary with the instrument being considered, just as it will vary with the quality of the human voice; and again, the sound of a group of instruments to which we listen or in which we perform has somewhat less externality than the corresponding solo instances, although when the individuality of each instrument in the ensemble is pronounced, because of low reverberation or differences in tone color, the tendency toward externality is increased.

Electronically originated tone is at the furthest remove from nature; it can easily be freed from transient components and from irregular cycle-to-cycle changes. Those that are sinusoidal, mathematically the simples, are actually the most artificial of all. But the absence of any purely acoustic source for all electronic tones, whether they are artificially abstract in structure or attempted duplications of the sounds of conventional instruments, is emphasized rather than compensated for by the unvarying impersonality, if not the invisibility, of a loudspeaker. Such tones tend to become immanent auditory objects, a tendency at its height in the case of pure tones, the immanence of which is anticipated by the relatively pure tones of instruments like the flute.

Noise that is electronically originated or manipulated, on the other hand, is similar to natural complex tones in its outward tendency. But the absence of a true acoustic source gives rise to a curious effect in the evocation of attention, for noise and abrupt sounds are automatically responded to as signs of activity and significant environmental events rather than for their inherent formal properties or sensuous attractiveness. Thus when we can find no source that gives this kind of meaning to such sounds, and when we cannot even imagine the nature of a possible acoustic source, we are subject to a strange frustration. We are forced back upon immanent objects and intrinsic properties, but at the same time we attend to our response itself and are unable to suppress the spontaneous suggestion of environmental objects and occurrences and the insistent demand that we identify and locate them. This problematical situation colors the whole character of music based on electronically reproduced noise.

Electronically generated or altered sound that does not resemble the sound of the voice or of known instruments obviously represents an extreme kind of musical material because of the absence of an actual or imaginable acoustic source; but within this field there can be found the polar contrast of pure tone and artificial noise (including so-called white noise, which is a more accurately defined opposite of pure tone). Pure tone is the ultimate distillation of musical material: free from any reference to empirical objects and almost entirely lacking any externality of its own, it exists almost exclusively as an object immanent to hearing. Nontonal sound produced electronically that is either unfamiliar or altered beyond recognition is its logical complement, and understandably a manifestation coincident in time, for instead of the minimum it possesses the maximum possible degree of externality and representational force, but it thwarts the perceptual reaction it provokes because of the factual absence of an acoustic source; thus in place of immanence and abstraction it contains a peculiar fusion of concreteness and abstraction.

The structural and significative potentialities of both these extreme varieties of artificial material are limited. This is true of noise because it is restricted in its susceptibility to types of order and in its capacity to provoke differentiated responses; nor does it compensate for this restriction with the meaning it could acquire through external reference. Pure tone similarly lacks the basis of a traditional acoustic instrument, and it is also limited by its restriction to a single frequency. The tone produced by an acoustic instrument is really part of a concrete complex that has a natural origin in the development within a culture of the sonorous capabilities of a physical device or in the similar development of a mode of singing; even when tone does not stand for the whole object or complex from which it is abstracted, it possesses a distinct significance or character because this concrete specificity adheres to it and endows it with a meaningful quality that can be applied to formal and expressive purposes. Pure tone lacks such potentiality for form and meaning. It also lacks the potentiality that is possessed by abstract complex tones, for partial frequencies produce intrinsic tonal properties such as timbre and the possibility of consonance, and these can serve as the basis of specifically musical structure and meaning. In the case of pure tone, however, intervallic quality is greatly weakened and tone color entirely absent.

Electronically originated sound is a striking example of the historical variability of musical material, which thus runs the scale—if we arrange the types logically—from noise to speech to tone and then to pure tone, manipulated speech, and synthetic noise: an increasing distillation to the point of complete

72

abstraction from acoustic sources, followed by a partial return with simulated noise. The creative freedom of change that selects the material of music is responsible for the significant variation within the larger areas of instrumental media and general mode of deployment of the voice; but it is striking here as elsewhere that with respect to these larger areas of possibility, history or human invention seems to proceed through the whole series of logically predictable forms.

Apart from the question of the different tendencies of various sonorities toward immanent or external objectivity, musical instruments manifest an inexhaustible variety in the quality, intensity, spatiality, and temporality of their sounds. The sonorous materials of a given cultural setting or social class, however, may be relatively restricted in their range and diversity, depending, above all, on the number and the variety of the musical functions and genres that exist. The characteristic sound palette of the culture or class will obviously be a fundamental determinant of the nature of its music, and will reveal, among other things, its relations and affinities to other cultures or classes, the influences that have acted on it, and the degree of continuity and change in its history. We may even learn something of the basic nature and complexion of the culture, of its moral character, and of its philosophic and religious outlook. Very much the same is true of vocal sounds, which are as variable as those of instruments; they can similarly range from one or a few approved qualities and levels of intensity and degrees of abruptness or prolongation to the astonishing variety found in the formalized roles of Chinese and Japanese musical drama. In societies throughout the world, from tribal groups to advanced cultures, the voice is subjected to every conceivable type of stylization, from unusual suppressions and distributions of corporeal resonance, through extreme degrees of loudness and rapid or disjunctive changes in quality, to the use of voice masks and ventriloquism and the imitation of the sounds of nature and animals.

As opposed to the character of individual types of musical material, the overall character of the material aspect of a work of music in its entirety is still more strongly dependent upon historical and cultural and even personal selective and formative forces. The traditions specific to social class and function and to musical genre are of decisive influence. At the same time, the overall sonorous character of music is correspondingly still less amenable than individual sonorities to schemes of classification and analysis. It can be considered as representing an ideal of sonority, and it depends, objectively speaking, not only on the material components of music but also on the details of its formal and expressive features. It will be realized through a selection of particular instruments, the mode of musical performance, the acoustic factors of reverberation and resonance, the properties of simultaneous sonority in respect of euphony, harshness, or blending, and even the relative interest or lack of interest in many of the properties of sonority altogether. The total sonority, nevertheless, is composed of overall quality, intensity, spatiality, and temporality, and manifests again a tendency toward externality of either type or toward immanence. Vibratory sensations obviously will make an important contribution. An emphasis upon the externality of sounds as properties of their sources, together with the precise localization of the sources that is facilitated by nonreverberant surroundings, will encourage the individuality of the constituents of simultaneous sonorities and produce an overall quality that is variegated rather than fused or homogeneous. The number and diversity of the factors entering into this comprehensive aspect of music make its potentiality for variety endless. Even the most casual comparisons of different manifestations of music with repsect to their overall sonority—of the Prelude to *Tristan und Isolde,* a medieval motet, a *gamelan* orchestra, a mass of *Palestrina,* Impressionist piano pieces—will reveal the incredible range of the material character of music.

We have been very little concerned in our present discussion with the question of meaning, which for the most part will be considered subsequently, but apart from instruments themselves, it is obvious that the overall sonority or texture of music, as well as the various individual sonorities of instruments and voices, will possess both a meaning and a fundamental formal aspect. Within this meaning, two interacting or fused phases can be distinguished: an immediate component, which is one of both biologically determined and culturally conditioned hearing, and a conceptual component, which involves basic notions of the nature of sound and tone and of musical experience. An ideal of sound is thus connected with the material of music as a fundamental determining factor that belongs to form in its most generally defining sense; and it often comprises explicit theoretical conceptions of the ontological nature of sound or tone and of the type of beauty or sensible quality that will correspond to or realize this nature.

Perhaps the most fundamental of the larger conceptions associated with sonority are those of animism, mathematics, and physics. In the animistic conception, sound of whatever kind is regarded as the voice of ancestors, divinities, or spirits, with a speaker or singer possessed by the supernatural being, or a performer who elicits the voice from an instrument. Such a conception of sound was almost certainly part of the musical outlook of prehistoric societies, as it has been of the beliefs of tribal societies of more recent times. That it underlies and accounts for many of the structural, significative, and functional features of the music of ritual and ceremony cannot be doubted. The magical efficacy of sound, for example, is clearly connected with its supernatural origin and status. The implications of an animistic conception for the ontological, local, and qualitative characteristics of sound are of obvious importance. An external source which can be located only vaguely or not at all is characteristic, and this adds a second and special type of externality to the location of the instrument, which may be the dwelling place of the spirit, or to the voice of the medium. The sound of the bull-roarer, mysteriously changing and of indeterminate location, is peculiarly suited to meet these demands. The human voice may call ventriloquism to its aid, and is capable of any imaginable transformation in quality.

In the mathematical conception of musical material—which applies specifically to tone rather than to sound in general—tone is considered to be the sonorous manifestation or embodiment of number, and tonal intervals the corresponding embodiment of numerical relationships. In the form this conception assumed from Greek antiquity to the Renaissance and beyond, the numbers were integers and the ratios relationships of integers, consonance, both as a rational property and a perceived one, depending upon simplicity. As a corollary, the fundamental relationships were derived from the first four integers, or in the Renaissance from the first six. This attachment of number and sense was regarded by Aristotle as indissoluble and inherent, while in the Platonic outlook number was the essential and sense incidental. But sound and audibility were in no instance the dominant component. Tone and music were accordingly known by reason, of which number and ratio were the exemplary objects; sonority, perception, and sensory pleasure were characteristically no more than means to the ends of abstraction and identity. The mathematical conception of tone was common to the Pythagorean, Platonic, and Aristotelian traditions, and remained the dominant view in the Middle Ages. To be sure, it admitted a certain amount of variety; the important treatises of Ptolemy and Boethius, for example, emphasized the cooperation of hearing and reason in the determination of tonal relationships; and they recognized a basic connection, grounded in number, between tone and the spatial dimension of length, and thus between music and geometry and astronomy. But a fundamentally different approach to tone—an appeal to hearing and to an innate auditory and vocal sense of tonal relationships—is found only in the subordinate tradition of Aristoxenus and Theophrastus, which discards mathematics as irrelevant.

A mathematical comprehension of tone is obviously favorable to the development of musical systems, which are conceived in the same fashion. Scale structure accordingly finds its first theoretical foundation in the Pythagorean consonances and their interrelationship. The connection of practice to a mathematical theory cannot be so readily determined, particularly before the use of musical notation became established. It is certain that the Aristoxenian tradition gave a better account of ancient practice than the Pythagorean, for it took musical experience rather than number as its point of departure in both melody and rhythm. And while plainsong seems to be based on a conception of tone as a useful and even divinely bestowed sensory pleasure, the dominant trend of medieval polyphony can quite justly be regarded as a counterpart of a mathematical theory of musical material. The simultaneous intervallic combinations of polyphony are based on the Pythagorean consonances, which are often presented in a rather static and individualized way. They are at times sounded together in apparent disregard of euphony, and they are propelled in their succession more by melodic forces than by "chordal progression." Similarly, the abstract and logical rigidity of modal rhythm and the speculative complexity of proportional rhythm and isorhythmic structure are consequences of a mathematical outlook rather than of an interest in auditory pleasure or kinesthesis.

Although the physical conception of material, like the animistic, applies to sound in general, it has been directed chiefly to tone, which more and more was understood to be complex in constitution. This conception is connected closely with the voice and with hearing, and thus with expression and sensation, rather than with number. It makes its appearance in the Renaissance, when it exists as a counterweight and a complement of the mathematical attitude, somewhat as a belated reconciliation of the old opposition of Aristoxenians and Pythagoreans. During the 17th and 18th centuries the discovery of overtones becomes an increasingly important factor of the physical conception, and leads to an emphasis on hearing as well as number in the foundation of consonance. Physics dominates mathematics in the powerful partnership of the two that seeks to control the domain of musical theory. The practical consequences of this outlook, like its systematic implications, are vast and ramified, extending from affective vocal expression that was quickly copied by instruments, to the important deployment of dynamics, timbre, and harmonic texture that become dominant features of 19th-century music.

A mathematical conception of tone, although not one based on whole-number ratios, again underlies the serial music of the 20th century, both in its systematic and its practical aspects. But this is a conception with a new breadth, and capable of encompassing not only relationships of pitch and rhythm, but also tone color, polyphonic texture, and dynamics—properties that previously were regarded as qualitative and physical in nature. Somewhat afterward, a physical view of sound becomes prominent also, along with the use of electronic amplification and the electronic generation of tone. Vocal expressiveness is not now a dominant concern, however, but rather the objective possibilities and scope of sonorous material as such, which encompasses modified and artificial types of noise, bands of frequency, and abstract wave shapes.

Clearly the large areas of animistic, mathematical, and physical conceptions do not in themselves exhaust the fecundity of history, for they contain graduations and subordinate types that are almost inexhaustible. The specific tonal ideal of Romanticism, for example, is a distinctive variety of the physical conception, which it turns toward the metaphysical largely by subordinating or eliminating the empirical externality of instruments. It is best considered, more accurately, to be a type of conception in its own right, a fourth or metaphysical type, which really fuses elements drawn from the three others with those freshly created by a new outlook.

It is not the case, however, that conceptions of the nature of sound automatically correspond to tendencies in sound itself; externality and immanence, overwhelming loudness or near-inaudibility, extreme rapidity or diaphanous quality—all are not necessarily counterparts in sonority of particular conceptions. The connection of practice and idea is certainly characteristic of a given manifestation of music, but it proceeds as much through a historically and culturally responsive freedom of association as it does in accordance with principle.

Our consideration of musical material has almost entirely excluded questions of form and meaning in the interest of distinguishing more clearly the various characteristics of material in its own right. While it is obvious that the quality, intensity, spatiality, temporality, ontological nature, and conception of sonority are already elementary aspects of musical structure and meaning, they are yet the most primary determinants of material that can be identified; they stand at the inception of the creative process that informs matter, and we can with justification call them prestructural or presignificative. They are nevertheless the foundation of the more sophisticated and properly formal and meaningful features of music, which will be examined presently. Even at this point, however, we are able to recognize something of the complexity of our problem, especially since musical form and meaning—like the selection and primary determination of sonority itself—will also vary with time and place and social group. The variation need not be synchronous with changes in material, of course; it can be much more rapid although hardly slower. In any event, music is clearly a multidimensional or multilayered phenomenon rather than a simple one; we cannot speak of a single definable course of change, but even apart from the interacting simultaneity of different cultures and social strata, we must deal within each type of music with a historical complex the components of which change at different rates but not without affecting one another or the properties of the whole; these range from the aspects of musical material and how they are conceived, through structure, significance, symbolism, and style, to the closely interrelated constituents of language, dance, and drama, the variously associated expressions and institutions of the cultural context, and the functions and philosophy and technical conceptions of the musical totality. If historical change is so deeply motivated, if its comprehensiveness and complexity comprise even the conception of sound or tone itself, and even the unconscious presuppositions and larger background forces that shape the whole outlook of a culture, our question concerning the nature of music can find no simple answer in the surface characteristics of a single musical style.

# CHAPTER 3

# Form

It is apparent that art arises through a process of forming material; but how this takes place, and the nature of the resultant form, are not easily understood. The very act of perception, or of the selection of material with perception in view, is inescapably formative; it is the form of an object that enables us to see it as an instance of a concept and thus to know it; even if we recognize its material, what we grasp is always some formal aspect of this material that serves to define it. Perception and knowledge are inherently abstractive in this way, and form stands allied to reason as matter does to sense. Thus we have seen that musical material is never really devoid of form; sonority can exist only with a particular quality, some degree of intensity, a certain extensive property, a quantitative relationship to the auditory field as a whole, and some measure of duration; it will also generally manifest a location. It is reasonable to expect, then, that properly artistic form will in some way be related to the formal characteristics of the material on which it is based. One approach to our problem is suggested by the role that premeditation and analytical thought play in creative activity. If sonority is not an undefined, malleable substance that is directly subjected without principle or guide to formativity—and this would obviously represent a very naive view of art—the artist may be thought to proceed by separating the dimensions found most amenable or suitable.

Now in the formative process of music, tone has been the most prominent substantive quality, and its attributes of duration and pitch the outstanding dimensions of structure; these are indeed justly considered the time and space of music. Their importance as coordinates of the musical field is doubtless due to the expressive range and force and to the precision they possess because they are attributes of tone in particular. They can be dealt with objectively, while the other attributes of sonority—which resist quantitative distinctions and are strongly influenced by labile subjective factors—cannot easily be arranged in definite patterns or cast into systematic schemes such as those of commensurate durations and scalar orders of pitch.

We may speak, then, of musical time and space as the basic dimensions or principles of aesthetic form, and to these outer dimensions, which underlie the structure of the tonal object, there correspond the dimensions or capacities of inner time and space, as principles of meaning, which can be thought of more concretely as feeling and formulation. The correspondence is actually an equivalence—almost an equation—since the music is taken up into inner experience, while feeling and formulation are perceived as properties of the musical object. Just as duration cannot be separated from pitch in the aesthetic object, of course, so feeling cannot be severed from structural formulation, as an emotive and volitional power from a purely intellectual one; for feeling is not a distinct division of consciousness, but really the sentient quality and emotional tone that pervades every experience, including even such analytic or comparative activities as the logical construction and detailed perception of formal interrelationships. Thus feeling and formulation are fused in experience, however distinct their anatomical and physiological correlates may be, very much as the senses are combined in organic perception, and very much as duration and pitch—or duration and structured quality—are united in musical motion.

If we examine in experience what is specifically epistemological, however, and leave out of account the matter of feeling and its contribution to meaning, perception and knowledge will still remain dependent on the basic properties and capacities of mentality. Musical form as such—and thus musical material also—will have its foundation in the unity of consciousness, in the temporally extended identity that constitutes the self and renders possible all perception. In an object itself extended in time, certain features—repetition, variation, contrast, synthesis—will occur universally; all of them, at any rate, can never be absent if an auditory form is to exist. There is in addition a second epistemological requirement, which has a spatial nature and which may be called "matrix": a diversified field of perception that is similarly a condition of possibility for form and that is again manifested in all music, predominantly as a collection of different pitches. The temporality of experience and of the identity of the self that underlies it doubtless rest on a succession of neural events along given pathways and on concomitant chemical processes of relative rapidity, while spatiality, which integrates the world and the self rather than distinguishing them, would correspondingly depend upon neural networks of a peculiar associative type and upon sustained chemical states.

A spatial matrix will contain certain intrinsic formal possibilities such as are conveyed in the notion "alongside of" or "surrounded by"; and time similarly presents inherent possibilities of repetition, recurrence, or a change of intensity. These belong initially to space and matter and energy and biology. A melodic pattern that is repeated a tone higher than its original pitch combines these intrinsic spatial and temporal possibilities and at the same time embodies them as properties of sound. But in becoming musical form they enter into a process which is centered in the shaping of sonorous material but which also involves new factors of meaning and of cultural and personal creativity. These appear to us, in accordance with a pervasive tendency of thought, in the form of dualities. Thus we have not only complementary principles of space and time, sound as a product of matter and form, and sonorous material as a compound of nature and artistic intent, but artistic structure as a composite of material and formulation, and formulation itself as a composite of intrinsic mental forces and configurational tendencies that are learned. In addition to this, both the formation and the perception of art proceed by uniting sensory and conceptual elements, so that sensuous and conceptual features are again fused in the meaning of aesthetic experience. Ingredient in the scheme of things, it would seem, and as though in conformity with some anatomical or physiological distinction, or perhaps with differences in function between the two cerebral hemispheres, are various strangely unified dualities—of world and self, nature and culture, the given and the novel, society and the individual. Our immediate concern in connection with musical form is with the paired properties of duration and pitch, and with the motion that arises from their union.

In spite of noise components and numerous complexities of constitution, tone is distinguished by regularities and recurrence in its physical structure and by a corresponding smoothness and constancy in its sensational quality. The perfect smoothness in perception is a more logical outcome of regularity in the acoustic and neural stimulus that it would be of irregularity, but it remains a surprising sensory counterpart of a provocation that is vibratory. It seems to be responsible for the unique quality of tonal duration, which contrasts with the temporal aspect of nontonal sound in the intimate union it forms with the sonorous substance; for duration permeates and saturates tone as it does no other temporal manifestation. The constancy of tone also contains its chief peculiarity, which appears in a paradox: for as a type of sound, tone is an indication of activity and motion and thus of a significant environmental occurrence, yet on the other hand it possesses a repose that can be hypnotic or at least intrinsically attractive to sensation. Tone is at once active and stationary, from no matter what point of view we consider it; physically it is motion that also possesses recurrence, as an immanent perceptual object it is at the same time both vital and fixed in quality. To a considerable extent music is an unfolding of this curiously equivocal and striking property, or perhaps more accurately, a play with this property—a development and formulation that variously enhances it and contradicts it.

Duration assumes its most concrete form in a sustained tone; it is acutally felt in tonal experience, but we are only aware of it, induce it, or deduce it in experience of other kinds; even purely inner experience such as pain is not so vivid a manifestation of duration because it lacks the objectivity of tone as well as its dense continuity. The perfect uniformity that a continuous tone presents to us has its image in both our memory and our expectation; what we hear as actually present is what we have been hearing and what we will continue to hear. But at any time, the phase of the tone we perceive has a certain temporal extension; this remains always the same, but we do not feel it to be exactly marked off or well defined temporally; we speak of the present but experience it as a certain space of time rather than an instant. Disregarding sensory fatigue, which will eventually remove a constant tone from consciousness or make it intermittently inaudible, a tone of any duration becomes a single object. Our experience of it, however, unites presence and passage; we hear something constantly present yet arriving and departing at the same time, or more precisely, we perceive a linearly extended entity that becomes audible one small section at a time, starting at the beginning and moving slowly along to the end. We remain stationary and the tone moves through our sensational field so that we become aware of its durational dimension. This is in physical fact, of course, more or less how the traveling energy of the tone in the air stimulates our ear, or in the case of a sung tone, how it leaves our larynx, but the apparent rate of travel of the immanent tone is too slow for it to be connected with the velocity of sound waves.

If a tone is sounded repeatedly, the silences that separate its recurrences will be measured by the tonal durations unless they are very different in length. The configurations that result will be shaped by the intrinsic structuring tendencies of auditory perception; silences will be heard as equal in duration to tones, for example, even if they are only approximately so. Very short silences will not be heard as such but merely as the occasions of renewed tonal articulation; very long ones will not be combined with tone into a configuration but will become separations of perceptions or of perceived patterns. But regardless of the lengths of the interposed silences or of the tone itself in its recurrences, a repeated tone differs from a constant one because the impression of activity will predominate over that of repose.

Patterns made up of a succession of different durations, perhaps with the inclusion of silences and the additional factor of different degrees of intensity, will give us more strongly defined meter and rhythm, especially in cyclical or repetitive arrangements. The temporal experience here ceases to be purely existential, to fuse simply with the flow of our awareness or to reveal the corresponding inner nature of the producer of the tone. Instead it becomes public time as well, in a sense spatialized or at least interpersonal, for it not only tends generally to identify the various subjectivities that are involved but to coordinate them, to lock them together in a definite form of experience common to all in spite of the individual differences in content that remain.

It is only when the pitch of successive tones varies, however, or when there are continuous changes in pitch of a gliding nature, that a feeling of motion arises in addition to the impression of activity and the objectivity of rhythm. This tonal motion affects by contrast our perception of a single tone, whether continuous or repeated, so that its active, moving quality goes unnoticed and its static aspect is emphasized. The motion produced by fixed pitches takes on a continuity of its own, rather than a disjunct quality, as soon as a series of tones is perceived as a configuration; then the sizes of the intervals in conjunction with rhythmic patterns of loudness and duration can produce a compelling and highly differentiated motional structure, with what we at one time feel to be contiguous steps and at another leaps, with more languid or more emphatic character, and with a speed that can vary from hardly perceptible motion to the utmost rapidity. Interspersed silences are destructive of tonal motion, which they reduce to a static quality from which even the feeling of activity is absent. The instrumental works of Webern provide classic examples of this effect.

Whenever motion becomes manifest, we are dealing with

spatial properties as well as temporal ones. Even in the case of a single tone, we would tend to characterize the level of tension and activity we experience as spatial or positional. But with variety in pitch, whether the change is continuous or disjunct, the feeling of highness and lowness becomes conspicuous and definite. A series of different pitches will possess spatial properties even if it is not heard as a pattern, although then the effect of motion will be absent even if the tones are not separated by silences. In the case of a perceived configuration, however, spatial and motional properties will always come into being together, the one or the other predominating in accordance with the nature of the pattern, for rapidity will emphasize motion and wide intervals space. Melodic motion and space are of course not to be confused with either environmental or physical motion and space, and in particular not with the motions and distances involved in the instruments and activities of performance, although these are closely coordinated with the intrinsically musical properties. Even the durational patterns of music have qualities different from the corresponding temporal patterns of performance; their very speed and durational extent are bound up with and influenced by the qualities of the musical totality. But immanent auditory duration—which can be taken most simply as the duration of a sustained tone—is so closely connected to the temporal flow of sentience itself that it becomes a natural measure of the temporality of relatively short-lived environmental events, and it is in particular the immediate basis of our perception of the duration of external sounds (somewhat as the temporality of external events in turn becomes the foundation of scientific time). On the other hand, the immanent space and motion that are found in melody and music are quite distant from environmental space and motion; they are in fact little more than analogues of these, although the analogy is sufficiently well grounded to entitle them to the same conceptual designations.

The spatial differences found in pitch have a physiological foundation in the literal differences of position and extent of the mechanical patterns of motion in the inner ear, and also in positional and extensive neural differences in the auditory projection patterns of the cerebral cortex. The neural events are ultimately spatiotemporal, of course, rather than spatial, since timed volleys of impulses are involved that are variously distributed among nerve fibers and progressively transformed in their trip from the ear to the brain; and there is no question in any event of a corporeal perceptual object either in the nervous system or in the cochlea which would replace the immanent spatial properties of pitch and thus reduce them to more literal external perceptions. The positional aspect of pitch is nevertheless unmistakable and in no way derived, secondary, or figurative; different pitches can be arranged in order unambiguously with respect to this attribute, in a way which is logically identical to the linear ordering of points or discrete objects in external space; they are also susceptible of simultaneous perception and appear separated by different immanent distances along the spatial dimension in question; the same positional relationships can even appear in various locations along this dimension.

At the same time, however, sound sets various parts of the body into vibration whether it arises from an external source or we produce it ourselves, and these vibrations may even be localized in the body by hearing as well as perceived by the vibratory sense. If we sing, the corporeal localization and resonances can be quite pronounced and are also accompanied by both a kinesthetic and a psychological sense of tension, strain, and effort. These factors, along with the intersensory qualitative attributes of brightness and volume that vary concomitantly with pitch, are responsible for our characterization of immanent tonal position as "high" and "low." These terms, accordingly, are not accurately described simply as metaphorical; more closely examined, they have an appropriateness that is ultimately literal, but that acts almost exclusively through various routes that are intersensory and associative.

Although motion seems to be a concomitant of spatial change, as we have mentioned, there is some indication that it is also a primary phenomenon in musical percepton just as it is in vision. Certainly it can be perceived when individual tonal positions are not defined, which happens in cases of gliding pitch. Motion along a dimension of near and far will occur with changes in tonal intensity (even if the pitch is held constant by compensatory changes in frequency), but the effect is slight and doubtless due to association with environmental sound; also it has little to do with the type of motion we are considering. At any rate, the relationship between the immanent motion and space of music contains the same problems that exist in other sensory modalities, in the multisensory field of environmental perception, and in the area of metaphysics. Place and position would seem to arise in a process of abstraction from motion, which is genetically and biologically primary. But motion is spatiotemporal, and any attempt to reduce it to or derive it from purely spatial conceptions of location and position leads to contradiction or absurdity. In the physical realm, strictly speaking, we never deal with position but always only with motion or with changes in motion and thus with force. Yet in the sensory realm, we can start with position and time, and synthesize motion readily, as in the case of successively illuminated points which are seen as a single moving point or in the more complex case of melody, in which the successive audible positions remain evident together with the new manifestation of motion they help to create.

It is musical time, rather than space or motion, that has given rise to the greatest amount of confusion and speculation, for this property is not so easily separated from other kinds of temporal phenomenon. That music or tone makes time itself audible is a notion without sufficient clarity of meaning to be examined seriously; it has arisen obviously because of certain peculiarities of musical experience which accordingly we must seek to describe more accurately. Now all experience is temporal, but music possesses a durational quality that is uniquely insistent; it also possesses a content that resists verbal characterization; and these two features taken in conjunction have understandably given rise to the belief that music is a manifestation of "time itself." What is called for instead is an emphasis upon the relativity of temporal manifestations. This may be fostered by the expression "musical time." Even though the durational property of music is embedded in the total musical phenomenon, it is a quality with a kind of autonomy in the sense that it need not be referred to any standard or any absolute entity in order to be measured, explained, or characterized. We do not intend to deny that temporality is inherent both in the outside world of physics and biology and in the very structure of our knowledge and experience. Indeed it is the interrelationship of these types of temporality that brings us as close as we can come to a final basis of explanation of the nature of experience. Our problem really concerns the relationship of musical duration to other temporal manifestations; and we wish to know the distinctive features of musical time, and particularly why it is so striking a property of music. Some of these considerations will come under the head of meaning rather than form.

The most immediate aspect of the temporal nature of music is comprised of the qualities of passage and duration that are experienced from moment to moment in an actual or imagined performance. These qualities rest on the unity of consciousness and therefore on the temporal nature of this unity—on a moving awareness that has a continuous identity. But our experience is also one of musical form in the making, in which immediate temporal qualities are joined by less vivid objects of recollection and anticipation. Thus in addition to immediate awareness, which in itself depends upon an automatic synthesis of instants, further powers of synthesis are called for—powers of memory and projection which unify the past and unite it with the present and with the possibilities of the future, or more accurately, which bring certain features of the past and the future into present awareness. The constitution of form in the making really depends jointly on two levels of synthetic activity: the automatic short-term retention and expectation that constitute what we feel to be the present and the immediate object of awareness, and the larger recollection and anticipation that permit us to constitute and to grasp entire melodies and other musical configurations of extended duration. Additional intentional mechanisms enter into the process of musical perception, both as inherent and invariant tendencies like that of closure and as culturally created tendencies that belong to style; conceptual thought plays a role in perception as well; but these are aspects more of meaning than of form.

89

If we now consider form as a finished product rather than as a process of formation, it will be seen to depend on no additional projective act (except for adumbrations of the possibility of future performances and of their nature), but will involve a final synoptic activity in what we can describe as a hierarchical group of syntheses. Temporal form clearly demands a special capacity of assimilation. We can conceive a temporal pattern and apprehend it only by means of an act which permits us to abstract the pattern from its temporality so that it is present to us in some sense all at once. This kind of integration gives rise to our knowledge of music, for knowledge involves a fixing or simultaneous presence of what is known, but it is also dependent upon our knowledge, for a totally unfamiliar style will restrict temporal integration to the most elemental perceptual processes and will therefore limit it to the most immediate and shortest span of time. Different types of integrative power are called for by time stretches of different lengths: as we have seen, the assimilation of an elementary durational configuration takes place automatically, that of a longer articulated pattern with the help of conscious recollection and forecast. But the creation or apprehension of a coherent durational structure of any length demands a simultaneous grasp of the whole. This knowledge of the whole, which is the finished form, and of the wholeness of each configuration, comes into being gradually, upon repeated hearing or repeated surveys, and during any hearing or creative endeavor after the first preliminary grasp of the totality has been secured, it coexists with the awareness of the changing temporal present and of form in the making. In an ideal performance, then, the full significance or apprehension at any time of the temporal present and of the form as it is being produced will include the comprehension and the import of the whole and of all the larger durational contexts, whether past, present, or future.

To facilitate the process of integration and the grasp of temporality in the production and apprehension of music, we make use of similarity, repetition, sequence, variation, or recurrence between sections of the form. The only alternative to this is the employment of some type of logical consecution, however

this may be secured. Doubtless both the similarity and the
consecution have other causes than the demands of the process
of assimilation—there may be a degree of delight in the quality
of a pattern that insists on its repetition, or a display of skill of
variation for its own sake, or a technical or perceptual enjoyment in continuity that is achieved through contrast, difference,
or balance, through habitual association, or through some relationship that cannot even be specified or identified—but the
comprehension of durational wholes would seem to be the most
constant and general basis of musical structure. In the simplest
instance, that of repetition at constant loudness, we are confronted most clearly with the reduction of change to sameness,
and thus with some suppression of temporality. A short tonal
pattern repeated continually will gradually lose its durational
qualities; we perceive more and more a constant presence than a
varied configuration.

The spatial aspect of musical structure becomes much more
pronounced in the resource of tonal simultaneity than it is in
melody alone. Simultaneous configurations bear a resemblance
to melody in that the constituents preserve their identity and do
not disappear into the new composite qualities. Somewhat as
tones remain perceptible in a melody even though their properties are altered by their context, so the various tonal components of a polyphonic texture continue to be heard individually in spite of the change they undergo in combination. The
effect of simultaneous configurations on the elements that are
combined, however, appears to be much more varied and often
more radical than the influence of melody on its component
tones and phrases. To be sure, a melodic phrase can be given a
very special sense by what follows it, for example; its
significance can be transformed in a way that is completely
unpredictable on the basis of the phrase known in isolation; and
in rapid melodic passages especially, the constituent tones are
often lost in the motion of the whole. But the effect of chords on
component intervals often completely alters their quality, and
the individuality of tones especially in complex chords can be
almost entirely submerged. Temporal patterns fare better in
polyphonic combination, for configurational qualities have the

perceptual interest and individuality that enable them to withstand suppression or subordination. Yet this obviously will vary
with the distinctiveness of the patterns and with their degree of
difference from one another.

In musical simultaneity the relationship of figure and ground
becomes much more complex than it is in melody alone, where
the melodic figure appears against a ground of silence. Two or
more melodic figures can be equivalent in prominence even if
they are different in pitch. In such cases, of which imitative
polyphony more readily furnishes examples than nonimitative,
the tendency toward the duality of figure and ground, which
constantly seeks to determine the basic organization of our
perceptual object, can often be held off indefinitely as far as the
polyphonic constituents are concerned, so that the melodies all
maintain the status of figures against a ground of silence. More
usually, polyphonic textures will resemble accompanied
monody at least intermittently, and a single line or more than
one will be heard against a chordal accompaniment.

But whether a melodic line is set off by a sustained tone or by
chords, enriched by parallelism, imitated strictly or approximately, or combined with other lines distinctly different in character, we are confronted in each case with a heightened spatiality that provides increased opportunity for structural interconnections and complexity. This is still more evident in Web-
ernian serialism, where the distribution of tones in the spatiotemporal field achieves a generality for which melody and tonal
simultaneity are special instances that are frequently inconspicuous; the connections of tones are thus not unambiguously
defined, and various patterns of relationship can be projected at
the same time. Almost every type of simultaneity we have
mentioned, needless to say, can be manifested also in terms of
nontonal sound; and combinations of noise and tone are also
not only possible but frequent. If tone is altogether absent, however, the spatial and temporal properties of music will be
completely different and in general less well defined.

Pitch and tonal duration are intrinsically amenable to the
formative interests of art, while other properties of sound, and
even other attributes of tone or of pure tone, cannot be so easily

or precisely manipulated in their physical production, nor are they susceptible in perception of such complex and subtle patterns or differentiated response. Beyond this, the other attributes of tone can be separated from pitch only with difficulty: they are concomitant variables of pitch in their instrumental and vocal production, and they recede behind pitch in our awareness even when we seek to vary them independently. Indeed the natural prominence of pitch and duration can lead to a mode of musical conception that suppresses the other tonal attributes; the result will then be an abstract kind of music, whether monophonic or polyphonic. Conformable textures in polyphony will be imitative or stratified; voices will tend toward equality in timbre, volume, speed, and so on; extreme registers will be generally avoided; and the emphasis will be on form rather than on expression. Bach's *Art of the Fugue* represents these characteristics with unusual purity; but to restrict music exclusively to the configuration of pitch and duration is of course hardly possible, since it is difficult and unnatural to isolate them either physically or perceptually. It is possible, in fact, only with electronic production of tone.

If we turn our attention to the other tonal attributes, the most important of which are loudness, quality, volume, and location, we find that expressive properties seem to be more of a guiding consideration than formal relationships. Nevertheless at least a few of these attributes are by no means incapable of being structured independently. Changes in loudness, for example, can be controlled, conceived, and apprehended readily; to a limited extent patterns can be made of them and these patterns can be combined simultaneously. Although its configurations are not highly diversified in character, loudness can qualify as an independent dimension of form, a potentiality demonstrated, for example, by its use in Beethoven's instrumental music. Loudness has its most obvious and frequent independent use, of course, as accent, through which it can become the sole determinant of meter and rhythm. It is controlled most readily by gradation of singing or playing power and only more rarely by changes in the number of voices or instruments

93

deployed (which produce steplike alterations more easily than gradual ones).

Quality, on the other hand, is differently flexible, for it is changed most naturally in a discrete fashion by changing the type of voice or instrument used and only with difficulty by variations in performing technique (which typically produce gradual and shaded changes rather than abrupt ones; the addition of a muting device is in fact comparable to a change of instrument). Again, however, quality can on occasion become an independent dimension of form, as it does especially in the serial music of the 20th century. Even the external location of instruments and singers, which is clearly not an immanent attribute of tone but a property of its sources, plays a central formal role in Baroque concerto styles and in medieval and Renaissance antiphony. In fact any property of sound or of its sources, provided only that it is sufficiently malleable and receptive to distinctions, is theoretically capable of becoming a prominent or sole dimension of musical art. This would be true of the spatial properties of environmental sound itself, if they could be changed and controlled with adequate flexibility and preciseness and if we were sufficiently sensitive to such changes. Indeed it is only the intrinsic limitations of hearing in respect of environmental spatial perception that make an art of moving sound unlikely, although an art of moving sources—which would allow the participation of vision—is much more of a possibility. We can even conceive of music that is based on a stationary pattern of distribution of sound or on stationary locations of continuously sounding sources; artistic configurations could then be created by a listener moving bodily about either freely or according to a composed plan. Such an art would be a kind of musical sculpture or architecture.

It is characteristic, however, for tonal attributes to act in natural conjunction, since they are physically and psychologically coupled; thus formal procedures are not abstractly grounded in the analysis of tone according to attributes—a possibility that electronic technology has only recently made practicable as far as the physical production of sound is concerned—but more concretely based on natural tonal sources and customary perceptual associations. Form will be created typically by the conscious patterning of pitch and duration, and to a lesser extent of loudness and tone color; the attributes that concomitantly vary with these, such as volume, brightness, or roughness, will generally contribute to the result incidentally; they may have played a role in shaping the prevailing musical style, but even in this larger and less tangible formative process, as in the individual creative activity of the composer, their contribution will not have depended on awareness and conscious employment. Indeed subordinate attributes, as we have mentioned, would seem to play less a formal role than an expressive or representational one, and even in these functions they are not singled out as such but act through various intuitive and subconscious processes that accompany the structuring of the conscious factors of form. Synesthetic connections are certainly important, for the subordinate attributes are strikingly intersensory and heterosensory. Since they are dominated in perception by pitch, duration, loudness, and tone color, however, they can hardly be patterned without simultaneously producing patterns in these more prominent attributes, which then become the ones we attend to. Graduated scales of volume, compactness, or brightness, which imply the possibility of detailed artistic configurations, are in fact no more than the product of abstract laboratory tasks; they suggest a search in the physiology of hearing for some tangible basis of each discriminatory ability, for the connections and associations of the tonal attributes with corresponding properties of environmental objects do not provide an adequate explanation; but as far as musical formulation is concerned, these varieties of differential sensitivity are essentially valueless.

The subordinate status of attributes such as volume or brightness cannot be the result of their intersensory and heterosensory nature, for duration and loudness and to some extent tone color and even pitch are also not purely auditory. What is doubtless responsible for the prominence of some attributes and the subordination of others is our greater sensitivity to differences in those that are prominent and also to some degree the superior ease with which these differences can be produced.

95

This is certainly true of the predominantly rational style of Western music, especially because of the importance of instruments, with their facilitation of precise tonal distinctions. But what seems to be crucial in determining the status of any attribute in music is the preference for constancy and definiteness in perceptual objects. If consciousness and knowledge tend toward durability and clarity in the constitution of immanent objects, if the production of these properties is built into the nature of intentionality, just as biological value and importance would seem to reside in constancy and definition; then a series of discontinuous and detailed changes in volume, for example—and those considerations will apply also to tone color or to physical location—will correspond to the same number of separate and different multisensory objects or to a succession of mutations (or of changes of location) in an environmental object; gradual changes will similarly correspond to strange transformations (or to external motion). This is the reason that Schönberg's *Klangfarbenmelodie* secured little importance in Western music, and Wagner's blending and overlapping of tone colors produced such an unusual effect. Changes in volume, tone color, and location thus contradict the intrinsic preferences of perception. Changes in pitch, duration, and loudness, on the other hand, will correspond to alterations in the state of a single object—in its degree of tension, for example, or in the duration or intensity of its activity. The effect of some tonal attributes will evidently depend on a constant level of prominence, or on the juxtaposition of two distinctly different levels, as in the case of separate environmental objects, rather than on transitions or on graduated scales. Thus changes in volume, tone color, and location are characteristically found in the form of contrasts, which are produced by abrupt and marked shifts of register associated often with simultaneous and similarly discrete shifts in loudness. Changes in brightness and sharpness similarly occur when strings are doubled by a flute an octave above or by an oboe in unison.

In terms of logical possibility in the use of natural sound sources, music can be produced either by changing the state of a single instrument or by successively activating different instruments. The resultant successive patterns of sound will be very much the same in the two cases if the instruments used differ only in size. A group of varied instruments, however, will produce a pattern that will have less perceptual definiteness and will reflect the multisensory or physical nature of the instruments. These procedures are not mutually exclusive, of course, especially if simultaneity be admitted, but in itself, a group of varied instruments is less compatible with the purposes of music than a homogeneous family or set; for art has tended more—and perhaps by its nature must inevitably tend more—to emphasize immanent rather than empirical perceptual values. Yet what we think of as the gradation of pitch in a set of idiophones is really the arrangement of a series of complex qualities intimately associated with the perceptual characteristics of the sources themselves as their acoustic manifestation. The gradation is one of sonorous volume or brightness, or even physical size, as much as of pitch; it is really a succession of total qualities according to their natural serial order, which is the joint product of separate analytical attributes that are for the most part congruent in their variation. This is especially true of metallic idiophones such as knobbed gongs, where the sound produced is extremely complex in terms of frequency constitution. What we conceive and hear as relationships of pitch in melodic succession is thus often by error construed provincially after the fashion of the analytical approach to artistic music in the West, where the wholeness of sonority is not sustained by animistic values or religious sanctity; the melody can actually be more a configuration of qualities than of pitches; it can, as a matter of fact, be a melody in a sense different from the accustomed one, for certain immanent dynamic properties, such as a variable impelling force connected with a functional differentiation of tones, may be weak or absent. There is a degree of resemblance in this respect between Indonesian gamelan music, for example, and many Western serial compositions.

The operation in Western music of a subordinate attribute of tone can be illustrated by the role of tonal volume. In the "Queen Mab" Scherzo of Berlioz, for example, the tiny volume is essentially constant and it is obviously part of a whole musical complex the effect of which rests on pitch, rhythm, speed, softness, quality, and so forth as well as on volume. But it is also evident that the composer need not have considered each analyzable aspect separately, any more than the listener will consciously respond in such a fashion; both are very much more likely to think in terms of the whole configuration and its overall character, of the concrete performing forces, and of what is being represented. The tonal volume is a concomitant and a factor of these larger conscious processes. And it remains constant, or at any rate, its changes are not attended to in their own right and do not constitute patterns that can be perceived, but are masked by the configurations of more conspicuous tonal properties.

The opening trumpet tone of Wagner's *Rienzi* is an example of gradually increasing volume rather than of constancy or abrupt change. But again, the increase of immanent tonal volume was not a consciously intended result, and similarly, we are much more aware of the concomitant growth in loudness. Wagner's intention, however, was actually guided by the environmental spatiality of the tone, for the sound is meant to expand and reach out into space and thus to advance toward the listeners. But this rare instance of a reliance on an extremely elusive tonal property is clearly not an example of a formal intention, even though the crescendo in question becomes a factor in the overall structure of the opera, but of expression and representation. We would also doubtless be accurate in saying that Wagner took into account whatever qualities the crescendo entailed, but that he thought of these qualities and their significance solely in terms of the instrument and its properties rather than as independent factors.

The Scherzo of Beethoven's Fifth Symphony will provide a final, nonprogrammatic example of tonal volume. In the false starts of the Trio, the dominant formal factor is the configuration of pitch and duration. But the large volume of the low strings—which remains essentially constant—taken together with the rapidity of the passage and the repeated efforts to continue, has a primarily expressive effect of amusing clumsiness.

What is the case with volume is equally the case with tonal compactness, weight, brightness, external spatiality, and so forth: they enter into both form and meaning, but as factors that contribute to the whole without generally being singled out or succeeding to prominence. There are exceptions, of course—Wagner's operas alone furnish a comprehensive inventory of conspicuous subordinate attributes—but most of these are found in the sphere of programmatic music and the composite musical arts. Some of the attributes of tone—even those of pure tone, which are most amenable to precise measurement—have been fractionated into constituent attributes, somewhat in the fashion of research on subatomic particles. As might be expected, however, these constituent attributes are in general no more susceptible of assuming an independent role in musical composition and response than their composites. The most notable instance of the fractionation of attributes has been the division of pitch into what we might call "height" and "tonicity": a continuously ascending positional component and a cyclical qualitative component. Pitch relationships are correspondingly understood as manifesting both distance and interval, so that a third, for example, can be described as smaller in high register than in **mid-range**. The separation of height and tonicity has been unusually fruitful, the psychological discovery coinciding in this case with a practical one in the realm of serial music, which separates intervallic quality from position both in practice and in its own theoretical conceptions.

The fractionation of tone color into component attributes is extraordinarily complex, related as it is to the physical makeup of empirical objects, the sonorous manifestation of life, and the qualities of personality. Even if nonperiodic components are left out of account, the dimensions of variation are almost impossible to define unequivocally and exhaustively. Something of the complexity that is involved can be seen in the instance of a human voice singing various vowels on a single pitch. The tone color changes with each vowel, yet not only does the pitch remain constant, as it also would if a succession of different instruments sounded the same tone, but so does the characteristic qualitative identity of the singer. Even in the instrumental realm, it would seem impossible for any scheme of constituents to encompass the bewildering complexity and interrelationship of qualities—the hollowness of the chalumeau register of the clarinet, for example, and its gradual transformation with ascending pitch into a hard density, all within the qualitative constancy of a single instrument. The intermixture of tactile qualities alone is complex enough to defy analysis. Nor does the analysis of component frequencies, in the tradition of Helmholtz, or of formants (which are regions of prominence in the distribution of energy according to frequency that remain relatively constant with changes in pitch) fully solve the problem, for it contains the danger of establishing abstract and arbitrary types and families of qualities that are only in part similar to those of the naturally occurring sounds of musical instruments. In matters of complex tone, not to mention markedly nonperiodic sound, it is obvious that the appropriate basis of definition is the source itself and that a referential tendency will always be present even if it is ignored in our concern with the immanent properties of artistic configuration. In any event, the analysis and classification of the qualities of complex tone were of no practical importance until the advent of the electronic generation and synthesis of tone, although their technical accomplishment of course brings into being their potential formal utility and musical value.

The comparison between the fractionation of tone into attributes and the analytical dissection of the atom is not based simply on external analogy, for what seems to be involved in the musical sphere is an attitude borrowed from physical science. But the rational and analytic procedures that are employed are humanistic only in the broadest sense of representing both a particular mode of thought with its own objects and a particular musical outlook (together with certain intentional structures of musical perception) as a cultural and historical manifestation. Beyond this they supplant more specifically humanistic values such as the traditional meanings and formal uses of instruments and styles of singing that reach back into the past, and in general the whole more intimate relationship between art and nature that this conception of musical material involves.

Even if they are not generally separated factors of musical conception, tonal attributes can play an unrealized role in determining the basic formal properties of music. Thus the apparent restriction of scales to twelve steps and the prevalence of those with five, six, or seven may be due to the limitation of volume discrimination, since distinctness in the quality of a scale degree will logically rest on the distinctness of all of its attributes. Similarly, volume would seem to be partly responsible, along with tonal weight, for the foundational property of low pitches, for the gravitational quality of cadences, and for the wide diffusion of drone basses, of the texture consisting of soprano melody and accompaniment, and of the slower motion and larger intervals of low voices. To be sure, the physical inertia of large sources of sound as well as the delay in perception to which the establishment and extinction of low tones are subject also contribute to the diffusion of these features of music, but tonal volume can undoubtedly be taken as a highly important determinant of musical form, although in a sense quite different from the conscious and detailed mode in which pitch and duration are determinants. In general, however, the attributes of tone other than pitch tend to be less specifically auditory and to have strong components of external reference (volume, for example, tends to be connected with the environmental spread of sound and with the physical size of the tonal source); they are thus chiefly amenable to descriptive and expressive purposes rather than purely to those of autonomous form; they also belong to a less analytical way of composing and hearing music, in which sonorous material is used as it is given in nature, with the concrete meanings of the instruments derived from it, of their functions, and of their corresponding tonal forms.

We must now proceed from the abstract formal possibilities of tonal attributes to more concrete considerations, for what we have been dealing with up to this point are more the principles of form than its properties. But the consideration of attributes other than pitch, duration, and loudness has already forced us to observe the limitations of an analytic approach to form. In actual fact, music does not arise, as though in a vacuum, from the realm of pure possibility that is presented by the attributes of tone. It has almost always operated instead with a composite material that is prestructured in many ways, or more accurately, with ready-made structural units that are built into sonorous material in its natural occurrence and social use. This preliminary structuring is the product of outer and inner forces: of physical and biological determinants on the one hand and of intentional and cultural ones on the other. These factors are indeed more fundamental than the attributes of tone, and more fundamental even than tone itself, for the formative purposes of music demand only sonorous material in general, and the limitless cultural diversity of art and of the creative imagination cannot be restricted to any preconceived class of sounds. But now we are concerned not simply with the nature of sound from these points of view, but with the nature of musical instruments and the voice and hearing, and with both their intrinsic and their culturally created characteristics and limitations. Theoretically established forms of tonal systems, scales, and melodic types, and the larger outlines and schemes of musical products in their entirety are also comprised in the notion of preliminary structures. In all of these considerations, however, it becomes extremely difficult to separate form from meaning, just as it was difficult initially to separate musical material from music by isolating a sonority that is formless and meaningless.

It will be helpful by way of introduction to examine again, from a somewhat different point of view, the two basic types of objectivity we have so far distinguished in music, and their contrast and interconnection. For although the essential nature of musical form is intrinsically auditory, it nevertheless cannot be fully understood without an investigation of its relationship to environmental space. It is obvious that dance and drama, for example, cannot be freed from their involvement with the multisensory world. A round dance and the sung text with which it is united are the embodiment of corporeal behavior and actual social relationships which thus become factual constituents of musical form; antiphonal or responsorial performance is no different; the alternation of two groups or the response of a group to a leader are fundamental modes of organization, for they are determined by the very nature of human society and ritual—even by biology and physics. Music can thus become a literally environmental formulation, and objects inherent to audition will be reduced to insignificance if indeed they exist at all in our consciousness. The fact that objectivity is coordinate with awareness, however, has implications of fundamental importance in a consideration of environmental space. For when activity and participation are in question—or indeed in any purely biological coordination of organism and environment—the notion of objectivity is not intrinsically applicable; musical form as an object, and therefore also the aspect of meaning that is perceived as residing in this object, may exist in a full sense only for an audience, or if there is no audience, only for an ideal observer. In considering occasions of musical participation, we must consequently make appropriate modifications in our conception of objectivity. Environmental objectivity, whether of multisensory objects or of sound itself in multisensory space, may at times be an altogether fallacious construct of our own deliberations—a danger that does not threaten either an immanent object or a conceptual one.

Antiphony represents an important and particularly striking external component of form that enters even instrumental and nonantiphonal music also, for it is a source of paired phrases which will have complementary cadences or may be in contrasted keys. In this causal sense it has an influence more or less equivalent to that of symmetrical paired structures in dance, which are similarly found in environmental space, and in which a coherent succession of steps and gestures is balanced by a repetition of this whole pattern, but in a direction opposite to the original. But antiphonal relationships are also a direct factor of form simply because they are an intentional and perceptual part of music. To be sure, antiphony is connected with repetition, which is formally effective without any locational contribution, and it also produces a kind of qualitative change that is closely comparable to changes in the immanent attribute of tone color (which is representing different sources, reciprocally tends to suggest differences in location). But these considerations do not negate the fact that with antiphony, changes in environmental position and changes in the identity of the source of sound become actual constituents of musical form. In doing so they tend to diminish and suppress the features of form that are immanent to hearing. It is as though the antiphonal interest is an alternative to the complexity of immanent configurations, which are then reduced to the simplicity of homophonic texture, for example, and repetition of phrases. Antiphony is grounded in basic physical and biological fact: in the experience of positional difference between environmental objects or between ourselves and others, in the perception of echoes, and in the combination of contrast and identity that is found in the relationship of an octave and in the relationship between male and female voices. If a tone or a musical phrase (whether purely melodic or more complex) is duplicated in another location, the identity of pitch permits the difference in position and origin to achieve its maximum prominence in perception; we are occupied to the smallest extent possible by the constitution of an immanent pattern of relationship when the two major components to be related are successive and exactly the same in pitch. As compared with exact repetition, repetition at the octave—which has a natural embodiment in the alternation of male and female voices—presents a distinction in pitch that reinforces the difference in the location and the intensity of the sources; but this reinforcement—which should perhaps be considered simply a lack of interference—succeeds only because of the qualitative identity of tones an octave apart. The fifth is also a characteristic interval in antiphonal repetition, although less so than the unison and the octave; and other intervals will obviously present varying degrees of interference. Still more will alternation be lessened in its effect when repetition is replaced by dissimilarity, and the answering phrase stands in a more complex relationship to the original one. Interestingly enough, the opposite seems to be true of responsorial form: intrinsically musical differences enhance the difference in the location and identity of the performers instead of interfering with it.

If we turn our attention from the succession of performing

forces that is found in antiphonal, responsive, and concerto forms to the simultaneity and interplay of positions and sources that is a more general feature of music, we find a situation resembling that of responsive types of organization but diametrically opposite to that of antiphony. For the incompatibility or antagonism of environmental and immanent form now gives way to conformability and mutual reinforcement. Simultaneous tones in various relationships of pitch, simultaneous melodic lines, and the distributed and interrelated tones and tonal patterns of pointillistic serialism will present differing degrees of tension or of compatibility between the intrinsic spatial properties of their specifically auditory configurations and the spatial patterns of their environmental positions. In general, an immanent perception of groups of tones or sounds will increase with their tendency to form immanent configurations. This tendency is obviously a joint result of culture and nature—a product of stylistic modes of constructing and hearing music but also of invariant properties such as the blending in perception of tones in simple integral relationships of frequency (or the separateness of those in more complex relationships). There is thus a fundamental connection between consonance and immanence, and between intrinsic and external disparity, so that harmonic music will more easily become an immanent object and polyphony an environmental one. The ensembles of opera buffa provide a striking example of the cooperation of polyphony with the interplay of external positions; each increases the perceptibility and effectiveness of the other to an astonishing degree. The single-channel electronic reproduction of such music, especially because vision is excluded, reduces it to the merest shadow of its actual nature; indeed this is to some extent the case for seats distant from the stage in a reverberant theater. It is not only in opera, however, that we can observe the mutual enhancement of immanent and external interplay; a Classical string quartet contains the same supportive interconnection: the listener perceives, with a division of attention so natural that it entails no antagonism between the two perceptual activities, a simultaneous and coordinated duality of form, two different but simultaneous objectivities that are coupled together in every detail of their structure to the benefit of both.

When we sing alone we do not become disembodied voices. The tone we bring forth is not only immanent to hearing but also a manifestation of corporeality that is located in our world. When we join with other singers the external objectivities will reflect the intrinsic intervallic and rhythmic relationships. Unison choral song will mitigate or cancel out differences of environmental location; melodic distinctiveness and contrast will emphasize them. Yet all music contains a general tendency toward unification, and one of the foundations of this tendency lies in the inability of unaided hearing to localize either sound or its sources accurately. For this reason and others of an emotional, vital, social, and ideological nature that we cannot properly consider in the present context, participation in music creates a stong communal bond; unison song in particular can efface individuality and its positional separateness, fusing the individual with his fellows through their joint participation in what becomes both physically and experientially a single tone or melody embracing all. Paradoxically, however, the peculiar kind of emphasis given to locational difference by antiphony, by the separation and alternation of performers or performing groups, is rendered more striking by close and conformable tonal relationships—by the unison, octave, and fifth and by rhythmic and melodic repetition—than it is by tonal contrast and musical differences, which evidently must be reduced to sameness if the antiphonal contrast is to become a conspicuous or predominant factor.

Not unrelated to antiphony is a basic tendency toward duplication in the construction of musical instruments, which also introduces literally spatial components into musical form. The production of any sound or tone—whether vocal or instrumental—can lead, on the most elemental formal level besides mere prolongation, to a repetition of the productive act and perceptual experience. But only a step more complex than this is repetition with a difference—the production of a second sound or tone in a comparable fashion, or of many other comparable sounds or tones. There is similarly an interest in literal duplication of an instrument, but a more particular delight in its duplication with a difference in size. To the acoustic novelty there are added the pleasures of the control of size, of the strange attraction of seeing and touching the same form in different magnitudes of realization; there is a conceptual element involved in such duplication, for it entails the separation of form from material, and therefore a type of knowledge and power. Symbolic values are also influential; paired large and small versions of an instrument often suggest or represent differences of sex, especially because the acoustic difference has a counterpart in the difference of male and female voices.

Long and short stamping tubes or vibrating slabs are widely distributed in the world, or large and small drums or bells, or double oboes or clarinets. Biological factors play an important role, especially the use of two hands and the motor impulse to alternation in the action of striking. Indeed alternation patterns are an important element of form in percussive instrumental music. Paired wind instruments, on the other hand, are connected with the combination of melody and drone, which substitutes a fixed tone for the silence that would otherwise be the ground of melodic figures, and at the same time sharpens the distinctions and relationships of function among the various tones of the melody by providing a standard of measurement for their individual values. Families of instruments are found as well as pairs: sets of gongs, of bells, or of wooden or metal slabs or tubes, as well as families of wind and string instruments, which call for groups of performers and combine positional distinctions with the differences of pitch that each instrument can produce individually. Even keyboard instruments—and also the panpipe, the Oriental *sheng*, and nearly all string instruments—are basically instrumental families, although locational differences, except in the case of the organ, here become so inconsequential that they are essentially equivalent to changes in mode or length of vibration such as those of the French horn, the trombone, the woodwind instruments, or an individual lute string.

Pairs and families of instruments obviously have a literal

counterpart in pairs and families of voices. But they also have a purely formal counterpart in monodic vocal music, where there is a natural tendency—although different in its motivation—to add a second tone to a first or expand the tonal repertory into a group of variously related members. These vocal manifestations, while comparable to those of instruments from an abstractly formal point of view, are nevertheless different from them in representing the change of state of a single source of sound; they have essentially no involvement with changes in environmental position as a constituent of form; and they arise instead through an interest in movement and articulation that is allied to expression—altogether a different source of form. Vocal melodies are very frequently centered on a single tone; they consist most essentially of an intoning very much like the repeated sounding of an instrumental source of sonority except that expressive and functional values replace or outweigh those of kinesthetic enjoyment and of sensible attractiveness and surprise. The elevation of a text above prosaic speech, both in audibility and in significance, is a purpose of outstanding importance, and it gives rise to additional formal features that mirror those of language in length, demarcation, parallel structure, and other relationships of phrases and sections. Often to serve this textual purpose, but also because of an autonomous interest in tonal variety, in points of relaxation or prominence, or in formal articulation, a second or auxiliary tone makes an occasional appearance; sometimes there may be two or three such tones, generally close to the predominant one so that they are felt to be adjacent or perhaps removed by a slightly larger step which therefore possesses unusual definition; intervals of a second and a third are characteristic.

The intervals of instrumental melody are often, by contrast, based on physical and biological properties. Differences of length or size in idiophonic pairs or sets will give rise directly to corresponding distinctions in tonal properties whether or not the physical differences have been determined by musical considerations. Similarly, the equal or comfortable spacing of finger holes, or the partitioning of strings at equally spaced intervals, provides a basis which is either directly expressed in

108

tonal differences or else artfully subjected to modification by blowing and fingering techniques to yield tones that conform to other types of musical requirement. The intervals of a fourth and a fifth—which, less conspicuously than only the unison and octave, have a distinctive perceptual character in successive as well as simultaneous realization—are often used as a basis for deriving a set of tones, either as a framework for the insertion of intermediate steps based on qualities of contiguity or to yield, by repeated applicaton, the whole set of tones used in musical practice. Overblowing and the harmonic division of strings comprise a third naturally grounded method—based on the regularity of shape of the vibrating source—of securing a group of tones in music, here standing in simple integral relationships of vibrational frequency and length. In addition to differences among tones in musical function and prominence, we frequently find, in both instrumental and vocal music, tones that not only have an auxiliary or occasional status, but also lack independence altogether, appearing as ornamental or even qualitative modifications of other tones that are more important; such transient existence is a characteristic constituent of melody as motion rather than as a configuration of precisely defined pitches. Indeed gradual alterations of tone, often at a rate that varies or in a course that wavers, can play a prominent part in the formulation of melody and even largely supplant individual tones. A more vivid and compelling type of melodic motion will be the result, with the suggestion of external motion (or even its literal representation, as in the case of the bull-roarer or the glissando) rather than the fixed distinctions in external location or size that are suggested by intervallic melody. Of the three basic procedures we have distinguished for determining intervals, the first and last are specific to instruments, and they may not in fact be taken over by the voice, which has its own sources of form and which may go its own way even when it is joined by instruments in performance, ignoring both the physical bases of interval and the kinesthetic bases of the rhythms of instrumental performance and of dance.

Clearly the most fundamental division of acoustic sources is that between voice and instrument, which are in many ways opposite in nature. To the contrast they represent, however, there must be added the compensating factor of mutual influence and imitation as well as the conciliating existence of sources of intermediate type (most of which use the body in what we may appropriately call an instrumental fashion), such as whistling, sibilant and other voiceless consonantal sounds, clicking mouth noises, fingernail clicks, clapping, slapping, and stamping. Megaphones are another intermediate instance, and so is the jew's-harp, in which an external vibrating tongue is used in conjunction with the variable resonating cavity of the mouth. Finally wind instruments are relatively close to the voice in comparison with the increasing difference of strings, idiophones, and percussion instruments in which pitch is obscure or absent; in some wind instruments the lips act as the primary vibrating source. Many instruments, of course, are essentially extensions of bodily capabilities—clappers are a good example—or in any event are intimately connected with the muscular and manipulative capacities of the body. Yet voice and instrument remain a significant duality, bringing their own distinctive formative as well as expressive and signifcative tendencies into music.

Both, to be sure, are dependent upon hearing, which imposes limits of perceptibility on sounds that keep them within a certain range of frequencies, intensities, and durations, and causes the differences between them to lie above certain minimal distinguishable values. And hearing is also responsible for the fact that comparable audible differences in any given respect that can be determined quantitatively will be produced by roughly the same relation of physical values rather than by the same absolute physical difference. It is well known, for example, that the difference in pitch produced by string lengths of three and two units will be comparable to that produced by lengths of six and four units. It is the relation between three and two that must be duplicated, not the absolute difference between them. This property of perception will obviously underlie the structure of the patterns and configurations of music, from the simplest conjunction of intervals in any quantifiable dimension of sound to the entire system of that dimension in musical use. Both voice and instrument are subject to these general psychophysiological conditions of hearing. And they are again subject—although in different degrees—to more specific configurational properties of immanent auditory objects, such as those of the intervallic qualities of pitch: of the fifth or the octave, for example, or of steps as opposed to leaps. Other formative influences that act equally on both are differences in external location—which suggest antiphony, repetition, and echo—and the reverberant and resonant properties of the rooms in which music is performed—which emphasize the prolongation and sensuousness of tone and the formal predominance of one or more particular pitches. Finally there are culturally created configurations of sound that are not specific to either voice or instrument, but that have succeeded—whatever their origin may have been—to a general currency in musical form; melodic cadential figures, for example, are usually of this nature, and we may place many other melodic configurations and even many scales in the same category.

On the other hand, the distinctive formal tendencies of separate acoustic media cannot be doubted. Within a framework of possibilities that is physically and biologically established, specific patterns are formed by psychological preferences, cultural traditions, and social functions. The singing voice tends toward sustained tone, a formal propensity that is furthered by the internal vibrations and resonances of the body. It has inherent restrictions (although even these are influenced by cultural factors and training) of its range of capacities in respect of pitch, duration, agility, power, and tone color, but within a culture and a given musical genre these features occur in types established chiefly by sex difference and age and they also manifest the characteristic variety of individual differences. Male and female constitute a natural duality of pitch and quality that is suggestive of antiphonal structures and supportive of the prominent place of the octave. Within each of these divisions there seems to be a bimodal distribution of range accompanied to some extent by one of tone color. Another significant duality similarly manifested in pitch and tone color is that of child and adult, although the voice of old singers also has its own special qualities.

Words that are sung or those that are intoned in some fashion intermediate between song and speech introduce into a composite type of musical art all the formal properties of sonorous language: the individual vowel and consonant sounds and the patterns of poetry and rhetoric as well as those of ordinary prose. The same is true of the speaking voice, of course, in all its varieties, for this too enters into various types of music. The duality of song and speech is fundamental to the nature of the voice, the distinguishing factor being definition in pitch; yet there are obviously many intermediate vocal manifestations that are partially tonal and partially nontonal. Within the range of song, apart from the presence or absence of language, the voice commands the opposed possibilities of gliding or stationary pitch, as well as the corollary possibility of employing different pitches either as shades of one another or as distinct and independent tones, these in turn being felt either as contiguous and equally spaced or as separated by gaps. The voice is also capable of producing remarkably accurate and subtle formations. The ability of a singer to compare and relate the durations of tones, especially those that are equal in length, may exceed in accuracy that of an instrumental performer. And the pitch, duration, loudness, and tone color of the voice can each be altered independently, either to a very great extent or in an only barely perceptible way, while the remaining properties are held essentially constant. Particular formal features are abrupt shifts of register as in yodeling, the special range and quality of the falsetto voice, the peculiar range and quality and sustaining power of the castrato voice, the glottal stop, particular effects in resonance such as nasality, and the subtle variations, often associated with one another, in pitch, loudness, and tone color that are found in periodic form in the trill and the vibrato or in progressive or irregular forms of cycle-to-cycle changes. Beyond this are the still additional ornaments of portamento, which subtly combines gliding and stationary pitch, intentional deviations or departures from norms of intonation, and *messa di voce,* which reveals the subtlety and extent of the gradual changes in loudness of which the voice is capable.

A final group of formal possibilities exists because the voice is flexible enough to adopt the features of external sources of sound and of theoretical tonal structures. In the assimilation of internal formal properties, the practices of ritual and the delight in imitation and parody are prominent motives for the duplication of animal sounds and bird calls, but vocal imitation extends also to the sounds of musical instruments, to other human voices and the sounds of foreign languages, and even to the imagined supernatural voices of spirits and deceased ancestors. Vocal signals and calls can also be stylized into melodic configurations, and so can particular instrumental patterns that are diverse in their origin, some arising from instrumental peculiarities and others from communicative, ritual, or ceremonial functions. Instrumental tone colors can be taken up by the voice, and even such mechanical character-istics as rapid and unvarying repetition or percussive qualities. Vocal imitations in general can be quite literal and thus clearly recognizable as such or stylized to a degree that conceals their reference or hides some derivation no longer known. The duplication of instrumental patterns—and to a lesser extent the imitation of vocal characteristics by instruments—also tends to increase the systematic unity of music. The singing voice is finally provided with a large stock of patterns and, still more important, with a structural foundation for all its artistic con-figurations, when it adopts from instruments various system-atic features of music such as scales and chords that have been theoretically defined, or basic intervallic relationships.

It is apparent that the forms of sonority produced by the voice manifest such remarkable variety in every conceivable respect that it is impossible to speak of any "natural" mode or type of song or speech or vocal expression. The naturalness of the voice as contrasted with instruments is a relative one, and consists simply in the obvious fact that it is a bodily source of sound closely identified with vital and personal expressive-ness. What is ultimately responsible for the forms manifest in vocal music, then, are cultural and historical peculiarities interacting with and shaping biological possibilities. But the culture acts through the creation of a variety of intermediate forms: those of language, of emotional expression, of cult and ceremony, of communication, and even of musical instruments— all themselves the product of the interaction of tradition with the natural world and with surrounding cultures or adjacent cultural strata.

Musical instruments have distinct formal features of their own that contrast with those of the voice and that are directly dependent on their physical constitution. This is at once apparent in the sonorous qualities of idiophones, in the melodic overtone patterns characteristic of brass winds, in the characteristic leaps of a twelfth on the clarinet or of an octave on the flute, or in the typical rapidity and mechanical patterning of keyboard figuration. In general, instruments make precise repetition of pitch and interval much simpler and much more accurate, they can be much more striking rhythmically, they can make simultaneous tonal relationships easily available, they bring into prominence the intervals of the partial series attached to regular physical shapes (particularly the octave, twelfth, double octave, and double octave plus a third), they provide vast variety in respect of range, duration, speed, loudness, and tone color as well as in respect of nontonal sound, and they suggest a host of external relationships of music—to various materials and physical dimensions, to muscular activity, and to the natural (and thus supernatural) world in general, including even the relationship to the human breath and thus to the voice and the sphere of inner experience. But as we have seen, the auditory perception of these possibilities is a determining factor in their musical use, so that instruments are subject to a group of physiological and psychological characteristics that is essentially the same as that controlling the voice—recognition of gliding and steplike change of pitch and successive intervals, comparison of durations, and so forth. They are also subject to the possibilities and limitations of muscular dexterity. Beyond this, instruments tend continually, through motives of assimilation and imitation, to adopt vocal tendencies—expressive tone colors and ornaments, for example, sustained tone production, and subtly transitional dynamics.

The voice cannot be accurately regarded as one type of sound source compared to the multiplicity of instrumental types. It is really in its variety more like an equivalent of the instrumental sphere in its entirety, especially if the subtlety and flexibility of the vice are added to its diversity. To be sure, the infinite variety of vocal properties takes into account the endlessly varied formative forces of different cultural and historical contexts. Yet if we are to consider a single cultural setting, it would inevitably limit variety in the instrumental as well as the vocal sphere, so that a certain equivalence between the two is more the case than a large disproportion of means.

In every instance of the formulation and perception of sonorous configurations we are confronted with a joint action of nature and culture, an interpenetration and intimate connection of the two that makes their complete separation impossible. To be sure, the physical nature of an instrument will produce or encourage certain sonorous patterns or types of pattern, and the biological nature of the voice will bring various tendencies, if more general ones, into the process of configurational formation. In both cases, also, the intrinsic limits and functions and capabilities of audition and the intrinsic nature of the constitutive activity of consciousness will shape the objects of perception if not determine their basic properties. Yet these underlying factors enter into larger complex processes and are absorbed and modified; the burden of artistic formativity is carried by society and culture. And it is a striking feature of the creation and perception of musical configurations that socially inculcated habits of hearing and singing and playing instruments, and culturally formed powers and capacities of constituting objects of perception, possess a natural and inevitable character, fully comparable to the automatic action of audition which is an inherent part of sense perception and of consciousness in general. There is a certain necessity and rightness to the sound of a chordal texture in a given style, or to the progress

115

of a melodic phrase, that is fundamentally as inescapable as the self-evident tonal duration or synthesis produced by the sheer activity of consciousness.

Besides the concrete tendencies of instruments and the voice, which comprise preformed sonorities, mechanically favored types of tonal succession, and traditional patterns, still other formal factors may intervene between sonorous material and its artistic use, between the dimensions of sonority and artistic form. These can be described as systematic structures, and they are variously designated as rhythmical patterns, melody types, modes, scales, tonal systems, chords, melodic formulas, harmonic progressions, generic styles and textures and forms, and precompositional series. They belong not simply to primary artistic experience, but to the derived realm of conceptions, of the reflective and theoretical ideas that guide and explain music. They are part of music, but they also have an additional and dual status as abstractions from practice that serve subsequently as conditions of practice. For they are all, not excepting even precompositional series, distillations of musical experience, rationalizations of artistic expression, reflective extractions from and generalizations of artistic form, but occurring within the sphere of music rather than as ideological pronouncements upon it. And they become in turn formal frameworks for more sophisticated composition and apprehension. They are abstract but natural patterns produced by culture—in the case of tone rows they may even be private rather than public—within which and in conformity to which the concrete and individualized structures of improvisation and composition are created.

Thus the rhythmical pattern or the melody type is a typical formulation of a traditional genre in outline that serves as a guide to future creative activity; the mode is a somewhat more abstract stage of the same process of generalization; the scale a still more abstract one that preserves only intervallic and functional relationships with few traces, if any, of actual melodic configuration; and the total musical system the extreme of generalization, at the furthest distance from actual music, which defines abstractly the whole range of available tonal material of which tone row, scale, chord, harmonic progression, mode, melodic and rhythmic type, polyphonic texture, and genre are selections successively more specific in form and character, the tone row being essentially an individualized substitute—but in its use a more general one—for the scale. In music of advanced cultures, consequently, musical form will be found to rest on a hierarchy of presupposed public formulations of material which belong to the basic determinants of the style of the culture. Musical practice will exist in every society, but the process of reflective abstraction and systematic formulation may proceed to various extents. (The two most powerful bases of this process that have made their appearance in the entire scope and history of music are the use of tonal sound and the electronic generation of sound.) The more thoroughgoing the process is, the greater will be the formal sophistication, variety, and individuality of the works of art it makes possible, and the greater the complexity and freedom of the activity of composition. Creative freedom is not restricted by a public idiom, which is an inescapable aspect of artistic expression, or even by the overall formal schemes of genre, but provided instead with greater strength and range of meaning.

Even in the material aspect of its nature, as we have had occasion to notice, art may be regarded as an activity of producing and apprehending meaningful form. The formative activity, however, is to a considerable extent the work of society and culture, and the receptive one is similarly outside the full consciousness and control of the individual. The form and the meaning are the joint product of nature, society, and the individual. The properly artistic levels of formativity, however, which involve purpose and conscious effort, bring into being an interconnected series of changes in the detachment, objectivity, and constitution of the formal product. Any artistic configuration becomes more thoroughly and essentially an immanent object of perception than is the material from which it is made. The interest it holds for us more emphatically detaches it from the environmental world—and this detachment is added to the initial separation from practical interests that is established by the very conception and nature of artistic material and

117

artistic purpose. The freedom of art from biological utility, and its basic independence of social and ritual function even though it coexists with these in mutual enhancement, are obviously characteristic even for configurations of an antiphonal kind, which are based on the externality and environmental location of sound, and even for the conspicuous externality of song and opera and dance; but it is also obvious in these varieties of music that multisensory objectivity need not be sacrificed to artistic detachment. Indeed a musical performance represents in general to the listener; and to a lesser degree to the performer, the simultaneous perception of two different kinds of object, environmental and immanent, each detached in its own way from everyday interests. The same duality is present, although less conspicuously, in an imagined performance, in one that is electronically reproduced, and even in the general conception of a musical work. The new prominence of detachment in artistic form, and the new enhancement of immanence, are corollaries of its complex constitution, for any configuration presupposes constituents which are in some sense definable and perceptible as parts, even though in their combination they give rise to a synthetic unity with novel emergent properties; and even if we set aside questions of meaning, it is the intrinsic formal interest of the relationship of part to part and of parts to whole, particularly with reference to the properties of the whole, that endows art with its own interest and value and removes it to a sphere entirely separated from outside purpose.

However small it may be, every articulated unit of form, whether a chord, a harmonic progression, a melodic motif or theme or phrase, or any other defined configuration of sound, will by the very fact of its articulation possess some degree of coherence and wholeness, just as an entire improvisation or composition does. Yet units and sections will in general be incomplete; their brevity and our musical expectations in respect of the overall form of a genre would ensure this even without a more tangible deficiency in completeness. Coherence will result either from the uniformity or the conformability of the constituent elements, unity in turn from their coherence or from their complementary relationship, and temporal wholeness from the definition of each stage of the duration in accordance

118

with its position. The unity of a theme, for example, may be grounded in a balanced economy of motifs which are varied in rhythm and in pitch configuration but which possess a vital connection that has the inevitability of organic form. But a dynamic quality that limits wholeness will be more or less conspicuous in every subdivision of an overall musical form; assertions will call for repetition, elaboration, or response; progressions to relatively unstable or unsettled states for continuation or complementation.

Starting from the traditional and public stock of configurations which arise through the combination of cultural idiosyncrasy with natural and biological properties and through individual additions to this material, musical inventiveness continues to create the numberless varied shapes of each type of formal section by alteration and analogy. The qualities and qualitative course of new configurations are the guide of this creative activity, so that form cannot be understood if meaning is left out of account. It is apparent, however, that the basis of the construction of form is given not just by what configurations already exist, but by the generalized residue of these configurations as relational properties and tendencies of the elemental sonorities of the musical culture. Each tone of a scale, each rhythmical pattern and speed, and each melodic and harmonic interval or chord will possess various affinities to every other element, various degrees of self-containment or various types of dynamic tendency that call for or suggest different kinds of succession or completion; and it is in the changing fulfillment or contradiction of these intrinsic forces, and in their novel combination, that the detailed nature of formativity consists. The process is guided by its result: by the new intrinsic quality or significance that has been savored and adjusted, perhaps many times, always according to a principle of comparison. The proposed formulation is is compared, explicitly and implicitly, with other individual patterns, some novel and some more familiar, and with established general modes of formulation and response. It is considered in the setting of the whole musical composition, of smaller contexts, and of other sections that have special relationships to the part being formulated.

Through repetition, sequence, variation, extension, and antithesis, and often in dependence on the structures and relationships of language, initial sections of form give rise to larger divisions. In articulated forms the hierarchy of sections, with smaller combining repeatedly to form larger, is often emphasized by a corresponding hierarchy of pauses or of cadential melodic figures or harmonic progressions. At times special styles, textures, tone colors, or tempos may define a division or mark its start or close, as in the episodes of a fugue or the divisions of a sonata movement, or the sections of an improvisation in Indian or Islamic music. The colotomic forms of gamelan music are punctuated by a hierarchy of different size gongs that mark off sections of different length, sounding simultaneously whenever sectional divisions coincide. A single and clearly defined articulation obviously represents only one formal possibility, although it is quite common in comparison with the opposite extreme of unremitting continuity, which is hardly possible to achieve, since it stands in contradiction to the inherent tendencies of temporal perception. But simultaneous patterns of articulation which are not congruent, and which are not defined with equivalent distinctness or by the same means, can be taken to characterize musical form in general, even in the case of purely melodic styles. The constituents of pitch and rhythm can establish contrasting or conflicting articulations of a single melody, and even the configuration of pitch alone can suggest or establish multiple articulations because of the complexity of its internal intervallic relationships, while rhythm contains possibilities that are at least equivalent, especially because of its complex basis in duration, loudness, subtleties of grouping, and even tone color. If the essentially endless varieties of heterophony and polyphony are added to the combination of pitch and rhythm, the formal articulation of music, even apart from the contributions of language and gesture, becomes susceptible of a complexity and subtlety that can easily exceed the powers of auditory perception or of auditory imagery and invention.

We are doubtless able to describe musical form without an appeal to the psychological and social processes through which it was produced, or to the process by which it is apprehended, or even to the significance that is attached to it; but our description and analysis will then fall far short of a satisfactory understanding. In the instance of artistic form, the nature of which is determined by an address to perceptual values and by its inseparability from the meaning it conveys, the description of purely formal features must remain very distant from the reality of experience. Yet it is well to realize that there exists an analytical possibility of examining form in itself, and that in principle form is not to be identified with its invention, with its perception, or with its significance. Formal properties thus objectively considered are bound up with temporality, simultaneity, and articulation. Music is essentially a type of motion, but as soon as we seek a closer description of it we prejudice our conception of its nature by the very descriptive terms we adopt, which inescapably reveal our model of thought, whether of exterior and contents, statement and meaning, or sensible manifestation and idea.

Now all of these characterizations of music, in their concern with the duality of form and meaning, neglect a closer examination of form itself, which presents not only a fixed aspect but also a dynamic one—a type of form in the making that is intrinsic to temporal form even after it has been completed and therefore has nothing to do with the actual process of its creation. In connection with form alone, then, we must recognize the existence of a fundamental duality of a moving or changing present and more persistent features that are less vivid and immediate perceptually. The persistent features are active as images or conceptions; they often have their moment of sensible realization as part of the changing present, but it is also possible that they may not be sounded at all, throughout the form they inform, like the A-minor tonic chord of the Prelude to Wagner's *Tristan*. The duality of form and meaning may seem applicable as a description of this situation, form designating the audible changing present, the meaning of which consists in or is given by the features that persist. But reflection will reveal that the meaning of a melody is attached to and dependent upon its

121

form as a whole, and not just the transient aspect of this form. Indeed the central fact of musical constitution that we are endeavoring to describe must be regarded entirely from the point of view of form, and more specifically as concerned with the structure of form, which we may characterize as a temporal simultaneity that is in some sense hierarchical if not spatial. The spatial notion of background and foreground, or (in the vertical direction) the idea of layers or levels, suggests itself as an appropriate description.

Even a single melody, then, which may be analyzed into a succession of tones, is not composed of equivalent elements: some tones are more prominent than others, they provide a framework or at least an enduring factor that extends beyond immediate perception to constitute an influence existing simultaneously with the changing detail of the temporal present; indeed there may be a group of such more enduring factors, acting simultaneously and, strictly speaking, imperceptibly, and with different degrees of insistence and different temporal ranges. There is thus an incipient or explicit dualism in musical form between function and decoration, and this distinction, which is intrinsic to temporal experience and is essentially a contrast of absence and presence, provides a ground for the separation of conception and perception, and thus for the existence of the whole musical work, which not only depends upon the activity of conceptual components, but indeed is largely conceptual in its entirety. But a functional tone remains present in a sense throughout our perception of detail, and its presence is not merely conceived but also actually perceived, as an active force that exerts a controlling influence over the course of the music, while "decoration" or "ornamentation" by no means implies a purely accessory status, but designates an essential part of the form and progress of the whole.

It is easy to see that in addition to melodic prominence other more palpable factors will provide similar formal properties; harmony and in fact polyphony and heterophony are obvious examples of simultaneous factors, and they also produce in general hierarchical relationships; thus in the fundamental sense in which these structures are relevant to the essential

122

nature of music, they are in fact no different from monody. Drones, for example, are simply an explicit version of the influence of a tonic or of other important structural tones in purely melodic styles, while from the opposite point of view figural melodic passages—in Bach or in Schumann, for example—often have conspicuous polyphonic implications. What is involved in every instance is an articulation, or a complex of articulations, that defines the temporal nature of musical form, or if we wish, a matrix of forces, not all of them literally audible, that shape the course of form as well as its totality. We can compare the perception of such a totality to a scanning process, in which the whole is constructed by a complex series of operations. There is first of all a synthesis of smaller sections—melodic motifs or phrases, let us say; this takes place at or near points of articulation; it consolidates what has been passing in our immediate memory and subsequently transfers the perception to a less conscious type of memory for longer retention and recollection. New syntheses are continually compared with those previously completed, but in an automatic way such that out of the distinct configuration in process of completion and the older ones not actually reinstated in imagery there nevertheless emerges an awareness of the relationship between present and past, of the similarity or difference of the novel with what has gone before. The whole we ultimately construct, of course, reacts in turn upon each temporal present, determining both its meaning and its form in terms of its place in the totality. It is this process of formal perception that musical structure subserves, just as it in turn represents the result of a process of imagination and speculation and comparison that along with social forces comprises the invention of form. Yet structure can be distinguished from both processes, and if form tends to be identified with perception on the one hand and with formativity on the other, the notion of structure can be taken to refer to form itself and to its objective detail apart from questions of origination or aesthetic properties.

There can be no doubt that musical form represents a paradoxical situation. It is not genetically different from spatial form, for this too must be created on the basis of historical style by the successive formulation of parts with the aid of imaginative projection and comparison; at most memory plays no vital role as it may do in musical composition. But in its perception, and thus in its objective nature also, musical form seems to consist of images and conceptions, very much as poetry and literature do, although the role of auditory perception cannot be said to be dispensable or even secondary. It would seem that music is devoted to the production of form that has merely an ideal existence in the sense that it cannot be perceived as a whole, or else that the art is dedicated to transient configurations that can be built up into a totality only by sacrificing their compelling and literally aesthetic character. To some extent, at least, music presents us with the alternative of pallid form or formless effect.

# CHAPTER 4

# Meaning

The meaning of music is indissolubly connected with its form; the two comprise a unity that is manifest even in the most elemental musical material. Indeed even the biological significance of sound that underlies musical material reveals the same intimate relation to sonorous form; for the form of sound—taking form in the wide sense of the total specification of sonorous matter—is a sign of the specific nature of some particular environmental object or event; tone in particular is a sign of life, and in the human sphere, it is consciousness made perceptible or concrete, as opposed to silence, which confines us to pure inwardness, inarticulate and unformed. But sound is also the occasion or specific correlate of an organic process of orientation and adjustive reaction, of localization and identification. These two closely interrelated kinds of meaning, each bound to the same specific form, have their counterparts in the detached spheres of artistic material. As belonging to an environmental musical object, the form of sound expresses the nature of its source: a vocal tone, for example, is the expression of a formulated inner state and bodily act, and an instrumental tone reveals something of the physical nature of the source and the bodily activity from which it arises. As belonging to an immanent auditory object, on the other hand, the form of sound provokes a corresponding response of distinctive feeling tone that appears as a property of the sonorous object itself. Thus the realm of art preserves the two interlinked meanings of biological interaction, but it removes the immediacy of these meanings and transforms them so that they reside less in the environment and in our subjectivity and more in the immanent auditory object. This change is especially evident in the case of music as opposed to musical material; artistic meaning adumbrates organic experience—its motion, mass, fragility, force, inertia, monotony, alarm, foreboding, or flight—yet these remain adumbrations of an object immanent to sense (or of objects, at any rate, that in spite of their environmental existence are without actual biological or instrumental significance).

The sounds used in music are in no case those that occur naturally; even when they seem to be, the process of taking them up into music endows them with a new meaning even as material. The fact that tone rarely occurs in nature in conspicuous form makes it particularly valuable among sounds in fostering the artistic property of detachment. And tone as it is used in music is not to be equated with tone as it is found in nature; the sound of the wind whistling through branches possesses an expressiveness and a significance that are fused with its form, very much, it would seem, like the sound of a clarinet; but the components and their conjunction in the one case are biological and in the other artistic. It is only in the artistic instance that the formulation is based on sensible properties for their own sake. Then the sound becomes a tone, and at the same time as it assumes the guise of form, it similarly takes on the aspect of formed quality and expressiveness. This is both the result of the selection and formulation and also their cause; to conceive of sound as a musical element is to endow it simultaneously with both form and significance. We could not hear it as an element of music unless it had meaning, nor could it be given a defined meaning except through the defining power of a selective or formative act. Outer and inner come into being together, so that when a sound is heard as material for music, it is also heard as possessing a feeling tone and expressiveness.

Again a wordless human cry is in the most immediate sense an expression of an inner state; the response it evokes is the other aspect of its significance; and there is no doubt that it possesses a natural form; but in these things it is not even elemental material for music. In order for human vocal utterance to become such, it must become the result of a formative or selective activity which is guided by and productive of its meaning. But our very act of conceiving vocal tone as musical material does exactly this; it converts the natural into the formal, the expression into an expressive element, and transforms the response—whether of arousal or of hypnotic attraction—from a literal to a virtual one. However great may be the aesthetic values of the tones found in nature they obviously are never the result of human formative purpose. They are almost all produced by animate beings, and therefore possess the additional significance of vitality that can easily be identified with human life; bird calls even have a complexity of structure that invokes the intrinsic constitutive powers of audition, thus producing a qualitative pattern of immanent perceptual interest. But lacking otherwise the expressive and responsive meanings of human formativity, the aesthetic properties of nature remain fundamentally distinct from those of art; they can at most give only the illusion of art, if they are perceived in anthropomorphic terms.

Tone has been the most prominent material of music not only because of its amenability to form but also because of its specifically artistic types and qualities of meaning. Of course pitch itself, because of its positional nature, the precision of discrimination it permits, and its ability to support distinctive intervallic qualities, whether successive or simultaneous, makes tone readily adaptable to the invention of diversified structures. This objective utility of tone, however, is really grounded in human physiology and response; the structures in question are determined by our perceptual apparatus in respect of frequency relationships. Intervallic qualities may have a foundation in mathematics and physics, but they exist only by virtue of perception. The very possibility that tonal structures can interest us at all from an aesthetic point of view must obviously be provided by sensational qualities and perceptive abilities. To create tonal patterns doubtless satisfies our constructive imagination and our desire to explore mathematical relationships, but these forms would not belong to music if they could not be heard; they would not belong to art at all if they could not be apprehended by any sense or projected or intuited somehow in sensible terms. And if feeling is not a faculty but a facet of all activity, it is not in any way strange for it to be attached to patterns of tone. Thus even the structural potentiality of tone as a musical material rests on properties of meaning and inner experience.

These properties are of remarkable depth and importance. Vocal tone in particular is an immediate expression of inner states of feeling much more than is clapping, for example, or even whistling. If we select the pitch capability of our voice for musical purposes rather than its power to produce varied complex sounds amenable to the communication of conceptual thought, we have at our disposal a medium of inherent expressive force that is at the same time adaptable to varied configurational and structural ends. Our utterance takes on form without losing its expressive character, or, if we wish, our structures, even if already aesthetic and qualitative, take on additional emotional strength and immediacy. Through a felt kinship with our own voice, then, not only are the tones of other voices and the sounds of animals endowed with greater interest and expressive significance, but instrumental tones and sounds also secure a vital intensity above and beyond their quality as continuous stimuli and products of continuous activity. We speak of "voicing" a piano or an organ in reference to a nice adjustment of tone quality, as though the instrument were being brought to express in sound its true or innermost nature. Ar d if a physical object or a machine is submitted to stress we hear the sounds emitted as shrieks or complaints; indeed if no sound results we feel that the object is keeping quiet, that it is undergoing silent suffering with endurance or fortitude; we hear the silence. In contrast to the connotation of *voice*, the word *sound* is further from speech, and suggests an inanimate and purely physical manifestation; the significance of *tone* lies between the two: it involves the notion of vital tension but not of utterance.

128

The process by which objective tonal structures are infused and fused with expressive values is abetted by the peculiar fusion of externality and immanence that tone manifests. For hearing is a distance sense only in part—only with respect to sources of sound and environmental adaptation. And this practical aspect of hearing is dominant only in the perception of tone color, of transient sounds, and of noise, where we seek to recognize or identify objects or beings in our vicinity. By contrast, tone is almost absent from nature, both animate and inanimate, and is of relatively little value in identification; indeed the attribute of pitch is essentially useless as an indication of the nature and location of a source of sound. Thus little remains of bodily orientation and equilibrium, or of environmental perception, and whatever is manifest of perceptual assimilation and comprehension is confined to immanent tonal patterns, where configurational tendencies of closure and so forth have no further significance in terms of environmental adjustment.

Hearing always has a mysterious nature as compared with vision, merely because vision is so much more competent a judge of the external world; we always seek the support of vision to come to grips with what we hear; indeed this adjustive process is an underlying cause of the existence and prevalence of the composite musical arts and persists even in absolute music. Yet taken in itself, hearing reveals many things about our world that vision can not; what it lacks in multiplicity of detail and spatial definition it makes up in telling us of the nature and state of physical material and animals, and of human personality, attitudes, feelings, and thought. To some extent also, the mysterious aspect of hearing is a prejudice of culture as well as a fact of biology. But with tone, the mystery that hearing possesses with respect to outside objects is deepened to such a degree that it easily gives way to a new kind of perceptual activity amenable to the purposes of art precisely because of its lack of utility in adaptation. We listen to the tones themselves, not to the sources from which the tones proceed. But although these tones are still objects, they possess a much less definite species of objectivity than their sources, for only the sense of vibration, but neither vision nor touch, can cooperate in locating them. They are in fact perceived simply as objects of consciousness with no environmental location at all rather than as objects in multisensory space. Quite unlike the objects of touch or vision, then, and unlike their own sources, tones are without external location, and—again uniquely—they appear as saturated with subjective qualities of feeling. With their internal objectivity and their strangely evident subjectivity, they present a phenomenal fusion of outer and inner that is responsible for the emotional force of music and for its freedom from conventional external attachments. The power of this fusion is due further to the paradoxical combination of an exceptionally insistent stimulus with an absence of practical import, for sound is by nature the most important sign of environmental danger; it is a descendant of vibratory sensitivity that puts us in direct, physical contact with any motion or threatening activity in our surroundings, even those that are not in our field of vision or that take place in complete darkness; and through the reticular formation, it awakes us to immediate reflex action, preparing our whole system for rapid defense and flight. With tone and music, the efficient protective stimulus that sound represents becomes at the same time totally deprived of survival value, and is not taken as a sign of external objects or activity at all, but rather for its own sensible and feelingful qualities. These qualities are then the more insistent in being attached to a stimulus with so potent an effect on our nervous system, and especially in that the stimulus is free from its practical urgency—free, that is, to turn its inherent force to a purely aesthetic service. At the same time, the aesthetic detachment of music retains a peculiarly contradictory quality that is due both to the biological values of sound and to its intimate connection with the fundamental features of consciousness and vital experience; for sound, however specifically artistic its use may be, will persistently attract and seize hold of every conceivable contextual and associative feature of music to extract meaning from them and identify itself with this meaning; thus the nature of sound and tone will make music seek complementation and fulfillment in the concrete meaning of composite types of art.

That the perception of any object depends upon the temporally persisting self-identity of consciousness is obvious; but in addition to this dependence, the connection of sound with consciousness has peculiar properties of its own, and is characterized by a unique intimacy. It is as though sound is the single adequate mode of expression of and therefore of access to certain areas of consciousness (and perhaps consciousness as a whole by means of these) that are ontologically central, primarily the durational persistence and thus the unity of consciousness and in close association with this, a basic species of vital feeling barely capable if at all of objectification in itself. Even noise and impulsive sound possess this peculiar capability, which would seem to be the nucleus of every type of musical meaning, but sustained tone possesses it in eminent degree. Tone is a concrete and vital manifestation of duration, and its vitality is certainly due in large measure to the readiness and self-evidence, indeed the insistence, with which it connects itself with the flow of sentience. Both are perfectly continuous, both possess a certain tonus, both depend on a constant expenditure of energy for their maintenance. Also tone can easily manifest itself apart from the sonorous material object that is its source, and the aerial vibrations that transmit it are altogether incapable of being perceived. Thus hearing a tone is often a perception of environmental events that it is an experience of immanent auditory objectivity; since this is not as objective or as separate from consciousness as the externality of visually and tactually perceived objects, tones and tonal patterns fuse more easily with the inner reactions they evoke and they tend to appear at the same time as manifestations or objectifications of these inner states and activities, to which they are after all formally similar and by which they are in fact constituted as immanent objects. In addition, through the sympathetic hearing that is part of our tendency to perceive and understand impressions in the most intimate and immediate mode available, that is, as expressions of life and especially of human life, instrumental tones that are not too dissimilar from vocal tones are heard as partaking of vocal expressiveness. These factors are not changed, but rather reinforced, by the vibrational sensations that accompany tonal ones. The result of the whole is to imbue tone with a vitality that often has an anthropomorphic character and almost always is felt as an objective counterpart of our inner life. For the same reasons as well as the obvious facts that it is subject to our will and reflects our emotions, the tone of our own voice appears as a direct externalization of our vital consciousness.

Much more than elsewhere, the durations and durational patterns of music are heard for their own sake; they have a prominence that is not easily suppressed by other aspects of musical experience, and an immediacy that is due to their close coordination with and direct hold on the inner processes of life. The immediacy of the temporal qualities of an experience would seem to derive from the ease and inevitability with which it is sensed and measured in terms of our responsive activity; in this sense the whole response to music never lacks temporal quality because it never ceases to be bound up with the flow of consciousness, nor does it contain meanings of a nontemporal kind that tend to draw our attention from its durational qualities, a situation that is characteristic in other types of experience. Indeed all the qualities of music are inherently durational, and the duration is a filled one, never absent from our musical response or expression. The force of the inner musical experience is such that it not only makes music the most vivid manifestation of temporality to consciousness, but also is responsible for the reciprocal facts that music provides a measure of inner duration in general and inner experience provides a measure of musical duration. Either can be regarded as the standard for the other, and it is probably true that there are no objects comparable to sonorous and tonal ones in the ease and accuracy with which they are measured by consciousness, but also true that consciousness can find no phenomenon comparable to tone and sound into which it so easily and accurately can project its own durational existence. Metrical and rhythmical speed, musical pace and tempo, the whole notion of fast or slow, indeed even the idea of long and short musical works: all have meaning only in their connection with vital processes, with heartbeat and breathing rate, with bodily motion and dexterity and speech and musical performance, with the capacity of rapid perception, the fatigue of sense organs, and the flagging of attention, with the cycle of the day, the round of daily activities, and the general level of animation of society. Music is in short a medium that is remarkably adequate to arouse and represent and articulate the feeling of inner duration, and its natural suitability in this respect is especially manifest in the case of our own voice. In this mirror of consciousness we have the most sensitive organ and the final court of appeal for the comparison of durations within a certain range of magnitude, so much so that vocal duration—sounded, heard, or imagined—could be regarded by Augustine as the path to the absolute standard of duration found in the soul—in its ability to discriminate and to judge its own discrimination. The synthetic action of memory leads the way. Ultimately the standard is timeless; temporality must be eliminated if it is to be known and judged; it must be reduced to simultaneity, if not to spatiality. In its metaphysical basis, Augustine's conception is close to that of Plato's *Timaeus*, which makes time the moving image of eternity.

Platonic and Neoplatonic types of meaning in music can be found not only in durational rhythm but also in the spatial relationships of pitch, which have been regarded as the counterpart of structural patterns in the soul or the cosmos or in the physical world of atoms or crystals. All temporal and spatial manifestations of equality and proportion become the sensible embodiments of eternal ideas or the emanations of a divine unity. Although metaphysical symbolism of this kind would seem to inhere less in music than in the whole theoretical system of music, it can be found in an individual musical work also, where it may be accompanied by other emotive and conceptual meanings: in a medieval motet, for example, or in a serial piece of Webern, or indeed in the hymn Augustine cites in the concluding discussion of his *De musica*. This is the opposite extreme of meaning from that connected with the aesthetic notion of detachment, which rejects the ontological indentification of music and the world and fosters instead the independence of musical time and space. Musical duration is abstracted from the astronomical and daily temporal framework, and from everyday temporal experience, whether externally directed or psychological; while musical space is separated from planetary relationships of distance and size and speed and from the position and volume and quality of environmental objects. The meaning of music changes accordingly, but it is an intrinsic meaning even before the unity of music and the world is disrupted, because the symbolism that is contained in this unity is necessarily an internal one: music is primarily not a simulacrum of the cosmos or of society but a part of them; thus it puts us in touch with the whole, it presents rather than represents, very much as it subsequently presents rather than designates the formulated inner course of feeling that becomes its specialized meaning. Thus music was apparently thought of in ancient cultures as a part and revelation of universal relationships, a microcosm of cosmic time and space, or conceived of as extending throughout the cosmos as a continuous manifestation, and it was related in ritual and religion and work and play to the annual cycle of the seasons, to times of day, to astronomical and meteorological events, and to the church year; but as an art in recent times in the West it has been divided up, as we might say, into monadic individual works, the historical peculiarity of which we are only now in a position to examine or to reject. Each of these became a world of its own with a hold on our feelings that had to find a new and appropriate explanation. Only the movements or sections of a larger composition—an oratorio or symphony or ballet of the seasons, for example—or a series of works such as *The Well-Tempered Clavier* or *The Ring of the Nibelungen*, could suggest something of a greater integration with the world and with life instead of a detachment from them. Aesthetics knows the alternative well: is art continuous with life or a special experience somehow set apart? It has of course been both and can be either, although some kind and some degree of detachment are obviously called for if art is to represent an activity devoted to its own ends

Both duration and pitch may follow either of two divergent

tendencies of meaning, the one an aesthetic route of sentience and expression, the other a route of reason and number. The specifically aesthetic meanings of pitch—as opposed to its biological, referential, and purely rational meanings—consist fundamentally in the fact that it is a positional auditory quality which represents on the one hand a concrete manifestation of human powers of response and perception, and on the other a particular expressive aspect of the environmental world—some multisensory object and the material and state or activity of this object. It also establishes or seeks to establish an equation between these two kinds of meaning, to set our experience into connection with the properties of our world. This is true of sound in general, of course, and of all its attributes; pitch is distinguished by its particular positional quality, which is really a distinctive part of the overall quality of a sound, but a part that easily separates itself from the whole and is perceived independently. To some extent the physical constitution of sources facilitates this separation. In any event, changes of pitch—whether disjunct or gradual and especially in association with rhythm—produce an immanent motion with various kinds of continuity, and also represent an external activity with similar properties, although in the case of motion the relation of intrinsic and environmental meaning is no longer so close or so obvious. The high-and-low component of pitch, which in contrast to its tonicity we have found to be strongly intersensory, must be singled out as responsible for referential or extrinsic meaning more than for the immanent and representative types.

This is also true in some measures for the other attributes of tone, although the particular kinds of referential symbolism based on number and connected with reason, cosmos, and supreme or divine being are not possible because of the inapplicability of numerical measure. But the significative implications of the other attributes of tone and of nontonal sound are in general more conspicuous than those of pitch, which being so eminently adapted to structure becomes prominent in meaning only in patterns, especially because it then acts as a basis for the combination of all the attributes. Duration we have already considered, but loudness, tone color, volume, compactness, and so forth also have striking qualities that have both an immediacy of involvement with inner experience and a powerful expressive property in conveying the nature of their origin. They have in addition, as we have had occasion to notice in the preceding chapter, a strong intersensory and referential tendency that comes into its own in the field of program music and the composite musical arts. Even biological meaning can become active: prolonged intensity can produce intoxication or dizziness, sudden loudness or prolonged growth in loudness can arouse aural pain, and penetrating tone colors can similarly produce painful tactile sensations.

These factors of meaning are again characteristic of nontonal sound, which further emphasizes expressive and biological types of meaning, although now at the expense of immanent significance. Noise is also intersensory and referential in tendency, and will not only represent its source but enter readily into the extrinsic symbolization of which music is capable. With speech, of course, the still additional meaning of conceptual thought makes an appearance, but this in itself really removes speech from music. Both nontonal sound in general and speech in particular must be taken up into music if they are to become part of it, or raised to an artistic status, just as tone is, by being conceived as musical material and thus subjected to a selective and formative or transformational process. They must be put into conjunction with tone, which already belongs to the realm of art, or removed from everyday life through stylization in accordance with sonorous dimensions. Oratory alone, therefore, is a type of music, for it attends to properties of duration, rhythm, tone color, and volume, and indeed to repetition and form as well. The same is more obviously true of various types of poetry, but not of the everyday language of communication. But besides exemplifying the significative features of noise, language as music and language in music—in their contribution of concepts and discursive thought as well as conative values— bring a new importance to the representative and immanent meanings of musical art and to the equation between the two. There is now a meeting of minds and of cultures, just as there is—although in a different way—in the purely tonal sphere of sonorous configurations, but not to a comparable extent in the sphere of sonorous material in itself.

If we turn from the principles of meaning that reside in the nature of sonority to the concrete significance and influence that are brought to musical meaning by sound sources of particular kinds, we find that the various sources have characteristic effects even on purely immanent meaning, just as they bring with them their own preliminary formal determination of sound and certain distinctive contributions to musical form; indeed the very choice of sonorous material is at the same time the selection of a certain tendency or range of possibilities of meaning as well as of form. A matter of fundamental importance is whether we originate sound ourselves or it arises from some other source. If we produce sound ourselves—by clapping, whistling, or vocal utterance—it will be primarily an expression of our inner life: of volition, feeling, cognition, and formative interests. Yet by the very fact of its production it will be projected or objectified, and take on a separate existence, both as an immanent and an external object. The properties of these objects, however, will be given to them by the action and functions of perception. In the opposite situation, when sound arises from some outside agency, it will be primarily an objective entity, whether self-subsistent or a manifestation of its source, and it will also become an immanent auditory object. The objective properties we perceive, however, are again the result of the nature of perception, and it is an understandable consequence that they cannot remain sealed off from our life of feeling; our inner experience is shaped by the qualities that we ourselves place in its object in response to a physical stimulus that remains imperceptible. The same relative weight of expression and objectivity respectively continues to characterize the auditory images of these two categories of sound; and it remains striking in both cases how much sound reveals of its source, how intimately and strongly it engages the flow of consciousness, and how prominently it is experienced as an immanent object.

The relationship in meaning between sound we produce ourselves and that which originates externally is as important as the difference. In both cases sound proceeds from the activity of some being, whether inanimate or animate; it arises from something that is active, activated, or alive, and is thus intelligible as the manifestation of the inner or nonvisible aspect of being—as the revelation of the intrinsic properties of a physical object or as the expression of animal life or human consciousness. But because we ourselves produce sound as a central natural expression of our ideas and feelings, hearing has a native tendency toward animism. The sound arising from whatever source accordingly seems to present the subjectivity of some vital being. On the other hand, the sound we produce ourselves endows us with another plane of existence, for it objectifies our inner nature and thus helps to build a bridge between consciousness and its world. In hearing ourselves—in some degree at least as others hear us—we become assimilated to the external objects of our awareness, and come to know ourselves as one of them, from the outside as well as the inside: as a physical and biological entity such as we see around us.

Thus whether sound is external or personal in origin, it possesses both objectivity and the marks of subjectivity. It is either external or an objectification, but in both cases it bears a significant relation to our inner life. We can describe this relation more closely by saying that sound makes us particularly aware of our consciousness, of its life and flow, and that it does this because it formulates and objectifies it, in a special mode, to be sure, which is that of audition, but in a mode peculiarly adaptable to the function it serves. By this very token, however, sound is also necessarily an otherness—a projection of our selves or a phenomenon that takes hold of our inner being, takes it up, and makes it observable. As an object of perception, sound could have no existence except for its constitution by consciousness, and it is this constitution that is responsible for its power to reveal our inner life.

An external sound, however, will express the inner aspect of its source as well as shaping and thus expressing our own; it will therefore tend to establish an equation between two subjectivities, to bring the course of our vital awareness into consonance with the nature of the being it reveals. In the case of

138

music, this being is ultimately the mind of its creator, but it is this mind thinking and feeling in musical terms. It is easy to see, therefore, that by a transfer, and especially in default of other knowledge of the mentality of the composer and performer, the music itself can be experienced as though it were an expressive organism with which we think and feel in sympathy. But even external sound, as a sign of vibrational activity or life, is clearly less a self-subsistent entity than a property or manifestation of its source, which is an object of visual and tactual perception as well as auditory; and music seems to extend and exploit this dependent status of its material, for it is a manifestation not simply of activity or life, but of mind and culture. In connection with sonority itself, we speak not only of hearing the sound of a voice and a violin, which implies the independence of the sound, but with equal propriety of hearing a voice and a violin themselves, or of hearing singing and violin playing, or a singer and a violinist. Sound will normally contribute to perception by providing knowledge of its source—by suggesting its approximate size and revealing the nature of the material that constitutes it. But in anticipation of the independence of music as an immanent and animate object, it also detaches itself from its source to become an external object in its own right—one which lacks the reinforcement of vision or touch and which bears only an indefinite relationship to the aerial agitation that supports it. (If we customarily designate the perceived sources of sound as physical rather than phenomenal objects, it is obviously not because we imagine that they are literally the objects of physical science, but only because their visual and tactual properties, and especially their shape and location, correspond quite precisely to the underlying physical events that go to produce them.)

A position midway between personal expression and outside phenomenon is occupied by the sounds arising from instruments we play ourselves. Such sounds are already approximated by clapping and even by whistling as contrasted with the directly expressive character of the voice; but a musical instrument or any sound producer that can flexibly register our intent becomes at once an extension of our natural expressive facilities and purposes as well as an independent external object. And similarly, the sound it produces will have not only an obvious origin in an external source but also a close connection—in the case of most instruments—with our corporeal sonorities and resonances, and we will feel in any event that our inner experience is finding a direct and immediate sonorous expression.

The relationship between personally and externally produced sound has a more specific and concrete manifestation in the duality of vocal and instrumental music. In the case of the voice, and especially the individual voice as contrasted with a chorus, meaning will derive mostly from inner expressive forces. In the case of an instrument, it will derive from the qualities and dimensions of a material object and its mode of activation. Yet the natural significance in each case is fully manifest only when we are the singer and some one else is the instrumentalist; the opposite situation will tend to reverse the meaning, so that the voice will in a sense resemble an instrument and the instrument a voice. Thus the expressive values that are perceived by the individual composer-performer in his own voice as an immanent auditory object are reflected back to reinforce and interact with the meaning that is their cause; but the voice of another singer becomes more of an external than an immanent object, and still more a manifestation of the singer either in his own right or as the representation of a dramatic character; the inner expressive values have shifted from the objectification of vital experience to the opposite extreme of the revelation of the nature of an external being. There is a similar reversal in the case of instruments, for their sounds are always heard to some extent as voices, particularly when they produce sustained tones, and thus as expressive both of their own nature and of the inner experience of the instrumentalists; this component of their meaning, then, will represent the expression and skill of another person revealed in an external object; but if we ourselves perform instrumentally, this outer representative significance will be transformed into the presentation of an immanent object which has captured our own expressivity and skill.

Each type of sound possesses its own inherent tendencies of meaning, but the most significant characteristic of all is doubtless the expressive quality of the solo voice. The voice is the single most important avenue through which we make known our desires and intentions; it is an almost automatic servant, compliable and highly adequate, of our emotive and intellectual life. Even if on occasion it seems unable to convey either the strength or the subtlety of our feelings, it is still the medium that makes our inner life audible, and manifest to the outside world. Thus in its own right, as a purely tonal organ and without the kinds of meaning contributed by words or functional context, the voice possesses a specifically musical range of expression. This can be seen in the wide diffusion and variety of wordless work songs and calls, and to some extent also even in melismatic sections of song with text, where the expressive values of vocal tone as such receive their due, although shaped in their feeling, of course, and directed in their meaning, by their textual and functional association and by the whole cultural setting in which they occur. European yodeling is a familiar instance in which harmonic values enter into the overall quality. The meaning of the plainsong jubilus, by contrast, became an explicit problem that called for elucidation in the context of patristic musical philosophy; it could not be readily sanctioned as a purely musical delight, but signified a rejoicing in the praise of God, as Augustine asserted in his *Confessions*, that because of its object necessarily exceeded the finite confines of language.

We hear our own voice not only as an immanent auditory object, but as an external sound also, with its particular qualitative and locational features—different to us, of course, than to everyone else because of the influence of internal vibration and of bone conduction to the auditory organs. Yet the sound of our voice in the act of singing is only with difficulty perceived as an external object; we know it more as an immanent object, and still more as an instrument of formulation and expression. Imagining music in terms of one's own voice is a creative or reproductive experience almost entirely without an aspect of externality. Indeed the object produced is immanent more in an abstract or general way than a specifically vocal one. When we hear another person sing, the reversal of objectivity produces an extreme of sonorous externality, but we remain aware above all of the expressive nature of the human voice; not only of the expressivity of the soloist but of the immediacy of inner force of our own responsive experience.

Choral music is much more impersonal; it demands that we participate in a group experience, or in a feeling common to all, and thus in one which is necessarily not of peculiarly subjective and individual quality. In addition, whether we participate or listen, the sound is not readily to be identified with our own voice; for the sound of a chorus, much more than that of a single musical instrument, resists being heard as the voice of an individual, partly because of the nature of its quality and the types of graduation of which its quality is susceptible, and partly because of its lack of external local specificity.

If we perform on an instrument, or imagine ourselves to perform, or conceive music in terms of an instrumental realization by others, the external objectivity is in every case more pronounced than in the parallel vocal situations, and the meaning correspondingly more tied to the nature of the source and the activity of performance. Both the meaning and the degree and character of the external objectivity will of course vary with the instrument being considered, and a basic determinant throughout is the amount of resemblance to the human voice, although the immediacy of the kinesthetic and emotional components of vocal performance or imagery is absent in every case. In listening to instrumental music we are impressed still more with the varying external objectivity of the different instruments and with the particular meanings each possesses. The tone of a harpsichord, for example, will insist much more upon its externality and its locational specificity than that of a French horn, a phenomenal fact that can be connected with physics and psychology: with the precision of localization the source permits, with the pattern and character of the energy radiated into the air by the plucked string as opposed to the wind instrument, and with the lack of a tone color and a subtlety of inflection that would relate the sound to the human voice.

The meaning is similarly peculiar to the instrument: to the action of a quill on a stretched string, to the manual act of employing a keyboard with particular characteristics of spacing and touch, and to the kinds of tonal patterns specific to the harpsichord and suggested by its physical nature.

Fundamentally, of course, the concrete meanings attached to particular sonorous media are historical in nature. They are based on a selection of sonorous materials that is bound up in instrumental music with the technological state of musical instruments as well as with a particular manner of playing them, and in vocal music with the tonal qualities conventional for the voice in its musical use, for the voice is no more than any instrument an unvarying medium determined by biological and psychological facts, nor is it again the equivalent of a single instrument but rather of all instruments taken together, particularly if the two spheres are compared in the larger scope of world history instead of within a single culture. In either medium, the musical significance is generally related to the whole range of uses and meanings that are connected with the sound producer, whether within music or outside it. Thus a ritualistic use of the drum gives rise to music that is informed with the emotional and cult significance of the whole occasion; the specifically sonorous aspect of the music is fused with the meaning of this sonority, the emotive and kinesthetic response to the music is not separated out as an experience in its own right, even as one characterized by traditional modes of response, but is an intrinsic part of a larger social experience. But the particular musical structures of drum beats can succeed to a use separate from this original context, and the point to be made in connection with such an abstract application is that the aesthetic conception of the music, and the aesthetic reactions to it, whether or not a stylization of the original patterns takes place, will contain emotive and cognitive elements derived from the original significance; it will be the exception rather than the rule for such music to arrive at a level of aesthetic abstraction in which purely artistic tradition comprises the whole meaning of the style, and for this to happen a whole new world of possibilities and a new freedom of formulation would doubtless have to be superadded to the earlier traditional patterns. The Western musical career of the trumpet from military signals and ceremonial patterns to a freedom of use in which its original emotive and social significance entered only occasionally (and then often with an attenuated or generalized import) is an instructive case in point. The French horn has a similar history that starts with hunting patterns. Other instruments, however, may have a specifically aesthetic career; electronic ones, not associated with familiar qualities of tone, are an extreme instance, although even "nonhistorical" instruments and styles are historical; but most of the earlier social contexts of string and keyboard instruments, for example, themselves comprise spheres of use that were artistic as well as social, so that the more concrete contextual components of meaning, already subordinate, easily vanish from present-day musical experience. A prevailing tendency toward detachment in art obviously entails a similar tendency in the meaning of individual instruments, of their tone color, and of their melodic, rhythmic, and dynamic patterns, all of which may undergo marked changes and manifest increased variety during the process of aesthetic stylization. But the detachment in meaning will have an important precondition in the original degree of interest that was directed to structural and sensible properties for their own sake.

The past of a musical instrument, during which its shape and material as well as its tone color were often of the greatest importance to its meaning, will generally tend to live on, together with various equally significant stylistic formulations, as part of later musical conceptions and responses that are more specifically artistic; but even when earlier meanings fade and disappear, the instrument is left with a definite physiognomy of size shape, and material, as well as of tone, rhythm, and melodic contour, all of which give it a more definite personality and character because they are a constellation of properties that have long existed together as a meaningful entity. To be sure, their connection depends also upon physical compatabilities; it is natural because particular materials lend themselves to particular shapes and possess inherent possibilities of tone color, and we are familiar with the associations from our more general experience of physical properties. For historical and natural reasons, then, musical instruments will possess a coherent concreteness that becomes part of the stylistic meaning of music; if we renounce this constituent of significance, as we do in the abstract tones of electronic instruments, where the acoustic constitution of the sounds is freely subject to choice and unrelated to the appearance and the material composition of the instrument, our music is importantly altered in its nature and loses a particular kind of emotional and conceptual specificity along with a corresponding visual component.

If it is often important to the significance of instrumental music that the drum, for example, is made from the skin of a sacred animal, it is still more often important in vocal music that the voice is an organ of speech as well as of musical tone and rhythm. Indeed in its musical use it generally continues as an organ of language as well as tone, and the linguistic meanings—poetical, dramatic, emotional—are used as a nucleus or as a foil for the tonal ones; there will in any event be some kind of relationship between the two. Here also, then, as in the case of instruments, the sonorous medium brings with it structural forces and patterns of various kinds—a limitation of duration caused by the breath, a differentiation of high and low based on bodily resonance and the feeling tone associated with muscular strain, culturally determined qualities of sound, the inflections and rhythms of speech in a particular language, and even the elementary melodic formulations of traditional calls and lullabies. But the verbal and musical properties of the voice seem more distinct from one another than do the ceremonial and aesthetic components of instrumental sound, even though in principle both voice and instrument possess the same sort of duality: namely, one of concrete meaning as contrasted with the formation and enjoyment of sound for its own sake. The resemblance of the two media with respect to this duality is apparent in music that joins instrument and voice, for the tendency then is to connect ritual patterns with verbal expression, or, on the other hand, freer instrumental uses with the purely tonal abilities of the voice. A basic distinction between the verbal and tonal spheres of the voice, however, can be found in the independence of vowel changes from pitch; all the vowels can be sung in turn on a single pitch, just as a series of pitches can be sung on a single vowel. Instruments have no capacity to change tone color that is comparable to vowel change. Thus in addition to the emphasis in speech upon variety of sound in its transient aspects of attack, noise components, and so forth, and the constrasting emphasis in music upon sustained pitch and definite intervals of pitch, the voice has the capacity for two distinct modes of variation in the acoustic structure of compound tones. Change of pitch can be regarded as its "instrumental," as opposed to its verbal, principle, although the comparison with instruments is not to be taken too literally; as we have mentioned previously, the mere fact that besides vowel and pitch changes there is also a quality in the voice tha is characteristic of each person shows how complicated the modes of variation of vocal tone are. It is also important that speech can make use of definite pitches and intervals, of rhythmic patterns, and indeed of the aesthetic values of sound in general, just as, on the other hand, vocal music is not restricted to distinct configurations of pitch, but can make constructive use not only of vowel color, but also of the indefinite pitch and intervals of speech, and even of speech it-self (although this obviously represents a realm of musical expression distinctly different from song). Fusion of the two functions of the voice can be found in the sustained pitches and formalized intervals of signals and calls designed to reach distant hearers, and in the speechlike vocal styles of 20th-century Expressionism. In its use of indefinite pitch and intervals, furthermore, vocal music does not always simply enter the realm of speech, for such configurations may have nothing to do with verbal intelligence, and may be employed for their own sonorous qualities and expressiveness, and shaped for their own sake, without words at all. A relation to speech may still obtain, of course, for the voice will remain the characteristic medium of expression for inner states of feeling as well as for thought; when the formative aesthetic processes of music are applied to speechlike tonal variation, and even when they are applied to the voice in its imitation or assimilation of the properties of instruments, the voice will still retain something of its nature as personal utterance.

Thus within the abstract possibilities of form and meaning that are given in the physical and psychological dimensions of sound and tone, each instrument and each historical guise assumed by the voice contain specific formal tendencies and an inherent meaningful quality. These are often additonally shaped by traditional functions and contexts into musical patterns with a more particular and detailed significance that is due in part to the occasion of use and in part to the intrinsic effective aspect of each configuration taken as a purely sonorous entity. The intrinsic sensuous-emotive aspect of a configuration, however, is only to a limited degree constituted by invariant psychological forces that endow each tonal stimulus with invariant specific qualities; much more than this, and like the patterns themselves, it is a product of a coherent historical or cultural mode of musical expression.

The quality of even the smallest melodic configuration within a given musical culture has two aspects. There is a temporal course of meaning, which contains momentary states of directional tendency and of degree of tension or rest—a moving temporal present the changing meaning of which is always a product of its place in all the larger musical contexts that surround it and of its relationships to these contexts. But there is also an overall meaning which consists in the qualities of the whole and which is especially evident to the synthetic grasp that projects the whole or that regards it in retrospect, when the progressive course of meaning has ended. This comprehensive quality is the kind of meaning also found in simultaneous configurations, where the qualities and dynamic tendencies of the constituent tones—here again each influenced by its position in the whole even though not temporally progressing—enter into an encompassing meaning without losing their individuality. There is thus a fundamental similarity between succession and simultaneity in music, for in both cases—and doubtless with comparable physiological correlates—individual components are united into a whole, but do not fuse in the sense of vanishing; their qualities are influenced, even determined, by the whole, but they remain distinct as constituents. It is for this reason that meaning always has a counterpart in form, even in the public stock of patterns that comprise the preformed material of musical style.

Prior to the operation of self-conscious artistic activity, then, form and meaning are to some extent given along with the sonorous material, inherent in its physical or biological nature and shaped by culture and social use. More sophisticated forms and meanings are dependent on this public stock even when they ignore it, for deviations from established patterns have effects that are correlated with the deviations. The dependence is greater than it might seem because new creative efforts, whether they belong to traditional or folk music on the one hand or individualistic art music on the other, constitute a second stock of larger formulated meanings that has a still more inescapable influence. But throughout the hierarchy of musical manifestations, from simple types to complex ones or from smaller to larger, the correspondence of structure and meaning follows from the same considerations that apply to a single tone, except that the historical and personal determinants increasingly dominate the constitutional ones. The correspondence may seem as enigmatic as that of body and soul, but only if form and significance are not seen as different aspects of a single realized entity. It is in fact not at all remarkable that coherent, significant responses are produced by the patterns of music, or that coherent, significant patterns of feelingful inner experience can be formulated in terms of tone, if we understand that outer and inner have grown up together from the beginning. Every tonal inflection, gradation, or relationship, provided only that it is effective biologically and that it belongs to a style that is known, has come into existence not by chance, but because of the musical meaning it brought with it; in shaping and forming it the artist was always under the guidance of the qualities and vital feeling it provoked within a given stylistic idiom (which can be thought of as the aesthetic counterpart of a logical universe of discourse).

There is nevertheless a distinction in principle between musical material and music. In the one we may still more easily hear a voice or an instrument as such, and certainly also an immanent sonorous object as an independent entity in its own right. There is a simple correspondence of inner with outer, and of subjectivity with immanent objectivity. In what we take to be music, on the other hand, the equation is more complex; we hear not only an immanent auditory object—no longer now an external one to any important extent—but also style; and not only our subjectivity is engaged, structured in conformity with the object, but our cultivation and knowledge, our whole sensitivity and human insight. We encounter a vital, meaningful form; there is a meeting of minds; for music is more than an auditory object simply representative of its source; it is the embodiment of feeling and imagination and a manner of formativity; it is expression perceived as such. Yet it contains its meaning in objective form; it is structured material—the product, that is, of intelligent shaping in a specific tonal idiom, not simply of unmediated emotion. Vital feeling is formed along with the sonorous material, so that the formulation is an appplication of intelligence and artistic purpose to a particular kind of emotive and volitional experience. Musical perception, similarly, is not a direct response of feeling to an auditory provocation, but a reconstitution of the formulated inner experience in which intelligence and understanding are active participants; the sensuous and emotive aspects of our perception are not autonomous uncontrolled reactions but the vital facets of an encompassing grasp of meaning that involves the totality of consciousness. Music in performance, or in creation that is also performance, is an objective embodiment of meaning in the form of sonorous material, but the meaning consists neither of the conceptualization of a defined course of inner experience nor of this course of experience itself, but of a fusion of the two; and contemplation and empathy do not represent two types of meaning but merely the polar extremes of a continuum throughout which they are combined in proportions characteristic of various styles of music and different types of personality; the one designates the component of thought, of the mind and the imagination, the other the corporeal and kinesthetic component of feeling and volition.

149

As flexible as its nature may be, however, musical meaning is not found outside music, but in it, so that music appears alive or charged with the experience it represents, and the separation of auditory object and meaning is more theoretical than actual. Intrinsically, therefore, music is symbolic only in presenting a formulation of vital consciousness that in form and feeling is closely similar—because it is so basic in nature—to numberless concrete experiences undergone elsewhere; it is symbolic in two special senses: simply as a formulation and also as an adumbration of a whole class of related formulations, both tonal and nontonal, or a specimen of a cultural and personal mode of thought and feeling. In no case, however, is there any defined denoted object that is essential, whether extrinsic or purely musical, or any necessary intrinsic object other than the internal musical connotations and the formulated vital experience. Any statement of the theme of the first movement of Beethoven's *Eroica* will signify as an auditory object the particular sensuous quality and feeling tone it formulates and the specific temporal course of this quality. It may also connote other statements of the theme or the movement as a whole. The idea or ideal of heroism, however, is in spite of its musical involvement and tradition not an equally intrinsic part of the musical meaning, and indeed would have no counterpart in numberless other musical compositions. Musical meaning involves essentially only two explicit terms: the music and the person who experiences it—composer, performer, or listener. The meaning includes no external reference, but inheres in music itself, and particularly in the sensible object of a specific experience. This is true in large measure even of the musical connotations of music, the relations between a present perception and the implications it carries with it of other similar experiences, or between a given work and its whole stylistic tradition and future influence (in so far as these are known); for the absent musical experiences are more suggested than specified, they are felt not as separate, represented objects, but as fused constituents of the experience that is present, which is therefore more than a part of the whole it symbolizes, since it really contains an adumbration of the whole. But it is more conspicuously the case that the distinct

150

forces, motions, and qualities we hear in melodic succession or harmonic progression are an intrinsic part of the perceived object. They are thus fundamentally no different from the forces and properties we find in the world in general; both are objective, and both are products not only of external physical events but also of our own patterns and modes of formulation, which are compounded of native and cultural elements and, with more or less difficulty, are teachable to people of other societies.

In its most common mode, musical composition consists of a spontaneous but controlled assemblage of public patterns; it is coincident with performance and not fixed in notated form. Either complete melodies, more or less well defined and belonging to a repertory of known types, or smaller melodic units belonging to a similarly traditional stock, are taken up by an individual or a group and performed with improvised modifications, small units being connected in a successive mosaic, to shape a total musical experience. To some extent this experience is unique to the occasion, so that the creative enterprise is very much like the performance of a composition belonging to the notated mode of music. Fundamentally, however, structure and meaning in a process of this kind are largely preexistent; but a purely auditory stylistic tradition can exist in no other way. Memory demands a stock of given patterns small enough to be learned, which can then be freshly molded on each occasion to produce a structure and an experience that are individual as well as closely similar to the other members of a whole series that extends into the past. These patterns—melodic and rhythmic—are in fact relatively few in number in popular music; in highly developed styles, however, such as those of Gregorian chant or of Indian classical music, which may demand a lifetime of concentrated study and discipline, the capabilities and resourses of memory are astounding, especially in nonliterate musical traditions, and the amount of preformulated material that may be mastered seems to have no limit. On the other hand, and especially in the performance of a classical Indian *raga*, for example, it may often be a misconception to think of a fully objective process of construction; the performance will be controlled entirely by its meaning and will therefore be best characterized not in terms of form, but as a prolonged devotional exercise, a slow and profound immersion in a state of revery and reverence that is formulated and defined musically by a given group of tonal relationships. These are reflectively presented and considered individually in an introductory section or *alap*, and their connections then revealed more and more definitively, first in a lower melodic range and then in a higher one. Throughout there is a gradual increase in speed and rhythmical complexity as the revery is transformed from trance to intoxication or ecstasy. The devotion may last for hours, and its cathartic power is an outstanding example of the ability of music to still the passions by arousing and purging them. However well its stages and formative techniques may be defined, this is above all a course of inner musicoreligious experience, a matter of feeling rather than objective composition. In such an art, repetition will naturally play an outstanding role, varied typically by gradual changes in loudness or speed, for changes such as these can create the sense of tendency, of direction from beginning to end, that will enhance the wholeness · of the performance and at the same time permit a constancy of melodic and rhythmic patterns—the factor that (even more than recurrence) will secure for music the greatest ease of assimilation and the maximum degree of coherence.

More deliberate modes of composition, whether they operate with the actual media of performance, with written notation, or with phonotape, will follow similar principles, adding to them more complex formulations and sophisticated relationships. In every instance, the actual medium that is manipulated—even if it is no more palpable than images of immanent sound in the composer's imagination—will exert an influence on the compositional process and its musical result. The voice in its various styles of use, particular instruments, the precise nature of auditory imagery and its reference to concrete sources of sound or media of composition, the kind of visual notation used, the properties of phonotape—each will contain its own musical suggestiveness and enter into the determination of form and meaning. Yet the inner nature of the compositional process will

152

remain fundamentally the same in each case, and equally hidden from view. Novelty of invention and new formal and expressive properties seem to arise in a variety of ways that range from sudden and inexplicable inspiration or discovery to diligent workmanship or trial and error, although the problem will always remain of the guiding principle of selection or the quality finally judged satisfactory. All we can say of the process is that it must have its basis in previous musical and sonorous experience and in an operation of mentality and muscular activity that goes on subconsciously as well as consciously so that the genesis of formulations that arise can often not be traced or followed. But the new forms and meanings created are without doubt combinations and modifications of those already experienced. Whether they are speculative projections of form, conscious modifications of known patterns, new combinations or mosaics of public patterned tonal units, or spontaneously appearing ideas, their value and acceptability will be measured by their precise relationships to previously evolved meanings.

Structural innovation will obviously bring novelty of meaning with it, and indeed apart from factors of chance, the new meaning will be an intention that dictates the innovation in form. If a phrase is changed somewhat when it recurs, the experienced change is simultaneously logical and feelingful: the second configuration bears definable relationships of form to the first, but these are inescapably connected with corresponding relationships between new qualities of feeling and the original ones. In every kind of musical manifestation, structure and significance remain inseparable. Yet it is possible for our interest to be directed to the one or the other more strongly, whether in composing, performing, or listening; and the musical product will of course reflect this emphasis. Varying attitudes in this regard are dependent upon personality and momentary disposition, and they are more generally fostered by different styles and cultures. To be sure, musical experience can hardly involve a complete obliviousness to either form or meaning; both phases are usually present, although to varying extents, and even when we apprehend music as an intricate pattern of formal relationships, or when the composer creates it as an objective formation or design, there is still an inner response or a shaping of vital activity, for the pattern, as a tonal one in time, stands in intimate connection with sensation, feeling, memory, premonition, and the human capacity to construct and assimilate relationships. The temporal range and tonal scale of music alone are evidence of this. And conversely, no matter how preoccupied the composer is with his expressive impulse and dispositional state, or the listener with his, they will necessarily deal with a formulation and presentation of structure, for pure inwardness cannot be art; if it is to be raised from the realm of a formless biology it must meet with distinctions and structures that can have their foundation and expression only in an objective world of sense perception. Even the most elemental and unstructured utterance is a manifestation and objectivation of an inner state; it possesses sensible form even though it has not been formed, just as the most elemental awareness of a sound is always an awareness, a specific response with its own feeling tone; and it is not only of voices that this is true, but also of the sounds of inanimate objects or machines, perhaps ultimately because these too are in some degree apprehended as voices even when they are produced by chance or in muscular play rather than with an expressive intent.

The unity of meaning and form has a corollary in the fact that the meaning of music is specifically musical. Artistic structure, like sonorous material itself, arises from inner experience of a particular kind, from the tendency of inner life toward expression and play as this is reacted upon by materials and patterns of sonority and their production. The inner is indissolubly connected with the outer: our emotion and manipulation are specifically tonal and of tones, sonorous and of sounds; they could not achieve formulation and expression except in terms of objective acoustic impressions, but these patterns would be devoid of significance—would not be music—without an inner aspect of sensuous and constructive experience that is a specific form of vital activity related to tone and sound. Thus subjectivity, we may say, is somehow susceptible of musical formulation, whether to produce a musical expression or in response to music we hear. This inner experience is both emotive and structured, and of course can be accompanied by feelings and ideas and conceptions that concern nonmusical entities. The emotive and structural core of musical creation and apprehension, however, is specifically musical; it is a play of feeling that is vital and volitional, and patterned in peculiarly rhythmic-sonorous terms, all of whih need be associated with no other aspect of subjectivity.

It follows from these considerations that the relationships involved in musical meaning will all exist within the world of music itself. The place of invariant and elemental features of sound that belong to environmental adaptation, vocal expression, and perception is ambiguous, since to the extent that such biological and psychological processes enter music at all, even as elements or parts of a musical experience, they would have to be informed with some significance, have some place in humanistic expression, and thus have a place in some cultural context of meaningful structures. Essentially unformed sound such as isolated tones will either be taken as a constituent of a significant pattern—will be heard or intended, that is, as part of a musical context—or will represent no more than a conjunction of biological stimulus and response that belongs to man as an animal and stands outside of social and historical consciousness. A similar situation will prevail even when the objective stimulus consists of a complete musical structure; if there is no inner constitutive and responsive aspect that is informed with historically evolved modes of tonal feeling and construction, comparable in this to the creative activity that produced the music originally, the response will belong to the sphere of biology and elemental psychology rather than to musical experience. And just as we can explain musical structure only in terms of human experience and stylistic patterns, we can examine the inner aspect of music only in terms of the same stylistic experience; to isolate purely psychological reactions, even without a concomitant attempt to break form down into elementary material constituents, will introduce unwarranted assumptions about the reducibility of musical experience and rob music of the meaning that makes it music. The structures found in music are in fact of such variety and complexity as to suggest at once, even if they are taken purely as structures, that their origin lies in the whole nexus of man's social-historical nature. But this is true of musical meaning also, which does not contain the interaction of organism and environment as such, nor the reaction to external objects and events or the response to laboratory stimuli, but at most may only build upon these things or take them up and transmute them. Nor does the significance of musical structure rest simply on feeling and thought, but on ways of feeling and thought; music is not merely expression and comprehension, but always a particular mode of expression that evokes a corresponding mode of comprehension; it is intrinsically cultural and historical. A change in the functional, social, or cultural context of a composition will accordingly involve complex relationships between the initial and later experiences; form and significance will separate; in an extreme instance, structural features may lose their meaning altogether.

The specifically artistic relationships entering into the meaning of music are consequently not environmental, but those of immanent perception; and musical formativity is guided and tested by perception. Within this immanent sphere, the specificity of musical meaning—which represents the most important aspect of aesthetic detachment—is preserved by separating the peculiarly musical features of inner experience from other vital and emotive and conceptual features. The composer, performer, and listener are all alike liable to a degree of empathy and generalized subjectivity that can threaten the very nature of art, although every aspect of the context of a composition is susceptible of transformation into a purely musical constituent and of course also susceptible of being joined to music to constitute a composite work. These distinctions are not always easy to make, but they are called for if musical meaning is to be properly understood.

The immanence of the musical object might seem to eliminate meaning from music altogether, and it does in fact confine it to types of internal significance. In the case of purely instrumental music, where it is possible to reduce any reference to nonmusical entities to the point of essential extinction, and the meaning of the immanent structures does not reside to any appreciable extent in their representation of instruments and performing activities, we would seem to have distilled art to pure appearance—to an ideal manifestation that apparently leaves no room for meaning. The appearance is no longer the surface of a larger reality that would qualify as the meaning, certainly not in the sense that an environmental object is represented by any of its sensible aspects. Yet the appearance represents the formative forces that produced it and the understanding it formulates and evokes—a productive and a receptive experience, however, that are both intrinsically musical. It has a meaning as well in the interrelationship of its parts and in their relationships to the whole, for the way in which smaller configurations contribute to larger ones, their relative conformity, and the fashion in which they produce the impression that accumulates with time: all are meanings that can be distinguished from the comprehensive significance of the whole even though they enter into this significane. There is meaning again to be found finally in the musical world at large that is composed of other specifically musical compositions and performances and experiences, for here we are confronted with various kinds and degrees of similarity and difference among which a given composition or performance takes its place, somewhat as a perceptible part of a single work has its place in the whole. But the reference of an individual work to others—in the case of an' older work also to those produced afterward—and to various musical styles in general, is a source of meanings—again purely internal to music—that are inexhaustible in their range of complexity and variety.

To maintain that musical meaning is internal and peculiar is not to insist that it is unconnected with other types of experience; indeed it cannot fail to resemble experience in general and even to suggest it; of this there is a guarantee both in its evolution from more comprehensive experiential modes to a specialized state and in human nature itself, which ensures the ingredience of certain fundamental properties in each area of experience, spontaneously relates and compares these divisions to one another, and fuses them into an encompassing whole in the unity of consciousness. The specialized auditory core of musical perception is obviously an abstraction not only from composite varieties of art but also from kinesthetic, tactile, vibratory, and visual experience, or in a word, from exploratory and adjustive behavior that involves the joint action of the senses. And the peculiarity of musical meaning, which consists in the logical consecution of sonorities, is clearly grounded in a comprehensive course of experience that involves rational comparative activities as well as a kind of volitional flow of feeling and vitality and a general dispositional state. The identification of tone and sound with consciousness connects music with the most fundamental aspect of vitality and with the detailed dynamic of emotional experience; but it is equally evident that the particular configurations of a given style involve the resources of intelligence and reason. Indeed the rational and emotional phases of meaning are difficult if not impossible to separate. Yet musical logic does not imply that music and language are the same; only that they have certain similarities. Above all, the relationships that can be created within musical style, like those that arise in language, seem to be spontaneous products of a mind in tune with its material of thought and capable of an inexhaustible number of fresh associations and transformations within an established idiom. Basic principles underlie all the compositions in a given idiom or style; the succession of subdominant, dominant, and tonic harmonies in major-minor tonality is a familiar musical example, and within this style it possesses an incontrovertible agreement with the natural tendency of musical perception and creation. There are even certain fundamental operations that recur from style to style. But the new meanings produced by structural innovation in music—like the meanings of musical configurations in general—are in principle intrinsic to the art, however much they may resemble those found in language, and even though they are sometimes actually derived from language. Thus when Schumann opens his *Humoreske* with a phrase that stylistically is a consequent rather than an antecedent, and goes on to answer it with itself, a curious quality of illogic is produced by an opening that is syntactically a continuation. The meanings created obviously depend upon previously evolved principles of melodic and harmonic formulation; but in this and in their temporally unfolding nature the resemblance to language is exhausted—and it is only a resemblance. There is a feeling of rightness and a conformity to the demand of understanding in the succession of music from moment to moment, but the feeling and the understanding are intrinsically musical; they comprise, in fact, the essence of musical meaning.

The essential meaning of music resides in the immanent properties of a musical object which is understood to have been produced by formative activity. The formative activity is guided by its perceptual results, which are both a response to the object and its constituting cause. Any external reference, whether of the perceptual or the formulative process or of the musical object, is a fortuitous or additional circumstance not affecting the fundamental musical relationship. Concurrent with this central train of meaning is a superimposed conceptual connection. An array of concepts and conceptions bear on the musical object and through this object for the most part on the social and cultural context of the formative activity, which similarly they both formulate and describe. An underlying stratum of meaning, finally, consists of an adjustive and orientational process that largely passes over the musical object and is correlated directly with the environmental acoustic events. This process, again, is both a reaction to and a factor constructive of our external world. It constructs in reacting to what it constructs, just as in perceiving a musical object we also constitute it and control the creative activity that produces it, and in conceiving the historical contextual factors of music we also bring them into existence within the sphere of our experience. The inner aspects of our experience—adjustive, immanent, and conceptual—and those beyond the musical object—environmental, formative, and contextual—act as magnets to which feelings are drawn, at times wedded or empathically attached to a particular factor, and at times in a connection that is more distant and conceptual. But even when a performer is convinced that he is expressing in an improvisation the very feelings he knows in life outside of music, these feelings are necessarily if unconsciously fused and identified with peculiarly musical ones. And the specifically musical core of meaning is always found in the interconnections of immanent musical objects with perceptual and formative experience and in the internal relationships of these objects with one another and of their parts among themselves. This meaning is only by exception intentionally symbolic or referential; essentially it is a special kind of meaning, as we well convey in our conviction that music is meaningful, that it makes sense, although also, in fact, it really means nothing.

# CHAPTER 5

# Style

The notion of style characterizes the whole range of the most properly humanistic meanings of music, those which reveal fully the scope and sensitivity of inner life in its fusion of logic and feeling; for musical style is the particular way in which we conceive and perceive patterns, the specifically human manner in which we endow sonorous structures with meaning and thus transform them into music; it is thus the musical characteristic that reflects personal, historical, and cultural idiosyncrasies—that mirrors the infinitely variable qualities of human disposition. Style exists not only at the level of the musical work of art; the improvised music of oral tradition possesses style also, and so do even the smallest melodic phrases extracted from any body of music. But properties become most evident when they are seen in different contexts, while things that remain constant often escape notice altogether. It is therefore only when we confront the music of a different time or place that style forces itself on our attention, for we are faced with the problem of a musical significance that is no longer as obvious as it was in its original cultural setting or that may not seen open to our understanding at all. For that reason—although style can become evident within a single culture, in the different kinds of music that coexist simultaneously—it is perhaps most logical to consider style as a manifestation corollary to the preservation and collection of music, whether in written form or as phono-records. As a matter of fact, the conception of style was first elaborated in the West about A.D. 1600, not long after the musical work, as a durable creation coordinate with works of art in other media, had succeeded to prominence. It may be relevant also that the word *style* has its origin in the writing stylus, and would thus have its most proper sphere of applicability in the products of manual shaping; and in the score music does at least in this sense become identified with writing, painting, sculpture, and architecture. The phonorecord does not present the problem of arriving at a performance that correctly reflects the musical meaning, but it obviously provides no more than an accurate acoustic pattern; the problem of turning this pattern into music, of responding to it coherently and appropriately, is sufficient to illuminate the presence and nature of style.

Even in the music of oral tradition, of course, we can always speak of a certain manner of composition or performance, although if older works are not preserved through artistic changes and if the culture is an isolated one, the current styles, as the only ones known, will be taken for granted. Yet even here different styles will occur, at least in connection with different musical functions if not with different personalities. Style is clearly a general property found in all music; indeed it is the central manifestation of musical significance, comprising every socially formed component of meaning and ignoring only the universal components that derive from physics and biology.

No elaborate demonstration is needed to reveal that music always employs a public idiom and that this idiom is always essentially a product of culture. Indeed a foreign or older style, like a foreign or older language, can be totally unintelligible. This consideration does not exclude the presence in any style of universal features of music such as consonance or tonal centers, nor does it exclude the presence of universal properties in the whole musical work that speak to the essentially changeless and biologically determined factors of human nature such as the response to insistent rhythmical patterns or to sudden loudness; but even universal properties are not correctly understood without a grasp of the specific and culturally determined musical idiom in terms of which they are conveyed. We are usually unaware of this fact partly because we deal most often with music of our own recent past, and partly because musical style contains its own coherence of principles, so that if we obtain only the slightest clue such as is given by the natural attributes of intervals and rhythms apart from any more sophisticated resemblance to known idioms, unfamiliar music may easily become intelligible at least to some extent through its internal consistency, and will leave us with the feeling that music is indeed a universal medium and that we have not learned a specific cultural mode of expression at all. The learning has been implicit rather than explicit; it has been accomplished by the work itself, and through intuitive processes that act with lightning speed. It would be an obvious error, however, to believe that a work of art could be independent of any formulated and public mode of expression, and that in addition to whatever features it might possess as a unique conception in a personal style, it had no basis in some larger established idiom.

Indeed the conception of style signifies that musical meaning is recognized to be intrinsically cultural and historical; personal style itself is not exempt from this larger determination. We may extend our notion of the biological meaning of music accordingly, and say in general that the largest function of music is to provide orientation in space and time, but not only in respect of physiological, equilibrium, environmental adaptation, and bodily security, which represent the biological substratum of music. The orientation reaches in addition through the temporal and spatial cycles of nature, the days and the seasons, to man as a social and historical animal: to his participation in rituals of passage and planting and hunting and worship, and his orientation in the world of style. History is thus an intrinsic dimension of musical experience and meaning.

How does a certain way of shaping and responding to tonal configurations originate? This is a question applicable to all the products of culture, whether physical objects, ways of thought, or patterns of behavior and speech. The answer certainly does not lie to any important extent in the world of nature; for music, like speech or visual art, makes what it will of overtones, ratios, physical sound producers, and physiological auditory capacities; it selects in the same way that it forms: in response to forces of expression and feeling which have their main source in the social constitution of personality and of which material and biological considerations are servants.

A single tone has inherent properties both as a structural element and in its sensational attributes; so does a particular degree of loudness, or a series of spaced drum beats of a particular speed. These properties are influenced only to a limited extent by associated conceptions of the nature or efficacy of sound and music. But why does a tone—or a succession of two tones—have the quality it does in the context of a melodic phrase? And why does a particular succession at a definite position in the musical structure come to be characteristic of a given style? The same questions can be asked about rhythmic patterns. It is of some help, and also of inestimable importance to realize the contextual nature of the meaning of such imbedded elements; a given melodic interval will of course have a meaning that is almost completely determined not only by its immediate rhythmic, melodic, and harmonic setting, but also by the context of the whole musical system; and this is obviously true also of a single conjunction of simultaneous sounds. But such considerations reveal the problem in its full complexity. What we are dealing with in music is obviously a way of hearing: a way of responding to sonorous patterns, or of forming them to project or evoke an experience that is an instance of this mode of response.

Yet there is a sense in which these things derive from nature; for we may take nature to be not only the physical materials available in the environment, but also the sonorous and gestural forms of linguistic communication, and the elemental patterns of sonority used in the normal life—small melodic formulations learned by everyone as part of various social situations, from the lullabies and taunting calls of infancy and childhood to the formulas used in signaling, in working, or in chanting ritual texts. But even the simplest melody or functional musical configuration—itself a second nature for more sophisticated musical expression—represents impulses of play and construction, of sensuous enjoyment and experimentation; and the creativity called for even in the most elemental production of novelty is a manifestation of the vital nature of the creator, which in human life is inescapably an embodiment of cultural and personal individuality.

Bamboo or shell or sonorous stone is not used as a matter of chance only, but of choice; metal must first be produced and then turned into an idiophonic instrument by specific intention. And the elementary functional patterns of rhythm and pitch are already particular manifestations of forces of physical and emotional disposition that are themselves idiosyncratic for reasons of biological peculiarity as well as the specificity of culture. Style is not the creation of a rational consciousness that is universal in nature; it is rather the opposite of this, the creation of concrete human being, and if we strip away behavior and expression and feelings and ideas by turning all of them successively into objects of awareness, what we are left with inevitably cannot be further characterized than as a moving, self-identical, constituting power; style will have disappeared entirely along with any possibility of explaining it.

At the present stage of our enquiry we cannot account for style comprehensively, but it is plain that it is not definable purely in terms of formal features, by the specification of characteristic melodic and rhythmic and chordal patterns, of textures and constructive techniques. A musical work transplanted from its time or culture can lose its meaning entirely or assume one which bears any imaginable relation to the original, from minor distortions of significance to complete irrelevance and travesty. This is a phenomenon we can frequently observe within a single time and culture, among the variety of styles available; for any arrangement or citation of musical material taken from a diverse style can easily assume a meaning foreign to the original; style can easily assume a meaning foreign to the original; the raucous convivial music inserted into the slow movement of Mahler's First Symphony takes on an entirely new aspect of significance. If historical disparity is added to the social contrast, the effect can be still more striking; a performance of a Bach fugue by a jazz group will sound very strange, partly because of the contemporary quality of sound but also because of the jazz that has been heard immediately before. With only minor changes, the response of the audience and the expressive experience of the performers will have little to do with the authentic significance and style of Bach. More subtle and legitimate influences on the style of the same fugue can be produced if it is placed in the context of a recital of 20th-century serial pieces. In this setting its actual sound may remain entirely unchanged, but it will be experienced in a way that will emphasize the effect of historical distance, both on present-day musical perception and on the meaning of an older composition. We cannot escape the conclusion that style does not rest solely on structure as such; it is rooted in the whole nature of music, which comprises both form and meaning; as a way of composing, and consequently of performing and listening, it can only be described in terms of characteristic structures together with the meaning of these structures.

Stylistic description must accordingly undertake to convey a musical mode or manner distinctive of a composer or culture. If it seems to do this in terms of formal characteristics alone it is necessarily elliptical, and based on the presumption that the response to these characteristics is familiar to the person reading the description. An extenuating circumstance that partly justifies such purely formal accounts is of course the imprecision of language in conveying musical meaning, or the often insuperable difficulty of finding words as all for this kind of task. Apart from structural and technical terminology, we can approach the significative aspect of music only in a general way, by calling a passage or a work graceful, for example, or tragic, or Mozartean. The failure of language to get at musical experience can be compensated for by adding a discerning performance to our verbal description. This will make evident to some extent the detailed progress of feeling the music seeks to convey, but it will do so simply by presenting the formal manifestation of the experience accurately, together with associated expressive and interpretative gestures, in the hope that it will convey its own message; the process is a kind of direct training with the aid of the visible marks of the performer's feeling; it is obviously something very different from the explicit but mediate description provided by language.

Yet the only adequate way to make a distant style intelligible is to combine performance with verbal circumlocution that conveys, however approximately and analogically, something of the musical feeling, and something of the whole mode of experience of the culture. The difficulty will find its fuller explanation in subsequent chapters, but it is due in large part to the fact that music is a subtle formulation of a specific variety of experience, which can only be approached but not duplicated by other manifestations of the same culture. Since it represents a way of feeling it cannot be translated or taught explicitly like a language, for example, but must be learned by a long process of ingrained response. Intuitive understanding may often be rapid, but it is rarely accurate and thorough. To the extent that musical style rests on physiological peculiarities, it can never be fully understood by outsiders; but even apart from this it often can be grasped only through conditioning and training that attempt to supply a substitute, in great measure conceptual, for the gradual formative process and the total experience of growing up in a given social and cultural setting, with all its modes of thought and expression.

The understanding of musical style in itself, leaving out of account now the problem of describing it in language, is an endeavor that belongs to history, ethnology, and sociology, and possibly as their most difficult enterprise. Such a process of understanding may begin with some feature of music that seems to be invariant with respect to culture, but since this can never be entirely true of its actual meaning in its musical context, our feeling of its quality and significance must be treated as a hypothesis to be checked by other evidence. How is this musical feature responded to? How is it thought of? How is it used in other musical contexts? Is our feeling confirmed by the conformability of comparable kinds of expression and response in other departments of the culture? In whatever way the qualities we have experienced may now accordingly have been

167

altered in our effort to justify them, we must take this adjusted hypothesis again to the same courts of appeal. Any kind of musical feature or pattern we may start with will call for the same steplike process; perhaps our intuitive projection of significance has been misdirected by what are only chance simil[arities to the sonorous patterns of the music of our own culture or social group. Even simil[iarities that are not fortuitous may represent very different meanings; the significance of a sustained triad in a work of Stravinsky, for example, will differ markedly from its significance in a work of Bruckner or again of Mozart. But the alternation of intuition and research, of hypothesis and verification, that constitutes the process of historical and cultural understanding can proceed at a rapid pace if documents and artifacts are plentiful or if the culture in question is not too dissimilar from our own or if we are dealing with a society of the present day which we can observe in its entirety or even participate in. Music adds a facilitation of its own, for more than other extended documents, its parts and aspects are mutually consistent and supportive; it provides not a few separated or discordant clues and indications, but a self-reinforcing texture of forms that all bear on a similarly coherent texture of significance. It thus tends to teach its own meaning even if it is unfamiliar. In spite of this, the meaning of a single specimen of music isolated from its culture can remain impenetrable to the most intuitive observer from a distant time or place; and even the meaning of older Western music has been astonishingly resistant to the understanding of subsequent performers and listeners, although this has been due mostly to deficiencies of realization that have misrepresented almost every conceivable aspect of form, from the medium of performance, the number and arrangement of performers, and the acoustic setting to the actual notes and rhythms and tempo, not to mention the very number and order of the sections of a compostion and its functional setting.

If we cannot readily account for the origin of musical style, and if we can interpret the meaning of unfamiliar styles with only varying degrees of success, we can, on the other hand, rather easily observe the transmission of style and its course and patterns of constancy and change. Music of any kind, together with the other aspects of the culture it represents, provides us with a particular way of formulating and responding to a whole interrelated diversity of sonorous patterns. The generality of this stylistic manner is such that newly composed works are more or less like previous ones; their creation proceeds by a combination of copying and innovation. It is obvious that works will group themselves in accordance with temporal and social structures. The most prominent groups of temporal extension are those based on genre and on the personal predilections of a composer. Genre is chiefly a product of social function and sonorous medium, as we can see in the case of marches, dances, work songs, or ritual chant on the one hand and the violin concerto or the piano sonata on the other. The degree of definition genres possess will depend on the importance of the functions they represent and the general interest of society in distinct, established, and formally elaborated functions. The constancy of genre will depend on the preservation of these functions and their formal manifestation and also on the general stability of society and culture, for dynamism can change the stylistic character of a genre even if the function it represents maintains both its prominence and its distinctness. The remarkable transformations in the style of the Catholic mass from medieval plainsong to Viennese Classicism are an excellent case in point.

But the definition and constancy of genre also depend on the general degree of interest in sonorous qualities and the specific properties of each performing medium as opposed to a more abstract interest in musical form and meaning, or as we might say with perhaps greater accuracy, on the degree to which tone color and manipulative techniques become dimensions of musical formulation and expression. They also depend again, however, on the general dynamism of society, for both changes in instruments and changes in the manner of their use or in modes of singing may radically alter the style of a given genre. It is apparent that a 15th-century chanson which permitted a considerable latitude—although within the practice and available means of the time—in the choice of performing medium, represents a genre relatively little defined by sonority as compared with a Classical string quartet or a Schumann piano piece; and it is equally apparent that the style of a Mozart piano sonata is very different from that of a mature sonata of Beethoven: both the instrument and the manner of use have undergone a striking change in a short time, although the genre—defined essentially by performing medium—remains the same.

With the acceleration of social and cultural change and novelty, such as we find in the 20th century, and the emancipation of aesthetic interests from functional ones, which took place in the 19th century and was foreshadowed by the related earlier development of an independent art of instrumental music, the most important foundations of genre were dissolved. The two factors were related, for the autonomy of aesthetic values made them all the more susceptible to the rapid change in society and culture, so that in the realm of art genre almost ceased to exist very much as a consequence of this additive effect of stylistic change and artistic autonomy. The accompanying changes in sonorous media (which were another manifestation of imaginative boldness)—the introduction of new instruments, new combinations or performing forces, and new methods of singing and playing—removed the second basis of genre, although certain preferences became evident that provided some definition; the "ensemble song," for example, as we may term the song for voice and a few diversified instruments such as we find in Webern's works, seems to qualify as a 20th-century genre based on performing medium. But the tendency in general was for works to stand alone, apparently unrelated to any temporal series of compositions of an established type.

The other obvious defining temporal structure of groups of works is the musical personality of the individual composer. This too is a foundation for style that can vary widely in its nature and prominence, depending not only on the developmental course of change of the individual personality, but also on the general prominence and value of individuality in society and on the subjection of individuality to the pervasive forces of

170

cultural change. Thus not only is personal style more constant in Brahms than it is in Wagner, but it is more conspicuous in the 19th century than in the 18th, and also more evident in major composers than in minor ones, or in art music than in the music of mass culture. And again it is subject to rapid change during the first half of the 20th century; the stylistic careers of Stravinsky and of Schönberg are probably the best known examples. Like genre, then, the definition of personal style can be lost or obscured in times of rapid change; compositions tend in this respect also to resist group membership; each stands alone or must find stylistic companions on other bases than genre and individuality.

Besides genre and personality, there are still additional structures that define temporal stylistic patterns or groups of works. Historical periods or cultural epochs are characterized by general stylistic traits: types of expressive intent, for example, or technical features of form. The Baroque was preoccupied with the dramatic representation of individual feelings associated with accompanied monody, 18th-century Classicism with clarity and motivic development, the 19th century with thematic transformation, harmonic sonority, and instrumental color. But cultures as a whole also have characteristic styles of singing, types of instruments, scales, musical forms, and expressive intent, essentially unchanged in some respects through the entire observable history of the culture. Sometimes even melodies and entire musical works have the same persistence. And finally formal techniques and expressive properties of style may have a continuity of their own, defining groups of works that exemplify them or acting independently as stylistic features that characterize only parts of works or that extend beyond the boundaries of a single genre. Imitative technique in Western music is a technical feature that is not confined to any single genre such as the 16th-century motet or the fugue, and the same can be said of thematic transformation or serial construction. Or again, the religious aura attached to trombones or the special expressiveness of chromaticism, while not entirely constant in significance, each has its own temporal career as a particular feature within individual works but not restricted to a single genre and persisting historically even across-cultural epochs. This is also true, of course, of many musical instruments and styles of singing and of an unlimited number of elementary configurations such as intervals, chords, rhythmic patterns, and melodic figures. Meanings change during the temporal course of stylistic traditions, but the later manifestations are variants and transformations of the old, and their richness of meaning grows with their historical depth.

The spatial or social structures that underlie the stylistic grouping of musical works are social class, artistic school, city, country, or really any defined cultural area from a small self-contained society to the entire world. Whether we consider particular significant features or the kinship of groups of works, the stylistic diffusion and homogeneity will obviously depend on social coherence and this in turn on geography and communication. Differences in style will become more likely with distance or with some degree of isolation. A musical academy or artistic coterie, on the other hand—confined to a single room and a closely defined social class and with the immediate communication of members of like mind who are pursuing the same stylistic objectives—can represent a maximum degree of musical uniformity. But whatever the spatial extent of the stylistic manifestation in question, it can never be strictly nontemporal, just as any stylistic manifestation extending in time—except for personal style in a literal sense—cannot entirely lack spatial or social diffusion. The string quartets written in Vienna in 1781, for example, could bear no stylistic kinship if they were a purely geographical and spatial group of works; even if they were literally simultaneous in composition so that mutual influence was impossible, they would all derive in style from music which preceded them in time and which was thus able to account for their stylistic interrelation; they would also be directed to the future in representing a formulation and a significance that would provide a basis for new stylistic change. In any event, it is obvious that style creates patterns of diffusion that are at once both temporal and spatial, following the structures established by social function and personal individuality, and by culture and its institutions.

The historical course of style within a given culture would

seem to respond to four different kinds of forces which tend to produce four corresponding types of change, even though they may well all act in conjunction. The first type of change is a pendular tendency and the second a cyclical one while we may call the third progressive and the fourth representative. Pendular changes in musical style can be found in the tendency of two formal or expressive characteristics to alternate: homophony and polyphony, for example, or symmetry and asymmetry, balance and dynamism, articulation and continuity, clarity and complexity, Impressionism and Expressionism. There may even be an alternation of formal and expressive interests in themselves. Stylistic alternation can proceed at the rate set by human generation, perhaps because of the juxtaposed and characteristically different outlooks of youth and age, or it can take place much more slowly, perhaps even over a span of centuries, for reasons that are much less tangible.

Cyclical types of change depict style as moving repeatedly— or once in each distinct culture—through a defined series of stages such as archaic, youthful, mature, and decadent. The conception of reaction that underlies the pattern of alternation is here replaced by the biological notion of life cycle, which is much less well founded and would seem to derive its applicability essentially from the single fact that both style and life exist in time. In the case of the style of an individual composer or performer, of course, the analogy becomes an intrinsic relationship, although even biological development shows considerable variation and the development of personality is subject to psychological and social forces that can produce extremely complex courses of change. Larger historical cycles, however, seem to have some foundation apart from biological analogy, in the human tendency to take up aspects of earlier achievement in a particular field of endeavor. The successive new forms achieved in this repeated process will readily lead to the elaboration of a suggestion, its ramified application, its overelaboration, and its eventual discard, simply as a consequence of a continuity of intelligence applied to a single evolving phenomenon.

Progressive types of change are grounded fundamentally in

human memory and records of the past, but more specifically in the tendency to build on the past and to project the future. A problem-solving mentality or speculative curiosity is a powerful additional force, as well as a belief in progress of some kind. In all this, an adoption of scientific and technological modes of thought also plays an important part. These underlying forces are not entirely dissimilar to those that may account for cyclical patterns. They are manifested in the development of imitative technique in the 16th century, for example, or in the culmination of harmonic ambiguity in Wagner's *Tristan*, or in the technical development of the piano during the 18th and 19th centuries.

Representative types of stylistic change we may consider those which occur as a result of social and cultural influences that are not specifically musical; the general intellectual and emotional development of a composer or performer has a similar status in producing change in style. In either case, the notion of a pattern of change gives way to that of a dependence on the background or context from which music arises. If patterns become evident as a result of this dependence also, they necessarily become manifestations of the congruent regularities that cause them or of encompassing regularities of cultural change in general which must find their own explanation. But representative change in itself contains no implications of patterns or regularities; it is a type due simply to the reflection in music of outside forces. The cynicism in the music of the 1920s, for example, is a stylistic quality that mirrors or is part of the disillusionment that followed upon the First World War; or similarly, the textural and harmonic simplicity that became predominant in music around the middle of the 18th century was an outcome of ideals of naturalness and clarity. Stylistic change in general, of course, whatever its type, is representative of the dynamic aspect of culture. There are doubtless periods in the course of any culture when tradition continues unchanged, and when innovation and personal creativity are values subordinate to stability; many cultures, notably those of the East and of nonliterate societies, seem as a whole to have changed relatively little or relatively slowly in comparison to Western civilization. There are also aspects of many cultures, and music is prominent among them, that are unusually stable in comparison to other aspects. Music itself, however, comprises a group of styles, stylistic features, and genres that manifest wide differences in dynamism among themselves. In the West, for example, performing media and musical systems tend to be somewhat more stable than melodic and rhythmic types of configuration, and secular genres more innovative and dynamic than sacred. In general, the historical types of change we have considered are difficult to discern outside of the literate Western and Oriental cultures that have continued to exist into the present; they are understandably obscure in ancient civilizations, still more difficult to identify in nonliterate societies, and a matter of conjecture in our incipient world civilization, for in these areas either the general course of social change or even whether or not appreciable change exists is essentially unknown.

Underlying historical types of change there may be not only an attitude toward the past in general, but the more personal relationship of a composer toward a particular predecessor, which in the fashion of filial reactions may be one of emulation, competition, or revolt. Individual psychology might then correspondingly be multiplied—by personal influence or prevailing outlook—into either a pendular, a cyclical, or a progressive pattern of change in society as a whole.

The cultural and geographical diffusion of all these types of change, or the diffusion of style in general, follows its own principles of regularity. The obstacle of distance has been overcome by the mobility of populations and the modern technology of transportation and communication; the interaction of styles depends not only on proximity, but also on stylistic affinity and compatibility as well as on the attraction of exoticism that is associated with varying kinds of dissimilarity. But throughout world history the temporal persistence and spatial diffusion of instruments and melodies and various other components of musical style have been remarkable. Indeed it is often difficult to decide between historical tenacity and acculturation on the one hand and independent origin on the other. The finite physical possibilities available in the devising of musical instruments or in the vocal production of tone, and the defined physiological and psychological capacities involved in the configurational perception of rhythms and tonal intervals make the spontaneous occurrence of various ubiquitous features of style more or less likely. Apart from the influence of foreign cultures, it is difficult for any society not to come upon the qualitative identity contained in the octave, the special quality of the fifth, the symmetry of literal or varied repetition, the effortless and enjoyable perceptibility of duple and triple rhythmical groups, the arousing impact of loudness and the soothing quality of softness and sustained tone, the stimulating effect of rapidity and acceleration in speed, the tonal possibilities of end-blown reeds or of bull-roarers, or the intrinsic interest of the different sonorous qualities of solid objects, especially as auditory manifestations of the other known properties and virtues of these materials. Given human powers of perception and the physical and psychological prominence of the fifth, it is no accident nor necessarily a matter of outside influence that pentatonic and heptatonic and dodecaphonic scales and systems occur so widely. Tempering of intervals has other equally fundamental causes, such as the equivalence of instrumental distances in strings and pipes and simple physical relationships in the graduation of size. Historical continuity is usually much less problematic than geographical diffusion, although the ancestor of a given musical instrument, or indeed of a given melody, is not always what it might seem. But cultural similarities especially among tribal societies must generally be tested by the specificity and details of the resemblance and by other evidence of transmission or contact. In prehistoric contacts especially, instruments may provide the only available evidence of musical relationships; but even if pictures and verbal descriptions of musical performance are available, actual stylistic features and thus stylistic resemblances are extremely difficult to define; even theoretical and philosophical discussions of music do not substantially alleviate the difficulty. Instruments in themselves, for one thing, without their actual mode of performance, are far removed from concrete stylistic properties, and descriptions and depictions of instruments are no closer. In default of notation and recording, then, and certainly of an accurate notation, only living music, or musical remnants of extinct cultures that have survived in some measure in current practice, will enable us to reconstruct concrete features of style and thus reliable patterns of stylistic diffusion. Otherwise spread of musical styles in the past must remain a matter of probabilities based largely on the diffusion of musical instruments and the mutual influence of cultures in general as determined by other evidence.

The spread of style from one social stratum to another is a related matter that—like acculturation and biological inter-mixture—is of great importance in ensuring stylistic novelty, variety, and vitality. If rural and popular and commercial types of music find their most useful source of style in the assimilation and adoption of all the properties and features of art music, which of course are necessarily changed both in form and in meaning in their new musical and social context, art music often takes as much as it gives in the use of popular dances, rhythms, melodies, and tone colors, all of which represent a kind of nature that provides material to be artistically stylized and detached from life or more accurately, further stylized and detached. The process of transfer in either direction from one social group to another, however, is often more one of stylistic transformation than of constancy; in contrast to the type of alterations style usually suffers in its temporal persistence and geographic diffusion over long stretches of time and space, the changes it undergoes in its short trip from one social milieu to another within the same culture more often seem abrupt and striking. The changes have more to teach us than the fact of transfer or borrowing.

In the historical and geographical and social continuities of musical style it is important to keep in mind the composite nature of style, for each of its factors and components, while bearing some indication of the quality of the whole, will in general have its own characteristics of temporal and spatial transmission. The persistence and diffusion of an instrument does not automatically carry with it the persistence and diffusion of a melodic style, a manner of performance, or even a musical system; while almost every feature of style can be transported successfully to another sonorous medium. Thus it is difficult, to take Western examples at hand, to identify the piano in Debussy's hands with the same instrument as Beethoven uses it, or the trumpet in art music with the trumpet in jazz, while the transportation of Vivaldi violin concertos to the harpsichord by Bach had surprisingly little effect on most of the features of style apart from sonority. Again the tonal quality and even something of the melodic idiom of the violin show a degree of continuity from the middle Baroque to the post-Romantic period that contrasts strikingly with the marked changes in most other components of musical style during the same period. And the persistence of melodies has been traced for centuries in Western music while everything changed radically around them, from tone color and polyphonic setting to rhythm, text, and even tonal system. Thus forms and meaning are transmitted historically and across cultures, in some ways the same and in other ways altered; but the features altered, if they are sufficiently changed or prominent or numerous, will change the overall form and significance appreciably, and in this way change the style even of the components that seem to have remained constant if they are considered in isolation; the influence of the musical whole on its parts is inescapable.

The endless variety of the styles produced by cultures and individuals and social classes in the course of time throughout the world makes any attempt at classification necessarily inadequate; indeed the description of the properties of a given style that would be presupposed by a scheme of classification lacks an exhaustive framework of dimensions even for technical features. Basic aspects of music such as melody or rhythm or polyphony, upon close examination, are not easily divided into types. What first seems obviously monophonic or monorhythmic will generally turn out to be compound—indeed often very complex—in constitution. As a corollary of this situation, our attention is naturally given to the unique properties of a particular style rather than to its kinship with others; and our description undertakes to point out—as a humanistic interest would dictate it should—what is distinctive in Schubert or Wagner, or in the Italian monody of the early 17th century. Yet the search for categories and similarities of style, for types of melody, rhythm, and polyphony, of structure and texture and tonal ideal, belongs to the natural tendency of thought and will doubtless never be abandoned. Personal styles give the impression of spontaneity or careful planning, national styles seem simple or complex, historical styles formal or expressive. There is the further suggestive implication that these categories rest on underlying types of personality and of national and cultural character, all of which unfortunately remain more arbitrary and vague than the musical distinctions. Styles that are continuous and that lack conspicuous repetition are certainly difficult to assimilate perceptually, while those that are articulated and make use of frequent and obvious repetition are easily accessible. But even here, where the psychological foundation is more secure, the consideration may still be urged that stylistic categories have very little relevance to the concrete qualities of the particular styles they subsume.

We may characterize a style, finally, by evaluating its various components with respect to their relative importance or elaboration. This may be done first of all with its formal components: with melody, polyphony, harmony, rhythm, tone color, antiphonal relationships, and the articulation of phrases. One or more constituents of this kind may have received the most attention and may attract the greatest interest, while the others will be relatively subordinate or conventional, and act as a ground for the prominent features. In Italian opera of the early 19th century, for example, melody became a dominant component of style, while harmony in particular remained unelaborated. But a similar evaluation may also be applied to the relative importance of form as compared with meaning, for at times the structural complexity of a style is predominant and it has only an imitative or routine significance, while at other times the most profound significance is conveyed by a form of disconcerting simplicity. Inequities of elaboration and importance among the components of style, however, are in no way a deficiency to be removed; they comprise instead a characteristic internal economy that in general represents the natural virtue of the style.

A consideration of types of style, of its characteristics of temporal and geographical diffusion, and of its compound constitution, with the differing characteristics of diffusion manifested by the various constituents, still leaves out of account what is doubtless its most distinctive and significant property, namely its composite nature—not in the sense now of a variety of constituents that all bear on the particular manner that is conveyed by a single type of style such as that of a composer or city or genre, but in the sense of a diversity of origin, a mixture of the various types in themselves. Stylistic mixture occurs both between coordinate styles belonging to the same type and between styles different in type. Thus Brahms' style is often Schumannesque and often Beethovenian, but it also contains frankly popular elements, Baroque melodic con-figurations, and a specifically Viennese tone. This does not pre-vent us from identifying individual characteristic features of his style such as types of sonority or chromaticism or polyphony, but it does imply that a stylistic analysis must determine the origin and nature of each characteristic with respect to its provenance; distinctively personal features represent only one possibility. Such a demand contains the presupposition that a determination of this kind is possible; but stylistic mixture can be a fusion rather than a juxtaposition, and the components that are yielded by a perceptual or a rational analysis of music may defy decomposition. It is evident nevertheless that pure stylistic types are generally more of an abstraction than a reality; the oratorio is characteristically operatic, keyboard music is often stylistically close to chamber and orchestral styles, Classical music borrows from Baroque, the violin from the voice. Some-times the result is the obvious mixture caused by simple stylistic transfer, as from the lute to the harpsichord; distinctions of national character, genre, and different personal or historic styles may be absent, although each of these basic stylistic types normally will be represented in at least the one species that is indigenous to the music in question. But at other times, as in Viennese orchestral masses, the Bach Passions, the Mozart operas, or the Mahler symphonies, the resultant style is a complex juxtaposition of incredible diversity.

There is an important distinction to be made between purposeful mixture of styles and the combination and fusion that occur automatically and are not part of the composer's or the performer's conscious stylistic intent. This distinction cannot always be made with certainty, but it is helpful to realize that there will be a certain combination which is characteristic of any given cultural setting and which will take place without special intent; typically a work will spontaneously unite styles that are representative of its genre, medium, composer, social milieu, function, local and national cutures, and historical period. In general terms, however, period, locality, genre, social class, and personality, and often the further multiplicity of different periods, different localities, different genres, different social classes and groups, and different personal styles may all act together, partly consciously and partly unconsciously, in producing the style of new works. A German opera of the 19th century may also be partly French or Italian in style, or may be influenced by 18th-century opera, or may derive also from symphonic style, from popular elements, and from the personal style of another composer. Times of great stylistic sensitivity and definition may also be those of bewildering mixture and interchange; Bach and Mozart are outstanding witnesses to the astonishing kinds of complexity of which the 18th century was capable; indeed stylistic mixture based on national diversity was an important German ideal. The cross relationships and intermixtures of style are endless, and they make both the structure and meaning of music endlessly fascinating although often extremely difficult to understand. They constitute the chief musical object of historical interpretation, and it is this tissue of musical ways of feeling that we must re-create in understanding, performing, or hearing a musical work.

The composite character of style would seem to explain how it may achieve universality, or more accurately, a wide diffusion socially or temporally. This is a stylistic characteristic that comes into question particularly with the preservation of music in a complex or changing world. It can have, in fact, two possible bases in style itself. Music of general value, broad appeal, and great durability may be either a combination of diverse styles: of different social classes, different genres, different countries, and even different historical periods; or it may achieve currency by a dependence on values that are fundamental or that occur very generally in space and time. The first basis of universality would appear to underlie Viennese Classicism, the second was sought by Wagner. But the explanation of stylistic universality and durability is not so easily found. Diversity of constitution in itself may be not a source of strength but the path to a valueless eclecticism, while stylistic properties occurring widely may not express profound human values but only superficial and colorless platitudes. A complex of factors must be held accountable for universality, and among them the channels provided by social homogeneity, such as that of European aristocracy, and by the constancy of historical tradition, such as the 19th-century German adulation of Bach and Beethoven, are of considerable importance. Also of undoubted importance are the general cultural status and role of a city or a country in the international or world community, and the consonance of a composer's personal style with the character and influence of the culture he represents. The belief that a particular style represents classical or definitive standards of beauty or expression is still another influential factor. But even the most successful conjunction of factors will produce only a certain kind and degree of diffusion or permanence. True universality consists not in the achievement of absolute or canonic values, and not in the simple agreement of a style with the modes of expression of other cultures and times and its consequent automatic intelligibility, but in fidelity to the deepest experience of a specific time and place; the universal is thus contained in the particular, although it is also necessarily no more than potential, and humanistic understanding will always remain the prerequisite for its vitalization.

We are concerned chiefly with the nature and difficulties of interpretation, but the preservation of music also gives rise to a very different problem, for exact re-creation may be either undesirable or impossible. It is difficult to know what we should preserve; the increasing quantity of music that is composed each year makes discard necessary even apart from questions of value; we obviously cannot continue to preserve, either in scores or in phonorecords, everything that is produced; even microphotography has its limits. But fortunately, while material of commercial purpose and mechanical workmanship may have its interest for the historian who seeks to construct a continuous narrative of musical change or a comprehensive story of culture as a whole, statistical records and summary descriptions of unimaginative works would be sufficient for such objectives, together with a few samples, which will fully represent a genre of a routine nature. Nevertheless, what seems valueless at one time may turn out to be crucial to later interests, so that considerable foresight and imagination are called for to project the essentially unpredictable creative and scholarly concerns of the future. That we should preserve the products of culture at all is scarcely open to question; indeed if we did not build upon the past to some extent culture would not exist and man would be something less than human; but the future may be much less humanistic, in the specifically historical sense this word has taken on, than the present; or if humanistic it may be much less antiquarian.

To preserve, in any event, is not the same as to keep alive. Here something additional is demanded: the ability to realize an older and different mode of musical experience, the precondition being that this historical or culturally distant mode will have some commection with present creative interests or at least some significance—as in fact it must—to a theoretical conception of the range and varieties and possibilities of human experience in general. To re-create the experience of a different time or culture exactly, however, is certainly impossible, for any given experience is only part of a whole which cannot be reinstated, but only approximated in imagination; and in default of this total context, the experience in question will differ more or less significantly from its original. We cannot revive the occasion for performance of Greek tragedy, or even the social context and attitudes that surrounded the performance of convivial music at an 18th-century court, and even if we could reconstitute the acoustic aspect of the music perfectly in such cases, which in itself is far from possible, we would hardly approach the 'experience these sounds originally formulated and provoked. We can of course still project such a literal reproduction as an ideal, to be approached with the aid of historical imagination.

On the other hand, since we are different from the courtiers of the 18th century, for example, why should we wish to duplicate their experience so closely? Perhaps this goal would serve the philosophic purpose or the large historical and anthropological purpose of studying man and culture in general, but it might not be the most conformable objective for the creative musical interests of the present, for the attainment of aesthetic pleasure, or even for the aims of the historian of music or the related ones of the historical epicurean to whom the past is a source of valuable and instructive enjoyment. But even for the philosophic goal of examining the range of human experience, a knowledge of the static entity represented by such a re-creation would seem less interesting than an understanding of the dynamics of musical experience in general. It follows, then, and with additional force when we realize that a past style will itself contain the historical depth of its own tradition and predecessors, that a more valuable and realistic goal for reviving old music is to experience it from our station point in the present, with an awareness not only of what it was but of what it has become. It was itself compounded initially of elements of the past felt to be relevant to the creative experience of the time it was written; it has also in turn been found variously relevant to musical experience since that time and up to the present. An ideal performance now would seem to realize something of this course of musical experience or at least something of its most important concretions at the original time of composition and the present day; and the ideal would seem best reached by a literal reproduction of the acoustic aspect of the music but a synthetic composite of feeling and thought on the part of performer and listener which represents in some degree the pertinent musical and cultural contexts that preceded and followed the composition of the work.

Is this too ambitious an aim? What it amounts to is the demand that we bring to a particular musical expression of the past an extensive knowledge of cultural and social history, including especially a historical knowledge of music itself. This is certainly attainable only in part and only with considerable effort, but it cannot be doubted that in accordance as we approach such an ideal our experience of a given musical work becomes increasingly significant, adequate, and authentic, both to the original intention and to the possibilities of our own position in history.

These considerations obviously will not apply, however, when there is no contact between a work to be revived and our contemporary musical experience. If a work is of sufficient importance and has entered into the historical course of experience that has led to our own, the meaning it embodied will in a sense be part of our present-day musical consciousness and there will be no question of its interest and relevance to our own experience and to what we create for the future. We might argue additionally that whenever we revive a work and re-create the experience it contains, we make it by that token part of our present and of our future; the revival thus belongs to a temporal counterpart of that process of mutual influence, mixture, and amalgamation that is tending to create a worldwide unity of culture; and indeed, if a musical work of the past was not in some way relevant to our sphere of experience we would not concern ourselves with it. But if we turn to music of a culture essentially isolated from our own, the situation is very different, and it might seem impossible even to arrive at any artistic understanding. There are, however, only rarely instances of complete isolation, and even here, common factors will exist in basic features that derive from human physiology and intelligence wherever found and from the physical world as well. For distant music to make sense, nevertheless, great effort and time must be expended, together with repeated verification of our musical responses against the evidence of other features of the foreign culture that are conformable or explicitly comparable to musical modes of thought and feeling. It is perhaps more puzzling that we should seek at all a knowledge of music foreign to our own tradition. The explanation of our interest, however, lies at hand in the very manifestation of this interest. If we do succeed in understanding and experiencing authentically the music of a distant culture, we must for some reason have found it relevant to our world, and by understanding it, performing it, and hearing it we make it in fact part of our history in the future. The process is clearly one that defines and shapes an emerging world community of culture. Our interest may be aroused for the reason also that we want to understand every available manifestation of human creativity, or because of the belief that the degree of truth we arrive at about the nature of man will depend chiefly on the range of our knowledge and our empirical understanding, or in fact be essentially coincident with this. Such a philosophical motivation is less specifically historical than a direct feeling that the music of a distant culture bears an immediate affinity with and relevance to our own present tendencies of creative musical thought and expression, but it is really also historical, in both its origin and its outcome.

The concept of interpretation is clearly central both in performance and in history; it has fundamentally, although not exactly, the same meaning in both fields, but the differences can easily obscure the similarities. The performer, like the historian, has generally to understand the meaning of a score in terms of sonorous realization; here he is dependent on the historian, who seeks first to establish an authentic text from the sources and versions available and then to interpret the meaning of this text with the help of comparison, written theoretical documents, the study of old instruments, depictions and descriptions of musical performance, and so on. The results of these preliminary efforts are incorporated in a more explicit and annotated score which becomes available to the performer as his starting point. The performer then continues this work of interpretation by an actual acoustic realization, bringing into play related but dependent faculties of musical imagination, and projecting styles of realization that will provide configurations of convincing significance.

186

At this point these various stages of external interpretation—which are more numerous in the history of a performing art than in other kinds of history—give way to a second level of interpretation which has played a role to some extent from the beginning, and which seeks to reconstruct the meaning of the sonorous forms as a historical mode of musical formativity and response. This internal interpretation is what we have discussed previously, and it concerns the complex significance of style. Again performance and history cooperate in a joint task, but performance acts again as a supplement or a complement of historical description. The reinstatement of meaning in its full complexity, with its varied origin and history, its social and cultural setting, and its course of historical change, is an achievement open only to discursive thought in language, and not in any adequate way to performance alone. Yet performance will again properly take up where history leaves off; it will implement historical insight by incorporating and reflecting to the extent it can what history has brought to conceptual life only. In both spheres the individuality of the interpreter, which is a particular manifestation of the outlook of the culture, will enter into the interpretation, and this fact, together with the recreation of a past mode of musical experience, is responsible for the fundamental identity of performance and history—an identity which extends to informed listening also, or also to the informed reading of history, both of which bring a third interpretive activity into the joint historical (and aesthetic) endeavor. A performer has a style as well as a historian; it is evident both in the choice of what he presents and in his manner of playing or singing or conducting. But his aim, like that of the historian, is fidelity to the past; his truth includes his own mode of experience only because this truth is his past as it exists in the present: it contains the intrinsic relativity that the here and now adds to every humanistic sphere of expression.

As compared with these historical considerations, questions of modernization in performance have a lesser importance and an extrinsic or practical motivation. It is hardly possible to secure a castrato singer for Baroque opera or to duplicate every obsolete and exotic musical instrument, for example; we must at times be content with substitutes and approximations. Nor in the pedagogical sphere can we expect that every piano student will be provided with a harpsichord. But often a rationale for modernization is sought in the conception of furnishing an experience for the present that is close to the experience of the past precisely because it deploys modern means. The use of a harpsichord to perform Baroque clavier music today, the argument might proceed, will only make an understanding and enjoyment of this music still more difficult; among other things the range of loudness will be insufficient for many large recital halls; but primarily, the sonority of the instrument will seem strange and not capable of sustaining a meaningful present-day musical experience, while a piano will provide a bridge to contemporary experience, and in fact the equivalent to us in terms of sonority and its emotional significance of what the harpsichord was to the Baroque era. This is a line of thought that can lead to an enriched orchestration or harmonization of Classical symphonies. The flexibility of earlier performance practice can also be fallaciously cited to justify changes which are totally anachronistic or outside the possibilities of the time or culture. It is obvious at once, of course—even without the amusing reductio ad absurdum of the contention that these are the instruments and harmonies that Bach or Machaut would have used if he were alive today—that equivalents of past musical means in respect of significance are not possible to find and that an endeavor of this kind can easily become ridiculous. To be sure, Renaissance harmonizations of plainsong have taken on their own historical value, but that does not constitute an endorsement of the practice at the time, which could have been justified again only by an extramusical motivation. Instead of questionable equations of significance, then, objective approximation of the original means is the only acceptable alternative course when the duplication of these means is either impossible or impractical. It is often well to forego accessibility and a wider audience in favor of aesthetic authenticity and historical accuracy, a decision which also has larger moral justifications and is especially called for in the case of music of complex significance or cultural remoteness. The problems have some resemblance to those involved in the translation of poetry.

The understanding of style in music is really the understanding of its specific kind of meaning, which is thus largely a historical one. What is preserved and what is discarded, whether consciously or unconsciously, tells us what is valued in a culture, in respect not only of its social function but also of the purely musical significance it provides. Within a single work, the stylistic components tell a similar story of preferences—of historical durability, foreign cultural affinities, the relationship of social classes, and of dominant genres and performing media and personal styles. But historical depth can reveal not only the conscious or unconscious persistence of tradition or cultural stability; it can also be revival, necessarily conscious, rather than continuance, and this revival can be very various in its nature—nostalgic or forward-looking, for example, or based on affinity or on satire. Stylistic mixture in fact contains an inexhaustible variety and complexity of meaning, often of baffling ambiguity, but all of a purely musical nature, all entirely within music and apart from any reference to nonmusical objects; a characteristically Beethovenian feature does not necessarily pertain to Beethoven the man, but can represent solely Beethoven as a distinctively individual but specifically musical intelligence—a particular creative manner of conception and formation and expression. The references of style are to other parts of music: to other genres, to popular songs, to foreign styles, to other composers and even to other specific compositions. Whenever a single stylistic constituent appears that is not part of the natural hierarchical grouping of time, place, genre and individual style which is proper to a composition, the possibilities of meaning undergo a sudden expansion. Are we dealing in a given case with an expression of reverence, with an acknowledgement, or with stylistic kinship? Is this an instance of satire, criticism, or witticism? Is it meant to be perceived or is it veiled or secret? Is it a juxtaposition that aims to produce a particular stylistic effect of coherence or of incompatibilty due to the contiguity of components with certain kinds of similarity or disparity? The meanings created when Alban Berg quotes *Tris-*

*tan* or uses older formal movements in *Wozzeck*, when Stra
vinsky adapts previous styles when Schönberg quotes "Ach
Du lieber Augustin," and when Richard Strauss quotes himsel
are not only very various but very different again from those
produced by the masked and ambiguous references of which
Schumann was fond, or by the manifestations of Bach's influence in Mozart or Beethoven, or indeed by the very use of the
fugue or the chorale prelude in the 19th century or of the song ir
the symphony or an Italian style in England. The manner o
citation or mixture, as well as the nature and source of the older
or unexpected features, will generally define the meaning
involved. We may say, then, that certain kinds of "statement'
can be made in music, although the meaning of such a statement is primarily conveyed by intuition and feeling rather than
by concepts, which have an accessory status. To a great extent
this meaning is also an embodiment of attitudes and intentions
that are often elusive, exceedingly complex, and of tantalizing
vagueness from a conceptual point of view. The formulation or
grasp of significance becomes a feelingful intuition of experience, not simply an interpretation of symbols. The reference to
the Western heritage of tonality that is found at the end of the
first movement of Schönberg's String Quartet opus 10 or at the
end of Stravinsky's Symphony of Psalms is a commentary on or
a play with the socially given; but both passages contain a
complex poignancy that cannot be translated into any other
medium of expression. The referential meaning is fused with
equally complex feelings and attitudes to form an intrinsically
musical compound.

   Although stylistic mixture and diversity has occasionally
drawn praise—in medieval cathedrals, for example, or in
Baroque architecture, or in 18th-century German music—it has
more often been the occasion for both moral and aesthetic
censure. The mixture of musical genres was viewed in Plato's
*Republic* and *Laws* as a concomitant, and even a cause, of the
general decadence of society. In the 19th and 20th centuries, on
the other hand, when the roots of style in social function had all
but withered away and its influence on character had corres-

pondingly very largely disappeared from view, the mixture of genres was seen in the light of copyright laws and the growing value placed on individuality; it became a matter of plagiarism, reprehensible again, however, not only morally, but also legally and aesthetically. The public idiom of melodic figures and structural techniques had receded in favor of individual creativity and private possession. And there were also new demands made on music for consistency and unity of style.

The recurrent moral cast of the objections to stylistic mixture are an indication that style is a matter of truth as well as meaning; it entails a fidelity to ways of feeling that are rooted essentially in culture and social function. To desert these underlying meanings, to fail to grasp them, or to confuse them or cover them over, is to desert their source in their particular historical social structure and the human nature it shapes and sustains. But there is an alternative to this truth in a humanity larger than a single culture, in a scope of style that will avoid both provincialism and the provincial error of construing local style as universal. To be sure, universality may always be found in the particular; but there is another route to the same end in an openness to the cultural diversity of time and place and class, in a wide horizon and a far-reaching sympathy and sensitivity such as we find, for example, in the music of Mozart. The human truth to be represented here, in spite of any superficial resemblance, obviously stands in the sharpest contrast to a virtuosic eclecticism of style, which is true to no significant mode of experience at all. And style also knows an empty truth, which is found in the repetitive imitation of mannerism.

From a larger point of view, it is we who create the nature of man (unless we observe rather than participate); we do not simply come to know the being of man *through* music, but come to know it *in* music (as we really do to some extent in every manifestation of humanity from language to society.) Thus the more music we create the more truth we have access to; the relationship is a direct rather than a conditional one, and even meretricious art would seem to have its place. But degrees and kinds of truth would still remain, even if not truth and false-

191

hood, with the related degrees and kinds of musical value that are attached to the wide diversity of styles, local and international, shallow and profound.

The basic public meanings of musical configurations that underlie every manifestation of style are so difficult to account for because the processes through which they came into being are rooted not only in intrinsic and invariant characteristics of man and nature but also in a series of antecedent meanings that extend far back into prehistory and are for the most part therefore hidden from view. But it is certain, and even intrinsic to its definition, that style is determined by human experience; it can be accounted for in no other way. The whole complex structure, no matter what its elaboration and abstraction, must grow (and proceed at each successive step by a derivation that is similar) from function, signals, the natural materials of the culture, rural song, and so forth; or in a word, from "nature," to which art itself is added subsequently and gradually. Eventually the roots are covered up and become difficult or impossible to trace. But play with sonorous objects, with sounds of the voice, with kinesthetic possiblities provides the discovery of attractive juxtapositions and patterns, and of utility in a variety of the activities of life; variation appearing spontaneously with no definable cause, or introduced by chance, has a part in this kind of production of sonorous form and significance, guided only by physical and physiological possibilities and the intrinsic perceptive qualities of rhythmical and tonal patterns. Such exploratory creativity added to configurations of known significance by way of variation or extension seems likely to be the central process in the creation of musical form and its meaning. The perceptual property of alterations of configurations, whether in tone color, pitch, rhythm, speed, or the deletion or insertion of elements, has an immediate meaningful measure against the original version as a standard, and therefore a palpability and meaning of its own that facilitates its assimilation. Thus if only we have some beginnings in music, the rest presents little difficulty. But this fact implies reciprocally that the beginnings are relatively unimportant, at least in their precise nature. The vital matter in musical meaning, as in all

192

meaning, is the accretion, the addition of new possibilities and interpretations to the old.

It is this process of the evolution of meaning, of the interplay and fusion of continuity and novelty to produce change, that constitutes the essential substance and the fascination of history, for here the process of alteration and transformation of meaning can be seen in the large, with a concreteness and detail that place its mystery within our grasp even if we never succeed in clarifying it completely. We are sure always, however, that stylistic change must have foundations of a certain kind: that it must be based on the past, on human psychology, and on our whole present world of experience—our expressive needs. In the conception and application of serial composition, for example, in spite of its apparently radical nature and absolute novelty, it is evident that the possibilities of sonority and configuration selected were not at all arbitrary nor based simply and directly on mathematical properties in themselves. The past was present throughout, joined to the inherent psychological qualities of auditory perception and to the ideals of sonority and form peculiar to the feelings and outlook of the time. Traditional consonances were avoided, along with melodic and temporal continuity. But disjunction and pointillism were preferred not simply in their contrast to melody and chords and consonant intervals, but because this contrast answered some otherwise inarticulate expressive need. And the particular arrangements of tones chosen—two successive widely spaced dissonant intervals, for example—were defined in their quality not simply again by their difference from traditional tonal conjunctions, but by the precise degree of this difference from specific older configurations and by the psychological quality of just this particular difference. Why neo-Viennese composers of the 1920s preferred exactly what they did prefer remained essentially unknown to them and has remained essentially unknown to us, with little detriment to either their music or its history. We are nevertheless sure of the bases of their preference and of its value in the production of stylistic change and new musical significance.

With this necessary kind of relationship to past and present styles as a basis, then, stylistic novelty will either be discarded or find acceptance, or it will be at first rejected and later taken up. What is involved here is clearly a coherence with the established body of musical style, an integration with the experience of music that is familiar and even with its history. This condition, limited by the realm of modes of musical organization and feeling that are possible or accessible to a given time and culture, and consonant, doubtless, with the modes of experience that are accessible in general, but also directed by current tendencies and expectation and projects, is really a condition of the truth of style. Radical change, such as that inaugurated by serialism, will create a new truth if it becomes established, both in experience and in theory. Thus major-minor tonality had to be taken up into a more comprehensive musical outlook with the advent of atonality and serialism; the absolute naturalism of the past became relative to a larger structure of the musical universe, it became a stage in a continuing process. The change is similar to the revision of the truth of classical mechanics at the beginning of the 20th century.

The definition of changes in meaning as derived from the nature of the differences between novel formulations and established ones does not in itself account for the consistency of a style or of a particular musical work. There are of course tendencies and types of preference that are characteristic of a culture or a composer or that belong to a specific creative project. But stylistic coherence is also illuminated by a notion suggestive of the situation of mathematical science, in which an initial correspondence between axioms and empirical properties ensures the applicability of successive theorems to a given physical model. Granting the correctness of the initial basic connections, counterparts continue to be found for whatever mathematical relationships we demonstrate or discover within the deductive logical fashion as the outer world of physics does in conjunction with mathematics. Initially established connections between tonal patterns and inner significance seem to ensure the meaningfulness of formal permutations and elaborations derived as deductions or consequences from the original axiomatic config-

urations. Thus a new style is significant and consistent throughout for a reason more fundamental, if more obscure, than the
perceptual testing of the qualities of each constituent formulation. There is always a logic to new art as well as just an extension of known expressive phrases—a logic of tonal interconnections. The inherent possibilities of the fundamental formal
relationships that become the material of a new style or a new
work are analogically extended and variously elaborated, and to
this evolution there corresponds a whole realm of feeling and
experience, in a kind of miraculous parallelism. The form as
formed is a world, but in its vital and human properties, and as
the creature of the cultural and personal mode of formulation, it
is a world that is alive, so familiar as to become intimately fused
with our own experience, but so individual and unified as to
confront us—especially in the durable form of a notated work—
as a separate independent being. In creating art we objectify
ourselves, and in perceiving it we become part of another
humanity. It is a corollary of this conception of style that in the
process of formulation, a musical work will have an intrinsic
genetic will of its own, a growth, nourished on the intellect and
feeling of the creator, which has a certain similarity to that of
some form of organic life, or in particular to the growth of one of
the composer's children. But the finished work will not only
arise from the endowment of the composer; it will also be a
concrete realization of the general conception that guided it,
which is composed of various concepts of genre, form, and
emotional quality, together with adumbrations and even
images and concepts of extramusical experience. The embodiment of the guiding conception, however, reciprocally transforms it into a concept, and it is this overall concept, fused with
a synoptic image and feeling of vital sensory experience, that
comprises the meaning of the work.

# CHAPTER 6

# Permanence

A fundamental distinction may be made in music with respect to its mode of existence. On the one hand, music is often best described as an experience or an activity or an improvisation; it is not committed to visual notation, and at times not fully planned in advance. Although music is always dependent in some way on preformed material, it can range as an activity from what is felt to be complete freedom of structure and expression to what is in fact a realization of a particular tradition—one that is defined in the storehouse of memory and skill, carefully rehearsed, and transmitted with little change from one generation to the next. On the other hand, music may be constructed with the aid of notation, fixed visually in notational form, and valued for its novelty and distinctiveness. The two types thus abstractly defined exist in song, dance, drama, ritual, and ceremony as well as in instrumental music. They constitute a contrast of spontaneity and prescription, of the momentary and the permanent. This is not to say that the greatest skill and care cannot enter into improvised music, or that the music of oral tradition cannot also represent the kind of continuity and permanence that inhere in relatively unvarying repetitions of

196

traditional secular or ritual melodies or in the successive occasions of elaboration of an established melody type; nor should we overlook, from the opposite point of view, the possibility that a notated work may be merely a fixed version of the most casual improvisation, or, in contrast, a routine composition like a thousand others and totally without the independent value that would make it worth preserving. What is more, the performances of a notated work are directly comparable to successive occasions of improvisation, with the musical score as the equivalent of the memorized tradition. It is clear that there is considerable overlap of the two categories, and considerable variety contained in each. In fact our typology really separates the sonorous existence of music from the form in which it is preserved. This distinction remains fundamental, and it will serve to delineate our conceptions of the musical work and its properties.

The contrast between improvisation and the notated musical work is very similar to the contrast between spoken and written language. Speech, like musical improvisation, must make itself as it proceeds, especially in dialogue, when the interaction and cooperative effort of two or more speakers is involved. It does so, however, out of known elements and formulated combinations of these elements, and even on the basis of a detailed plan of the succession of topics. In addition, speech not only operates within a given language, but also within a given idiomatic tradition; it can even be endowed with the permanence of phonorecording; while written language, from the opposite point of view, can be no more than the record of an improvisation, just as a drawing can be simply a spontaneous and unrevised sketch. But in no case (except for memorized orations) are spontaneity, creativity, and novel combinations excluded from speech in favor of preexistent formulations. Written language, on the other hand, represents the final product of a more conscious, reflective art, behind which there may exist many complex and successive processes of creation and formation and revision.

This polarity of types, however, is perhaps more accurately described as a multiplicity, for in music, at any rate, it is difficult to discover principles or features that characterize each type unequivocally, and the diversity we find cannot be quite so neatly divided up into categories. The musical work of art (and indeed even the literary work) may be no more than a particular historical manifestation found in a particular cultural setting; just as it has come into being it may also die out or be superceded by other modes of musical existence. The work of art nevertheless represents an intrinsic potentiality of music, and is therefore in that sense universal; it has brought with it, in any event, a ramified significance and an impressive range of values. But it is obvious, for example, that human memory in a culture that is nonliterate or that employs writing only for special functions rather than as a general facility useful in every aspect of life can accomplish prodigious feats in respect of the retention and preservation of detail. These accomplishments can be more readily understood in music if we remember that they take place not in the sphere of abstract instrumental art but in that of the composite arts of song and dance and drama, where sonorous and tonal experience is united with the concreteness and definition of multisensory and conceptual forms. The limitation that does exist in the absence of musical notation is in the time taken to learn a multiplicity of complex works and therefore in the size of the musical repertory. It is also not possible for music to disappear entirely from unrecorded tradition and then to be reinstated or revived after considerable time has elapsed. Yet the distinction between oral tradition and notated work of art is not as great as might appear in the factors of durability, complexity, and workmanship; and this is also true for other properties of music: for detachment, wholeness, and value, and even for individuality. Nor is the relationship ˙between the notated score and its various performances entirely different from the relationship between the traditional form of music—preserved in conception and habit—and its various realizations; indeed conception and habit are also connected with a musical score.

The difference between written and auditory culture is certainly a profound one, yet it is not properly expressed in terms of a contrast between "historical" and "nonhistorical."

Written words and music are not the only access to the past. We can, for example, disover a remarkable amount from excavation, preserved physical objects, pictures, and the changing style of artifacts. The history we write is in fact a construction whose nature depends quite exactly on the nature and quantity of the evidence available to us, but not simply on the existence or non-existence of written records. There is really a kind of technological basis to this consideration, partly in the sense of the technology available to us now in archeological and historical discovery, restoration, decipherment, and interpretation, but more fundamentally in the means of formulation and expression available to the cultures we investigate. Phonorecording, for example, has given rise to libraries of "oral history." And it is clear, similarly, that musical phonorecords can be equated neither to oral tradition nor to visual notation. Phonotape shows us, in addition, how the whole nature of art can be changed by a new medium, for here music takes on not just a visual but a literally tangible aspect; the material and manual operations that can enter the compositional process have a profound effect on the character of the artistic result, and the particular technical facilities of splicing, superimposition, speed change, and so forth also have their manifestations in terms of the resultant qualities of the music.

In spite of its varied forms, visual notation, as a medium handled by the composer in his creative activity, has implications that are of great significance in determining the nature of music. An instructive comparison can be made again with writing, which brings about a radical transformation of verbal art, for literature is clearly identified with its medium; it is essentially a product of written language. For the effects of notation the involvement of the sense of vision seems largely responsible; the complexity of interrelationships it makes possible within the composition is the foundation of most of the aesthetic properties of the musical work of art; this is in fact a striking example of the influence of an artistic medium on the nature of the work of art and of the intimate connection between the two. Even though the medium is an intermediate one it participates directly in the creative process and also in the creative imagination. Much of the advantage of visual notation is present also, as is quite readily realized, to the musical analyst, historian, or connoisseur; the score reveals many things that are not so easily heard; it gives us a more distinct appreciation of the form of the whole, if not of its aesthetic meaning, and it immensely facilitates comparative study both within the work and among a multiplicity of works.

Musical notation not only provides the permanence and textual authenticity that artistic composition deserves, but much as written language alters the nature of linguistic art, it changes the process of composition itself so as to foster the very properties of unified diversity and qualitative interest that it permits us to preserve. The objectivity of music is supported by the visual and tactile externality of the score; the shaping of the composition in complete independence of its transience and its temporal course permits continual adjustments of every part of the whole, along with deletion, enrichment, extension, and in fact a total freedom of formativity that exceeds even the flexibility found in the visual arts. Although the score is a concrete object, it yet can be subjected to every alteration conceivable with very little effort and without affecting the final qualities of the musical work. Composition thus operates with a thoroughly tangible medium that is present simultaneously in its entirety. But this is true of the musical work as well, since the score is a representation of the work. The wholeness of the work becomes literal; it is present all at once in visual form; repetition in time becomes repetition in space, and complex structural interrelationships are able to take on a clarity which can inhere only in visual objects. But also the feelingful course of experience that constitutes the inner aspect of the music is given a corresponding objectivity. The work assumes lasting existence independent of composer, performer, and listener; the experience it formulates is transformed into a relatively permanent object that can be brought alive in an unlimited number of performances for an unlimited time, but which need not, on the other hand, achieve such realization to exist. The objective nature of the score pervades the smallest musical units of the work; the very thematic patterns are rationalized and objectified in accordance with the natural capability of visual notation; there is a characteristic definiteness about the themes of a notated musical work which makes them comparable to the motifs of visual art or to concepts and which stands in sharp contrast to the fluid character of improvised formulations; notated thematic alteration and variation also manifest the same relative precision. An immense power of manipulation and retention resides in the auditory imagery and imagination of a great musician, but the subtleties, the interrelationships, the complexities, and the intricate web of emotions and ideas that make up an achievement such as Wagner's *Tristan* seem hardly to be possible apart from the practices and conceptions of composing a permanent, unified, important, and unique work cast into written form. The vast dance dramas of nonliterate societies such as the Maori are products of communal tradition rather than creations of the individual imagination and they are part of life in general rather than autonomous works of art.

It is notation, then, that ultimately underlies the conception of music as a coordinate member of a group or system of arts, which implies also some degree of similarity between music and visual art. Composition renounces something of the inner aspect of music, of its generalized emotive impact and its involvement with motor activity, and stresses rationality and structure. Music becomes more specifically auditory; it is able to discard text and dance and drama; but it adds to the ear something of the capability of the eye, and it comes to exemplify the characteristics that are emphasized by general aesthetic theory, which are especially adequate to the visual arts: detachment with respect to the observer and autonomy with respect to environment and function. Thus the musical work of art represents a paradox: it is a stable form possessing complex interrelationships that is created in an evanescent and inward medium—a durable spacelike structure built of transient durational constituents. Aesthetic notions arise that connect it with architecture as well as with oratory. The nature of musical material—of sound and hearing—must obviously provide the basis for this: in the span of the temporal present, in memory, in pitch, in the possibility of simultaneity, and in the musical

201

system. But composition develops these features of auditory perception to the fullest extent to create a simultaneous as well as successive whole, detached but still saturated with vital qualities of feeling, mood, and volition; independent but still immediate in the involvement of consciousness and in somehow incorporating or urging our bodily as well as inner participation.

Notation brings still other musical values into prominence, for without the careful workmanship and detailed interrelationships it makes possible, many aspects of novelty and personal style could not develop; without the value permanence suggests and fosters, the necessary care would not readily be taken; and without the preservation of each achievement, no measurement of change would exist, nor could a rapid course of development take place if the novelty of each new work were not available for inspection so that its features could be extended or modified and in general become new points of departure. The value found in novelty and personality leads to the creation of an individual style for each work, as in Verdi's *Otello* or Wagner's *Tristan* or especially in the music of the 20th century. This has other causes than the appearance of the notated work of art, for a culture that is musically literate may still follow an unchanging tradition; general conceptions of the value of progress are influential, especially as exemplified in the achievements of science, and the role of theoretical speculation is of considerable importance; but notation provides an indispensable basis. The radical effect it can produce on the course of historical change and in revealing aspects of music that might otherwise go undiscovered can be seen if we compare the musical art of the West in recent centuries with what we can discern of the history of the music of auditory tradition. Indeed we can say that the full value of which art is capable could hardly reveal itself without notation; man could not create such a world of sonorous experience except through the visual instrumentality of written records. This is true not only of the richness of significance that an extensive and varied past adds to new creation, but of the depth and dimensions of the artistic experience itself. The complexity, or perhaps more accurately, the intellectual concentration that gives music its universality as a self-contained world, is almost an inevitable consequence of visual notation and permanence, the one permitting the flexibility of thought and the analytic penetration required and the other providing the necessary incentive and the models for emulation. Only in the work of art can man create the full humanistic truth that is to be found in music, for it provides the personal complement to the general style produced by the culture.

The significance that notation has possessed during the centuries of its use has often been very different, of course, from the meaning it has now for musical aesthetics and philosophy. It seems to have been for some time a practical adjunct of an auditory musical culture, aiding in the recollection of known melodies and in learning new ones, and subsequently supporting the construction of carefully integrated polyphonic works. At the same time, its ontological status rose as it changed from a dispensable accessory to a representation of the essence or ideal form of music itself; during the Renaissance it often seems to occupy a position separate from and superior to its realizations in sound, which took on the various colorings of the subordinate realm of the senses and confronted the lesser problems that arose there, such as those of ornamentation, instrumental setting, musica ficta, and other practices of performance. The notated score became more the province of the *musicus*, its varying realizations the province of the cantor, even though theory and practice were often combined in the person of the composer or theorist or singer. But it obviously calls for historical study in any given case to determine the relative weight and kind of importance that resides in the score and in its performance, or whether and in what respect the one or the other has an accessory rather than a primary position.

Notation does not in itself account for all the aspects of the musical work of art, but it does underlie most of them, and it is certainly the single most important foundation of the whole. The definitive and versatile notation of pitch, by representation on a staff, was developed during the 11th century, and a similar achievement for relative duration during the three following centuries, while in another two hundred years, during the sixteenth century, the vertical alignment of polyphonic parts in a score format seems to have come into general use by composers. During the 18th century, autonomous instrumental music achieved an increasingly impressive status, coincident with the development of aesthetics as an autonomous division of philosophic thought, and in the 19th century, musical aesthetics in particular underwent a similar development. We are now able to survey the whole process, to secure historical insight into the nature of the musical work, and at the same time to examine and question each of its properties and to describe or envisage alternative forms. The manifestations we have mentioned extend over a millennium; they are all related and they all bear on our subject; but the basic conceptions that define the musical work of art and the expression of these conceptions in practice belong to the 16th century. It was then that the fixity of notation and the artfully composed work were explicitly contrasted with improvisational practice, that individual genius and personal style became conspicuous as musical values, that the musical work of art was regarded as a self-contained and perfected entity, and that music was thought of, like the other arts, as a creative, or "poetic," endeavor based on science, with products that merited preservation and imitation.

What has brought together and what binds together the accretion of features that have been found characteristic of a work of art is their common dedication to the end of aesthetic experience for its own sake and its own properties; the goal is variously conceived as beauty, expressive quality, moral influence, style, or truth, depending on the general outlook of the culture and the prevailing philosophy of art. To the (historical) observer the artistic achievement is one of style, to the composer the values sought for—beauty, expressivity, the structural elaboration of particular tonal relationships—appear in a more "absolute" light. In any event, each of the typical features that have seemed to define the work of art is to some extent independent of the others and calls for its own characterization. What comes to mind first in the context of a temporal art is the property of definition. Certainly the musical score seems

204

to possess a definiteness as compared with music retained in the memory, and the performance of a musical work would again seem more defined, if in other ways, than an instance of music-making in a culture or social sphere that is musically non-literate. This is, however, not at all the case. Each copy of a musical score is definite as a physical object, and all the copies are definite in that they agree or correspond to each other (which we can assume for the sake of simplicity to be the rule); in this sense a score is certainly more definite than the music retained in memory, and the difference is even greater for the copies of a score as compared with the music in a multitude of memories. But the musical work is a conceptual object, not the score itself, and whether we consider one person or many, the work is thus hardly different in the property of definiteness from the tradition carried in memory. Nor is a performance of a work necessarily different in this respect from the performance of traditional music; it is only in respect of its duration or length that traditional or improvised music is in general much more indefinite than a performance of notated music. To be sure, the conceptual framework in improvisation or the elaboration of a *raga* or a *maqam* often permits the widest latitude to spontaneity and inventiveness, much beyond what the conception and image of a musical work of art permit by way of interpretative freedom, but this is not true of the most defined products of a nonliterate musical culture. Successive performances of an Indonesian gamelan piece or dance drama, for example, much as they may give way to other versions in the course of time, can have a precision and exactitude of resemblance among themselves in spite of their complexity that easily exceeds the similarity of successive performances of a Western musical work, even by the same instrumentalists or singers.

The definiteness that apparently characterizes a literate musical culture would seem to reside in the relationship of the score to its performances. The music of a nonliterate culture, then, since it makes no use of such a relationship, would appear to be poorly defined. But the definiteness of a score with respect to its realization—quite contrary to what one would expect of a visual notation—has been very variable and is intrinsically limited. The score is in fact a locus of possibilities, usually of so great a range that it requires historical supplementation even with regard to pitch and duration, and especially with regard to medium of realization, number and arrangement of performers, loudness, speed, ornamentation and subtleties of tonal inflection, and appropriate acoustic setting and functional occasion, not to mention the separability and independent performance of parts of the work or its coupling with others in a larger musical whole. But even the most complete visual notation and the most detailed supplementation would not remove the indefiniteness of the score with respect to its sonorous realization. This can happen only if performance is eliminated from music and realization assigned to machines. The score would then be able to provide complete specification, but it would cease to have any place in music after the phonorecords derived from it had been produced. The mediate interpretation of performance would disappear, together with the additional expressive component of music that originates with the performer, and the aspects of historical interpretation that would remain would be those of the historian and the listener. Music here would acquire its most definite form, although the definitional difference between the preserved specification and the realization cannot be removed whenever any music is subject to repeated consideration or listening. Except insofar as the score in itself is concerned, then, the property of definiteness that is associated with a musical work of art—in the historical sense in which we are considering this conception—does not seem distinctive.

It is worth remarking that both score and work of art at times make considerable provision for spontaneity and creativeness on the part of the performer, so that the musical work encompasses a freedom beyond that of interpretation which corresponds to the freedom often found in music without a notational basis, such as improvisation, folksong, and the elaboration of melody types. But what is common in nonliterate music is rare in the work of art. Here the freedom is attached to the latitude of the score, and this is mirrored in the musical

work itself as a conceptual object. Thus the selection of performing forces, of repetition schemes. or of dynamics can be
open to the performer, as in the Middle Ages or the
Renaissance, or the realization of figured bass or the addition of
ornamentation, as in the Baroque, or the improvisation of
cadenzas in concertos, as in the 18th century. There are works of
Schumann and Chopin that the performer may repeat as many
times as he chooses, and in the 20th century, doubtless in part
as a reaction against total specification, the score can devolve
into a general plan for licenses of different kinds: the order of
sections of a work may be optional, or an improvised section
may be called for, or only a range for pitch given, or merely a
certain type of melodic agitation or rate of speed outlined. But in
these things we are also dealing with a reaction against the work
of art itself—and against features other than the definition of
the score—so that we are really considering not the variety that
can be accommodated within the bounds of the musical work,
but music of a different kind.

Similarly, but for contrasting reasons, the definition achieved
by music that is produced by synthesizing sound electronically
and making use of phonotape is no longer a feature of the
musical work of art in its accustomed sense; many features
remain, but the change in definiteness, which has become
essentially that of a single performance, or more exactly that of
an electronically reproduced performance, is coupled with a
change of basic importance, for the composer now works
directly by the manipulation of sound, whether with electronic
synthesizer or tape, instead of indirectly with notation
accompanied by imagery; his working medium has a
concreteness closely comparable to that of the painter and
sculptor, who also shape the actual perceptible medium of their
art. This is approximated when we record an improvisation on
conventional instruments, especially if alterations are made and
passages redone, and it is also foreshadowed by those
composers who have worked at the piano, particularly in the
composition of piano pieces; but recorded improvisation at least
pretends to spontaneity, and composition at the piano has had

its destination in the score and the conventional properties of the musical work.

Within the apparent definition of the notated musical work, in any event, there obviously exists an area of freedom and creativity for the performer, as there is for the historian and the listener. Novelty in this area of interpretation would continue to exist even if music were restricted indefinitely to an unchanging group of notated compositions. Performance, very much like acting and dancing, may be considered a separate art, somewhat related to the art of the historian, although it is obviously complementary to composition; indeed it not only consummates the work of composition but is frequently joined to it or fused with it in the activity of a single person.

The definition of any sonorous realization of music, it may be added incidentally, is also in its own way subject to limitations, for what the listeners and performers perceive even in the same performance varies from one to the other; each has in some measure both his own external object and his own immanent one, not only in the dependence of these upon his conceptual contribution and intentional predisposition, his musicality, experience, and emotional state, but also in their dependence upon his physical location. A final aspect of definiteness is presented by recorded performance, but it is apparent that this represents the proliferation of the definition attached to the original performance itself; the external multisensory objects either vanish or exist in imagery, with consequent increased variety among the listeners, and there are other lesser modifications, but all of the changes can be mitigated with sophisticated reproduction techniques and videorecords. In any event, the significance of electronic reproduction in music clearly does not lie in its effect on definition.

If the definiteness of the musical work of art is not the characteristic feature it appears to be, and in fact has its distinctive manifestation in the negative form of the indefiniteness that inheres in the score, a second feature—durability or relative permanence—is doubtless well founded. As a matter of fact, it is durability that is probably responsible for the notion of the definiteness of the musical work, for the constancy of persistence in time is indeed an entirely legitimate instance of definition. Durability is also closely connected with value, both as its expression and as its justification; and it relates music to the spatial arts of architecture, sculpture, and painting, in part simply by making it permanent and in part because permanence represents an enhancement of value. But the nature of durability calls for some examination, for even in the spatial arts it can be emphasized to varying degrees; the Egyptian pyramids are an example of the extreme value that is at times placed on permanence, and in the same art, the architecture of world expositions represents the opposite extreme and that of American skyscrapers an intermediate example of a life span with an estimated limitation in length. But the material spatial objects of these arts can be distinguished not only from each occasion of viewing with its attendant object of immanent perception but also from works of art as conceptual objects; and to the works of art the decay and restorations that the material objects undergo are not applicable. Yet a work of art is not absolutely independent of time; it does not exist before the period of its origination, and it may eventually disappear forever from human awareness, while its properties and values are subject to continuous changes in estimation and meaning, however slight or gradual they may be, in response to all the forces of history. It is unaffected in principle, however, by the changes with time of the material objects that constitute its starting point and its foundation.

In music the situation is somewhat different, for durability is founded not upon perceptible sonorous configurations themselves, but upon their visual symbolization in the score, which can be saved from decay or change by copying or reprinting. An analogy can be found, however, in copies or photographs of spatial objects (although these really resemble phonorecords more than scores), which similarly permit reconstruction or duplication of the sensible originals. But in music there really is no sensible original: neither the sonorous image in the mind of the composer nor the first performance will qualify as such.

There is always only realization, increasingly reliant with time on historical knowledge and insight. The outcome of these considerations with respect to musical durability is that it again seems to be a property most directly applicable to the score and its formal reproducibility; it is primarily the score that persists, as the basis of both the musical work and its performances. Thus the score serves the same function as the literary text and the material object of spatial art; and historical interpretation must act as an adjunct for all three. The score is peculiar along with the text of a play only in its distance from the object of aesthetic experience, for it must be converted into the musical work and the individual performances, while the printed copy of a literary work and the material object of spatial art are as such the immediate foundation of individual readings and viewings; the true musical counterpart of these would be the phonorecord.

With the property of permanence the cultural and historical nature of music comes into prominence, along with the significance of the style of an epoch or a culture as a whole; for the reproducibility of a musical work, as we have indicated, is not a matter that is self-understood; it is by no means the case that the reproduction of the objective structural aspect of a work will bring with it the corresponding inner experience it originally externalized or evoked; indeed the acoustic reproduction of a work is in itself hardly possible except as the expression of a course of feeling which may have become foreign to musical experience. Apart from its difficulty, however, the reproduction of a musical work under new conditions of time or culture may not be desirable in every respect; the very concern with immortality or durability may be in some way mistaken or naive; and in fact the same possibility exists for history or humanism in general. What are the values of studying man as we can know him in history and anthropology (for this is ultimately the outcome of the preservation and understanding of works of art)? The permanent work is very much like an embalming or artificial preservation of a course of inner life, and thus an instance of the paradoxical effort of man to keep the past as a part or a determinant of his present and future.

There is a middle course in this endeavour, deviations from which in either direction are destructive of value, for what we are dealing with in the retention of the products of culture is a contest of past and future, of tradition and creativity. To be concerned with our heritage to the point where no energies or time are directed to the exercise of our own creative spirit and the expression of its unique outlook is as little a fulfillment of the possibilities of life as to seek complete novelty and construct a future in disregard of the past; the one error is scholarly, the other vitalistic. But to use the past creatively as well as contemplatively, and in this use to enrich the significance of what we create, demands a nice adjustment of our interest and activities. In spite of technological aids, of digests and statistics, and even of improved educational processes and a longer span of mental life, it is plain that the recorded wealth of culture must easily outstrip our capacity to revitalize and experience what we preserve and to turn it to account. There can be no end then to the ever-new conception of history that is demanded by each generation and indeed by each individual—to the sifting and selection and varying foci of interest dictated by the feeling of relevance attached to each manifestation of creative vitality. The immediate past will serve one generation as a point of departure, but represent for the next a completely alien spirit to be overthrown, while some preceding era or exotic culture becomes a model for the qualities now sought after.

In a similar fashion, the written musical work will have the effect of uncovering and illuminating every aspect of the nature of history. The general problem of the relation of past and future, for example, includes the more specific question of the pattern or course of historical change. Here the notated work of art emphasizes the departmental and atomic constitution of the movement of culture; it reveals history as a building upon the past in discrete efforts, but also within distinct fields of endeavor; as a varied group of serialized accomplishments belonging to separate departments of expression or utility. Often a series may take on the aspect of successive solutions to a problem, at least for part of its course; but whether this problem is made explicit or remains implicit, it really is something of an

211

abstraction or fiction. For one thing it keeps changing with each new solution, and for another, it can never define the whole nature of a work of art, which may encompass the solution of certain problems but is always much more than this no matter how generally or broadly any problem is formulated. In any event, the notated musical work occupies the foreground of consciousness for a composer engaged in an enterprise of the same genre; other influences—even musical ones but certainly those of other areas of culture—are only by exception comparable in importance. If this is not the inevitable nature of history, it is the nature of history that is based on recorded achievements; the general form of history is as much a product of culture as any of the individual events that constitute it, and we may correctly say that the recorded work gives rise to a certain form of history—doubtless to the most characteristic form that has been known. The notated composition focuses future efforts so that they need not begin again from the whole complex of culture and function, but can arise from music itself and within a specific genre. It also frees the historical process in its temporal career, for successive members of a series of compositions are not limited in their spacing by human memory, which controls oral tradition. Instead a tradition may lie dormant or be taken up only occasionally, with long intervals between successive works. At other times, by contrast, the members of a genre may bunch together, even to the extent of arising simultaneously, so that no influence is possible of one upon the other, but only a common ancestry. The spacing of compositions will depend only upon interest or upon new developments, whether within music or without, which may have the power to revive an inactive genre or cause a flourishing one to fall into obsolescence. A general change in the organizational principles of music, for example, can deprive a genre of its vital force until a new foundation is devised; the course of the symphony or the fugue in the late 19th and early 20th centuries is a case in point. Changes in social and religious functions and in institutions can have an equally drastic effect both in extinguishing a genre and in calling one to life. In the initiation of a genre, however, contextual factors will join musical ones as

212

significant determinants of historical novelty and change; the character of new religious conceptions and liturgical practices, for example, can exert a formative influence as powerful as that of other conceivably relevant musical genres, older styles, or the prevailing general idiom.

Coherence would seem to be another distinguishing feature of the musical work, for we would expect a work of art to be unified, and its parts to hold together or really belong together. This feature is difficult to justify and to define, however, for it can be found outside of works of art and it is apparently not always manifest within them. It is obvious, for example, that folksongs often manifest little variety either formally or expressively, that they consequently may possess a maximum degree of coherence, but that they lack notation, definition in length and in melodic detail, and other properties that would permit us to designate them as works of art. The performances of a *raga* or a *maqam*, and of many kinds of functional music such as that for dancing or marching are often also indefinite in duration, variable in melodic detail, and without a basis in notation, yet they may similarly represent the highest degree of coherence. On the other hand, the stylistic diversity often evident in music that indisputably belongs to the class of works of art would seem to undercut the criterion of coherence from the opposite direction. No one would deny that Bach's *St. Matthew Passion*, Mozart's *Zauberflöte*, or a Beethoven symphony was a work of art, yet each in its own way comprises an extreme formal and expressive diversity of style that certainly places the requirement of coherence in question. The same apparent contradiction can be found in the simultaneous coherence of texture, which ranges from the uniformity of monophony and imitation and the fusion of concord and of blended tone colors to the disparity of drone accompaniments, nonimitative polyphony, discord, and variegated tone colors. Are there perhaps deeper factors of coherence in each case beneath the conspicuous diversity that redeem it as a criterion? Or are we subject in our belief in coherence and indeed in our view of the work of art to the particular historical prejudice of classicism, in the sense in which the 18th century conceived the

213

properties and values of the art of ancient Greece as an ideal, or in the sense in which "classicism" does represent a recurrent but nevertheless particular possibility for artistic style?

Coherence, however, is not necessarily uniformity. Perhaps what one would demand of a work of art is the unification of variety, at least as an alternative to uniformity or even as an alternative higher in value or more characteristic. Thus the criterion can be saved if it is conceived as the coherence of diversity, with uniformity as a limiting case. In respect of coherence, then, musical works of art would still overlap with music as a relatively spontaneous activity, but the overlap would not be significant and other features would easily sustain the distinction. The problem of how diverse parts can cohere and of the nature of that coherence will remain to be solved, of course, but solutions can be sought in a variety of unifying forces and perhaps found in more than one: in factors of personal style, in the logical character of psychological reactions to sequences of formal change and contrast, in the common devotion of diverse elements to a function best served by their planned succession (such as a dramatic action or a religious service), and generally in a rationale or emotional pattern that gives meaning to diversity; the coherence can even lie in conceptions of universality or divine governance of the world, as it does in the symphonies of Mahler.

Closely allied to coherence is the important characteristic of wholeness; the one asks of a work of art that it be unified, the other that it be a unity. A work that coheres, or is unified, will tend by that fact to be marked off to some extent or in some way from its context; but the requirement of unity or wholeness transforms this tendency into a necessity. What wholeness still more than coherence represents in a work of art is the property of being fully or carefully prescribed or designed rather than outlined or planned in general. More specifically, wholeness demands not just design but unity of design—a unity of conception that in a temporal art is manifested most clearly in the fact that the start is a beginning and the end a conclusion. And for a temporal experience to have a wholeness and unity it is necessary that relationships exist between various moments;

the recurrence or constancy of rhythm or melodic patterns, or even of the systematic features of music such as scale or key, are features most commonly found, but juxtaposition or novel succession can also contain a logic that will make for wholeness. In the first instance, repetition enlarges upon the chief phenomenal feature of tone: a dynamic constancy based on the ever-new provision of what is falling away into the past. In the second instance, change rather than constancy furnishes the basis: the innovation of a new kind of material and the associated feeling of freshness. Underlying repetition, however, there is also the novelty of temporal context that justifies it; it is not just sameness and constancy that are deployed, but also the dynamic effect of increasingly later positions in time. And similarly, novelty and freshness will never make up wholeness if there is no background of constancy underlying the change; the relationship supporting the difference may lie in the logic of experience rather than structure, almost in the simple psychological identity of the perceiver, but something must bind the succession into a whole if the result is to be unity rather than confusion. Yet these are as much factors of coherence as of wholeness, for unity contains the additional requirement of orientation within the temporal course of the work.

Not only beginning and conclusion must appear to be such, but intermediate sections of the whole must be calculated, in structure and in significance, to reveal that they are intermediate, and in addition to reveal their precise role in the economy of the totality. This is, accurately expressed, a requirement of consecution, and it is again a matter of coherence as well as wholeness, but the coherence involved is of the particular kind that constitutes a temporal unity. Thus we know in a musical work of art or a performance of one, the stage we are considering in the work or the stage that fills our temporal present. We know that we are experiencing a reiteration of the opening, for example, and of whatever expressive significance this reiteration may carry with it; we know when we are then departing toward other formulations or are suddenly immersed in them and whether the transition and the fresh material have

215

a character of inevitability or abruptness, of expansion or contrast; and we know some time before the conclusion that we are reaching the conclusion (unless it is designed to appear as one only in retrospect)—that we are approaching it in the fashion distinctive to the genre or to most of the music of the time, inexorably, dramatically, sadly, objectively, or routinely, be it signaled by a pedal point, a crescendo, a subsidence, or a turn to the subdominant; by a quality of apotheosis, or a backward glance that is expressed in a nostalgic transformation of initial material. But each genre has its own varieties of wholeness, its own forms, with their characteristic tendencies toward sectionalism and the characteristic marks of each stage of their temporal course. The Baroque fugue and the Classical sonata are remarkable examples of these properties, achieved without external support such as drama or ritual, but solely by means that are specifically tonal. Even the most monolithic and uniform works of art contain something of this feature of wholeness, which helps to distinguish them on the one hand from music that behaves and starts and stops as the performer desires, with a consequent fluid and variable definition of its temporal phases, and on the other, from sectionalized and episodic compositions such as instrumental dances or the short canzone and ricercari of the early 17th century, in which the forms and qualities of the individual sections often do not reflect the position of these sections in the whole. Like serially published novels that are conceived and written in installments, successions of musical compositions such as instrumental dances or the short piano pieces of the 19th century do not constitute a coherent and unified temporal whole, but merely fill in a framework of duration that remains external to the musical contents.

Indeed music not unambiguously formulated in a single movement presents a problem of peculiar importance that brings into question not only unity but the very nature of the musical work. Even the fugue and the sonata, which are taken as exemplary instances of works of art, confront us with this difficulty seen in its two opposite perspectives. The fugue is often coupled with a movement of contrasting style that is unified and a whole in itself, while the sonata, or any of its varieties from chamber music to the symphony, consists of movements which again are unified and wholes in themselves. The performance of an individual movement has at times been an accepted practice, and composers on occasion have discarded a single movement and substituted a new one considerably different in character; indeed multimovement works have at times been created by assembling previously independent compositions.

Is the fugue a work of art, or only the totality of prelude and fugue, or toccata and fugue? And is it the symphony or the quartet that is a work of art, or really each of its movements in its own right? In both cases the way the movements are articulated is obviously of central importance. The composer may prescribe that the following movement is to begin directly. But the articulation is typically secured by a pause of unspecified duration that permits considerable differences in length and character. The performer may therefore determine the quality of the connection of the movements with a latitude that includes the integration of the silence into the form of the whole by an appropriate and precise definition of its length. But he can also interrupt the continuity of the encompassing work drastically, even permitting applause and reflective evaluation and the intrusion of feelings and ideas extrinsic to the music; or he can create a quality of consecution between movements which has some special character, such as the feeling of removal to a very distant sphere of expression that can be produced by a prolonged pause before a slow movement (reinforced by conformable bodily gesture and behavior), or the brusque dismissal of an introspective mood produced by starting a loud and vigorous movement almost directly after the preceding one (again reinforced by conformable gesture). This is really an aspect of interpretation or even spontaneity remaining in the musical work that easily escapes notice; the same is true in a rather different sense of the whole physical behavior and visible expressiveness of performers; and formal articulation in general represents another opportunity for interpretation within an individual movement, but on an extremely subtle scale of duration.

With the more conspicuous unity that was introduced by

217

Beethoven, movements are interconnected by transitions, and they contain interrelationships of thematic material or of significance, whether the sequence of meaning is one of continuation, complementation, or progressive succession. Single movement works eliminate altogether the spontaneity represented by pauses between movements, although long pauses often make their appearance within the composition as though to provide a substitute. Composed transitions have a still wider range of meaning than pauses; their significance can vary from indecision and foreboding, through conventional expectation, to relief and happy surprise. But any tangible interconnection of movements defines the unity of a musical work unambiguously. It is the movements of Classical instrumental music, which characteristically end in a definite fashion and appear to be self-contained, that present the problem we have been considering: is the musical work an individual movement or the totality of them? The comprehensive conception of the genre provides an answer, for it becomes the basis of a hierarchical relationship. The totality is obviously a unity, but it is a unity composed of lesser unities; each movement is less of a whole than their sum, which has the greater degree of perfection and wholeness.

In general we seem little troubled by the question. After the prelude that precedes a fugue of Bach's, or after the first movement of a Classical symphony, we do not have a full sense of totality, largely, perhaps, because of conceptual factors connected with genre and a sense of musical history, but doubtless also because of intrinsic formal and significative properties—a stylistic or emotional incompleteness or a concentration or uniformity that within the context of the style similarly calls for complementation for its full meaning to become manifest, together with the meaning of the whole. To be sure, there are a curiously large number of equivocal instances. We cannot always tell a collection of pieces to be drawn upon at will from an encompassing work. And what are we to say about *The Ring of the Nibelungen* or *The Art of the Fugue*? Or the practice of performing separate movements of symphonies in 19th-century concerts, not to mention arias and sections of operas? Yet there was doubtless a tendency to emphasize the unity of the musical work in the 19th century, as is clear from the logical and psychological course of the succession of feelings that was found to be of such epochal importance in the Beethoven symphonies and later sonatas, and also from the interest in one-movement compositions and in the thematic interconnection of multimovement works and operas. This is a corollary of the new independence and importance of aesthetics and especially musical aesthetics. It is part also of the new independence and importance of music itself and especially of the musical work of art and its individuality as contrasted with its conformity to genre.

But if we consider music in general we are struck by the ubiquitousness of multipartite and multimovement compositions. It is as though most paintings were triptychs or most sculptures friezes; indeed part of the explanation may be sought in such multiple spatial works. But the compound constitution of musical works is without doubt a phenomenon of intrinsic importance, bound up somehow with the very nature of music or with the very nature of a temporal art. We cannot understand it fully without a consideration of the composite musical arts and the whole cultural context of music. But it is clear that the unity of a musical work of art is generally achieved in spite of, or at least without the abandonment of, a series of interconnected and variously related movements. The chief specifically musical way in which this is accomplished is by making the movements logically or psychologically complementary in a given sequence. They may also be interlinked by means of common or related material.

In so far as the occurrence of multimovement works is an inherent tendency of music or of temporal art in general, it would seem to arise partly through the limitation of our span of attention, particularly in connection with complexity of form and intensity and depth of meaning, but still more importantly through an intrinsic conflict between the nature of music and the conception of a work of art. What the work of art calls for most fundamentally is an apprehension of interrelationships; each of its characteristic properties and values rests on this

219

perceptive and intellectual capacity. But the demand for an apprehension of this kind is also a demand for simultaneity; even the temporal course of our experience of a work of spatial art must arrive at the simultaneity of a synoptic view, an achievement which takes place in this sphere, however, without difficulty and even as a matter of course. But the simultaneity implied by the apprehension of interrelationships stands in opposition to the very nature of specifically temporal experience. Music can achieve it only by integrative devices of form and meaning, and by integrative perceptual capacities, that succeed through a constant combat with the transient and continuously vanishing character of its material. On the other hand, relative uniformity of form and meaning avoids the conflict only by reducing the values and canceling out the properties of the work of art; it proceeds by deploying and indulging the direct connection of consciousness with extended tonal duration and repetition in themselves, shaped solely perhaps by gradual cumulative changes of loudness or speed. Within the framework of the work of art, however, uniformity entails boredom and a consequent reduction of our span of attention for this reason. The highly multisectional character of early independent instrumental music in the decades around 1600 testifies to the need for frequent change when each section is uniform. Compositions that were quite short were also typical of that period, many of them transcriptions of vocal works. Others have simply been freed from function—from the social occasion that would bind dances together, for example, in an encompassing contextual unity, or the religious service into which a toccata was integrated—and are not correctly regarded as wholes in themselves. Even those that might pretend to artistic autonomy tend also to be brief or multipartite. But this is simply a historical manifestation of a dilemma difficult to avoid: musical works of art tend by their nature to be either short or sectional. Ritual that lasts for hours, on the other hand, does not meet the criteria of a musical work of art, and neither do social or ceremonial events; the music included in these is certainly an artistic activity, although not in itself a work of art.

Closely related to the occurrence of multimovement works is an opposite phenomenon: the integration of works into larger wholes. This may take place for external reasons, as it does in discharging a commission for instrumental works in the 18th century, where six or twelve compositions became a single opus. But the musical relationship then remains as external as the cause, although diversity was certainly a guiding principle even if there was no further intention such as mirroring the four seasons or temperaments. Groups of twelve also ocur in a pedagogical framework connected with temperament, as in Bach's *Well-Tempered Clavier*, where the principle of diversity takes on a cosmic connotation of universality and perhaps also of the annual cycle of months.

In the early 19th century the social basis of groups of six or twelve works disappeared, and the growing unity and importance of the individual work was uncontested by group membership. But new tendencies appeared to replace the old. The last quartets of Beethoven seem to be related in their thematic material and to carry out a single encompassing conception. This is certainly true of Bruckner's symphonies, especially of the last three. In Wagner's *Ring*, the unity and integration of the whole involves not only common thematic material and a single dramatic narrative, but again conceptions of universality and of ancient Greek dramatic cycles. In the string quartets of Bartok or of Schönberg, along with the individuality of each work there is the suggestion of an overall course of development, largely of personal style in the case of Bartok but also of historical and general validity in the case of Schönberg. And in the 20th century subsequently, as the conception of the musical work as an unequivocally defined masterpiece recedes, compositions often become examples of the personal or historical development of style and technique. They may then be thought of either as different versions of a single work, all equally valid, or as successive sections of a vast encompassing work that is composed over a period of years. In either case it is clear that the older notion of the definitive version of a perfected masterpiece that is abstracted from

221

historical time has given way to more flexible ideas of compositional activity that connect music with the temporality and general course of life.

The detachment of a work of art is to some extent a consequence of its wholeness or unity, for to be a totality is already in some way to be demarcated from an environment or a context. Of the several aspects or kinds of detachment, the chief one is probably the separation of the work from activity—in the case of music, from the activities of composing and performing—and its consequent ability to serve solely as an object of perception. It can then be conceived for that end, composed and performed with an audience in mind, dedicated to its role as an aesthetic object. No matter how immediate or sympathetically participative our experience of listening to such a work may be—in dependence upon the type of music and the type of listening that are involved—and no matter how inclusive of strong kinesthetic or even adjustive and orientational bodily components and of strong feelings both associated and specifically musical, the music will remain distinct from that literally participative type which consists essentially in creative and corporeal activity and sonorous expression. The performance of a work of art is devoted to the production of music that is eminent in its properties of auditory objectivity, even if the performers themselves comprise the only audience present; and the work of art itself has no existence at all other than an objective one—its nature is wholly and specifically that of a conceptual object. The central auditory properties involved in a musical work of art are the configurations and stylistic meanings of an immanent object; externality may also be involved, but it is not the essential artistic manifestation; nevertheless detachment from the listener is as clearly applicable to an immanent mode of objectivity as it would be to an environmental object; the listener becomes comparable to the viewer in visual art—even to the viewer of a painting, for whom bodily motion and change of position have the fewest perspectivic implications and the elapse of time the smallest significance—and notions of disinterest, passivity, and contemplation become as relevant to music as they are in other areas of aesthetics.

Again it was around 1600 that the audience became a distinctly more conspicuous factor in music. In the performance of opera during the following three centuries the separation of performer and audience doubtless had its most striking manifestation; public concerts secured a comparable importance in the later 18th and 19th centuries; and it is only in the mid-20th century that ideas of participation were entertained that began to bring into question the exclusive position of both the passive audience and the musical work of art. Yet there have been many kinds of audience and many kinds of listener. Performers can listen to themselves to varying extents, and there have been select aristocratic audiences very conscious of their role, private bourgeois audiences of one or a few people, and public audiences of every conceivable constitution from conservative annual subscribers discharging a social duty to avantgardists avidly pursuing a novel style or a new conception of music. There are composite audiences and mass audiences, and even participating audiences such as those in the time of the French Revolution or those engaging in community singing or joining in the refrains of commercial folk music. The distinctions are numerous and they obviously correspond to distinctions in types of listening, social varieties of music, and various genres and styles, all of which are interrelated and connected with different cultures and historical periods. For our present purpose, however, the variety may be overlooked; it is the mere existence and the conception of an audience in themselves that bear on the definition of detachment.

Doubtless the extreme of detachment, which made its appearance when most of the other features of the musical work of art had also reached their most fully developed form, is represented by the "audience" of electronically reproduced music. The fact that externality is here subordinated or essentially eliminated is paradoxical in its significance. To be sure, one cannot be detached from something that does not exist, but it is the immanent rather than the external musical object that is essential. The individual listener to a phono-recording or a radio program—who is also simultaneously a member of a mass audience—is able to achieve a maximum degree of disinterested contemplation and adequacy of musical understanding, by virtue of the very absence of performers and of other listeners. Alone with his electronic equipment and undistracted, he seems to represent an ideal relationship of consciousness and its object, in their interaction and their separateness. The detachment defined by the isolated act of listening and the role of passivity is here at its height, although it necessarily carries with it a social and functional detachment that calls for compensatory imaginative and conceptual activity. Electronic reproduction also fosters a deeper comprehension of music through the increased availability of music it brings about and the possibility of repeated hearing, yet these very factors tend also to produce a casual and superficial experience. Which of the two con-tradictory tendencies will be the more effective one will de-pend upon the general musical attitude of each listener, although the effect of removing all music, whatever its type, from any literal representation or suggestion of its functional and social context will be present in any case. The use of music as a background for other activities and for the general business of life should not really be characterized as a type of listening at all. The minimal or flickering awareness that is involved also calls into question again the very applicability of the notion of detachment, for the musical object is not posited as such. Instead the music is simply a constituent—by its nature not perceptually singled out in any way—of a general environmental tone or ground upon which other events and objects are projected. "Listening" of this kind can often be found among individuals in other audience situations, but it is the flexibility of electronic equipment, and the ease with which it makes music available and the same works repeatedly available, that encourages the background function. There are also, of course, characteristic musical styles that are associated with the varieties of background music intended for different situations, and the practice obviously represents a significant social and cultural phenomenon. As far as detachment and musical aesthetics are concerned, it is a borderline manifestation, encouraged, rather oddly, by the same technological development that is re-sponsible for detachment in its most striking form.

It is of importance to note that the detachment defined by the distinction between audience and musical object contains all the implications and significance that reside in any· instance of purely mental experience. A genetic process is suggested, both in evolutionary history and in the life of the individual, which transforms a biological interrelationship into a mental one—which replaces activity and physical interaction by a specifically contemplative attitude. The most complete detachment implies immobility on the part of the listener; everything is internalized; the body is apparently set aside and functionless. But is the inner experience correctly conceived as implicit behavior? Is it in fact a contained and transcended version of adaptation and overt activity? Such a characterization will obviously apply to the whole intellectual and cultural life of man. The aesthetic detachment of music provides evidence to support it. Explicit gestural participation in music, and often singing or humming or whistling as well, continually break through the corporeal passivity of the listening experience, and not only for young people listening to dance music or for pianists, conductors, or singers who are particularly familiar with the physical activities of performance. Musically untutored and insensitive listeners in general seem to find it especially difficult not to participate corporeally, and apparently are unable to find meaning in music in any other way. But even in thoroughly passive listening, the body is not so much absent as held still; there is even a state of tension involved in this constraint; and it seems to occur only to make possible an inner bodily participation that is a complex composite of semi-conscious patterns of breathing and pulse changes and kinesthetic impulses, all of which may be an intrinsic part of the creativity of listening. It is not clear at all that only a bodiless and isolated consciousness is at work. Yet there is at least a relative autonomy in purely inner experience—in conception, reasoning, cognition, speculation, and even imagery—that cannot be reduced by deriving its novelty, let alone judging its value, from considerations of overt behavior and organic adjustment. Language and art and thought obviously cannot be accounted for without a detailed study of the properties they possess as autonomous and independent departments of human expression.

In removing the listener from even the social occasion of a concert or operatic performance, electronic reproduction really carries a step further another kind of detachment that the concert hall and opera house had already largely consummated, for these institutions had gradually become counterparts of a museum, in which the original functions and contexts of art were cast aside in favor of a uniform setting that embodied the attitude of "art for its own sake." But this is clearly of major importance in the conception of the work of art, for it represents a detachment from function and original cultural context and thus from purpose, which is taken to mean extraneous purpose.

To view freedom from function as an essential condition of a work of art, however, is an oversimplification; this species of detachment is a less stringent requirement than separation from the perceiver, or objectivity. Art in its essense is purposeless, but this entails only a certain degree of detachment from function, or a freedom from subservience. The two requirements—that art be purposeless and that it be functional—are not mutually exclusive; a work may meet functional demands perfectly, but these may affect only certain of its larger characteristics or more extrinsic features; it can still be purposeless and autonomous within this framework, in how it fills out its general requirements. In addition, the function can become part of the aesthetic conception, part of the circle of purely artistic demands, and in doing so it is transformed from an external requirement to a musical one. That there is a core of musical experience which is unaffectd by function, or at least not adversely affected, can be seen when music is transferred successfully from one purpose to another, often with a concomitant change of text that is fully compatible. Indeed function can exercise a positive rather than a negative influence upon the work of art, for it can act as a stimulus evoking musical consequences of unusual quality or expressiveness. There are occasions, finally, when the relationship is reversed and music becomes the purpose that is served by function. In elaborate funeral or cremation rites, for example, or in ceremonial processions or cultic drama, it may be difficult to decide whether it is the ritual or the music that is the overriding interest; the two may constitute, in fact, a composite enterprise in which ceremony and music fuse to produce a joint result.

What functional and social detachment mean fundamentally is conveyed in the notion of self-containment, and it is nothing less than the center of the quarrel between aesthetics and history that we discussed at the outset of our inquiry. This kind of detachment is made possible by preservation, but it imposes the necessity upon the now unavoidably less involved or more passive recipient of reconstituting in imagination, through conception and imagery, the contextual circumstances and meanings that have been stripped away by the very process of preservation and transplantation. The durability of the work of art permits a decision to preserve, but the decision to preserve implies the duty not to falsify, for what is preserved is only the isolated work which in its original setting may really not have been a work of art in the full sense; indeed even the work in itself, as we have seen, is difficult to preserve, and brings up problems such as textual interpretation and modernization. To preserve is thus to destroy also, in the sense of the context in which the work existed. The chief danger, which lies in a certain self-contradictory nature of the work of art, is the implication that musical compositions exist outside history. There are, to be sure, fundamental kinds of formulation and meaning that reside in universal features of human biology and consciousness, but configurational significance and style are specific to culture, and what is more to the present point, they lose much of their meaning if they are known purely as separate from their social milieu and functional role. On the other hand, those compositions conceived as works of art are amenable to the very treatment that can be criticized for other music, and we can say that it is part of the nature of a work of art to possess an initial detachment that can be described as a certain independence of function and social purpose.

Indeed the notion of detachment can justly be taken as the

central characterization of traditional aesthetics. The work of art and the aesthetic experience are disinterested, purposeless, even isolated, and thus sharply distinct in nature from experience and objects in general. The contrast has without doubt been exaggerated. They are certainly distant in principle, however, from the practical purpose of the perceiver; will, desire, and practical advantage are ideally irrelevant, although there can be no doubt that they in fact often impinge upon the aesthetic realm and color the artistic experience, especially in the case of composition and performance. Doubtless the belief in the isolation of art is nourished by older and recurrent classical conceptions of beauty as ideal and mathematical, which look to Greek antiquity and Neoplatonism as sources of inspiration. If the conception of beauty is enlarged, on the other hand, to comprise expression, character, style, and thus culture, it will necessarily entail various types of context. The work of art may lose some measure of detachment, but the artistic experience can remain essentially disinterested. Historical relationships, however, along with many other kinds, will bear upon and enter into the qualities of the object. The same considerations apply to conceptual thought, which really cannot be excluded from perception, or from creation and performance. But even economic purpose and social function are at least at times an intrinsic part of beauty and of aesthetics, as we can see at once in pedagogical or occasional or liturgical music. If purpose is nevertheless entirely excluded from art, the appearance of purpose, or the property of purposiveness, as Kant emphasized, remains central. This characteristic is similar to that of expressiveness without expression, and is connected to some extent with a confusion that is fostered by language. It is clear, however, that a musical work is intrinsically expressive even when it is not literally a personal expression of the feelings of a composer, performer, or listener. And it is clear also that it has a quality of purposiveness or rightness, of the accordance of parts with the whole and of the whole with contemporaneous potentialities of musical feeling and conception—even with invariant capacities of inner life—although it obviously need not present or serve any literal external purpose. It is in fact this relationship of art to life that underlies the conception of the work of art as a symbol, as the embodiment of meaning or truth or as containing the very essence of moral and religious aspiration. Music in particular, however, is at least a valuable guide and a touchstone for aesthetic theories in respect of detachment, for even in its material—especially if we take this to be tones in defined relationships—it is radically detached from the environmental objects of external experience.

A type of detachment related to that of function or society can be found in purely instrumental music and still more in music made up of electronically generated sound. The term "absolute" has often been applied to instrumental music in particular, if it is free of programmatic representation and strong extramusical implications as well as from text, dance, drama, and ritual. Detachment of this kind tends to carry with it detachment from function, which is also responsible for the notion of absolute music, although self-containment is perhaps a more appropriate designation for functional detachment. In any event, nonprogrammatic instrumental music is a manifestation concomitant with the growth in importance of the musical work of art. It has been taken as the object of speculation for musical aesthetics in the 19th and 20th centuries, when it had already ceased to be a predominant variety of music, but at no time in its history, from the Renaissance to the present, did it ever represent the leading or most common variety, and it is similarly subordinate in earlier times and in most Oriental and nonliterate cultures. If it represents an ideal of detachment—or perhaps more especially of purity—for music, this stands in contrast with practice, which provides striking evidence of the greater popularity of composite musical art. This may, to be sure, be evidence simply of the greater accessibility of certain kinds of meaning rather than others, or perhaps of more conceptual kinds of meaning or those more bound up with varied or general experience rather than those peculiar to sonorous configurations and works of art; and it may represent also a contrast of practice with speculation, or of language and gesture with mathematics; in the dialogues of Plato the one artistic sphere, largely in *Republic* and *Laws,* is connected with the realms of ethics and politics, and the other, largely in *Timaeus*, with mathematical cosmology.

There can be no doubt that purely instrumental music, separate from social function and from language, will be detached similarly from the obvious bases of moral value, for nobility and depravity of character, revelation and corruption, as well as the vigor and justice of society or its opposite, are clearly not products of specifically aesthetic properties; it would not be possible to produce such effects by the merely biological impact or elemental constituted properties of sonority, either in rhythmical or qualitative patterns. They can be due only to style, and most conspicuously to those meanings of style that are ideological and contextual in origin if not in fact. For if detachment removes music from its place in artistic composites and social and religious function, the moral force of musical style in itself will be due still to the imprint of those absent factors on purely tonal configurations, and often in quite concrete components of meaning such as the implications of melodic formulations and harmonies. It is to these that the proscription or praise of music is generally due, and with them either the low regard and inferior social status that is often the lot of musicians or the adulation and special esteem they at other times enjoy. Conceptual factors play a large role. The position of instrumental music in ancient Greece as a manual endeavor inevitably barred the professional performer from the status of a poet. And again, the connection of instrumental music with pagan worship in late antiquity and the Middle Ages turned its low value into rejection and the low esteem of professional performers into disdain. The 19th-century composer, on the other hand, conceived as an inspired poet and evaluated in the light of Greek social ideals, became a divine prophet of a new order. With explicit functional and contextual factors eliminated, however, and even if no associated or conceptual factors of a moral nature exist, music still retains an ethical force of a different kind in the experience it represents and calls for when it is properly understood, for the truth it possesses to particular modes of thought and feeling is simultaneously aesthetic and moral. In music of distant provenance,

even the negative moral values that were originally manifest—like the positive ones—can expand the tolerance and
humanity of later performers and listeners.

A final kind of detachment is the separateness of a work from
other works of art, which again is self-defeating and really
self-contradictory, for a work cannot be known in isolation; its
meaning would vanish if we had no experience of other music
that was stylistically related to it in some way. Yet a tendency
toward independence of this sort became increasingly
pronounced in the 19th and 20th centuries; it is an aspect of
detachment that is synonymous with individuality, which is a
property of the work of art we shall consider in its own right.

Although we have regarded the detachment of music
primarily from the point of view of the separation of listening
from participation, it is a feature of the specialization of
composition and performance as well, for both of these
activities may become quite distinct from other types of
experience; indeed detachment is a consequence not only of the
wholeness and unity of a work of art, but also of specialization
itself, whether of artistic activity or of any other. Notation and
permanence doubtless foster the specialization even of musical
composition, but they obviously have their chief effect in the
areas of performance and listening, where apart from the unity
and wholeness they encourage, they entail an effort of
understanding which calls for the interpreter to project himself
into the original cultural and social setting of the work and acts
to remove him in some measure from his own environment. In
the case of a historical or foreign work, therefore, as opposed to
a traditional or contemporary one of the performer's or
listener's own cultural circle, an environmental displacement is
added to the detachment entailed by absorption in the world of
the work of art, by dedication to its intrinsic forms and
meanings and to any representational content. The detachment
of the work is clearly both complex and fundamental; it gives
rise to dualistic notions of art and life, or illusion and reality; and
the separation of the two becomes the ground of new referential
and symbolic relationships that replace the alternative or
preceeding state of integration. Stories within stories and plays

within plays, at times manifested as dreams or dreamlike qualities, constitute a recurrent pattern of artistic form and significance that merely makes explicit what is inherent in the nature of art. But the complexity is compounded by the fact that reality also possesses the same constitution; our experience in general reveals both separateness and unity, the many and the one, and the demarcation of any object or person—even of ourselves—is necessarily accompanied by problems of the nature of the demarcation and of the consequent relationships of what has been marked out to the world as a whole and to other entities.

The individuality of a work of art is a feature that distinguishes it in form or in meaning or in both from any other. It is embodied in a style that represents not a cultural, local, historical, or personal mode of formulation or expression, nor one specific to a musical genre or medium of sonority, but one that is peculiar to the individual work. Distinctive concrete subject matter in the composite musical arts can make an important contribution. In the individuality of a musical work the nature of music as a world or being in itself becomes most fully evident, alongside its nature as a language or as an expression or statement or experience belonging to an individual or a culture. The work becomes a living entity that we can connect or identify with ourselves; both in its genesis and in the durational existence of its performance it formulates and projects its course, and the past and the future are always active in its present. The truth it presents is contained in its own nature as well as in a reference to the experience of its composer, performer, culture, and listener. Fundamentally, however, this novel ontological character of the work of art rests on the archetypal formulations of the general musical style, which like those of language, constitute a world we live in and explore and extend and cannot easily break out of.

The unique style of a single work has its closest relationship to the style of the composer and more distant ones to the style of the genre, period, and the locality. We would normally expect a

Beethoven sonata, for example, to resemble most closely other works of Beethoven, but less closely other sonatas not by him or other compositions of the time or other works composed in Vienna. If we consider his late piano sonatas, however, when the characteristics of the musical work of art and especially the characteristic of individuality became more pronounced, the whole texture of resemblances will be seen to change: the uniqueness of each sonata will become more striking, and most of its resemblances to more general styles will recede; it will be correspondingly more difficult also to define a personal style peculiar to Beethoven's late works than it is to define his personal style in the middle part of his career. This difficulty is often encountered in the early works of a composer, but then the apparent individuality of the works is shown to be false by their strong resemblance to the works of other composers. In a case of individuality that has been somewhat exaggerated—the remarkable uniqueness of style of Wagner's *Tristan* and *Meistersinger*—it is quite clear that even genre has given way before the unique qualities of form and significance of the single work; the only stylistic tie that remains visible is the personal style of the composer, and even that is astonishingly subservient to the artistic demands of individuality.

It is apparent, then, that the style of the individual work can become prominent only at the expense of types of style common to groups of works. Individuality is also essentially equivalent to novelty, and therefore readily construed as a manifestation of progress. Both its reciprocal effect on other types of style and its equivalence to novelty can be seen clearly in music of the 20th century, where together with the appearance in music of modes of existence alternative to the work of art the work itself tended to manifest exaggeration in all of its features. Stylistic individuality and novelty often seriously reduce the meaning of a composition: it will no longer represent the idiosyncrasies of a composer or a given genre, no longer bear any marks of locality or definite characteristics of a known or contemporaneous stylistic idiom; lacking any orientation in historical time and any context in a cultural or personal mode of expression, what significance remains is deficient in humanistic value. As we have seen in our discussion of style, novelty must have some relevant background and frame of reference to give it meaning and permit it to be measured; it must give rise to a revised or expanded truth; otherwise it destroys itself. Thus the exaggeration of the features of the work of art does not by chance coincide with the appearance of other musical modes of being.

An additional property of works of art can be designated by the notion of craftsmanship, which is partly a cause and partly a consequence of other properties. Craftsmanship is not to be understood in the sense only of technique, or of workmanship in itself; it comprises this but represents more generally the idea of concern, which includes any careful and sustained attention to aesthetic values, whether or not complexity and speculative or facile techniques are involved in either conspicuous or concealed form. There is craftsmanship and care not only in a fugue of Bach, a quartet of Beethoven, or Wagner's *Tristan*, but also in a simple orchestral piece of Debussy or a simple song of Hugo Wolf.

With this feature of careful attention to aesthetic qualities of form and significance is coupled the feature of value. This is essentially the manifestation of humanistic truth. It is also, with respect to its objective characteristics rather than its significance, very much a summary property, although again it is partly causal with respect to others. The value of a work is a result of, or resides in, its durability, coherence, unity, detachment, individuality, and craftsmanship, but it is also in reciprocation responsible for longer preservation, additional attention to coherence, unity, individuality, and craftsmanship, and further emphasis upon various aspects of detachment. The value that comes into being as a work comes into being is indeed a fundamental motivation of the process of composition and thus enhances the very properties of the work that create the value. It is specifically tonal, but like musical meaning, it grows from a context of general human experience, and it takes up and reveals the deepest nature of this experience. Ultimately the value takes the form of perfection or a certain classical quality. This consists essentially in the embodiment of definitive degrees of every artistic property, or of degrees that are conformable to the character of the totality. It is the achievement of a constellation of aspects that represent the highest conceivable level of artistic understanding and formative powers. We may speak in such cases of art rising above history, or of representing invariant truths of human experience, which are not dependent upon time and place; but more accurately described, what the composer has done is to discover the universal in the particular, to discover and uncover the deepest qualities of a given culturally formed mode of human life. It is in this paradoxical sense only that aesthetics can take issue with history and that art can become transhistorical—by a sufficiently perfect and profound embodiment of a specific manifestation of experience, of truth in its cultural particularity, which is its only form.

There is a sense, then, in which Palestrina and Mozart and Bach represent a permanence of value in Western history, even in principle a value that is eternal or ideal, as opposed to one that is temporary or what has been called slightingly "historical." It is indeed obvious that the influence of certain composers has remained limited, their value has been apparent or their music found exemplary only once in the course of time, usually when it appeared, and perhaps also only within a more or less restricted locality or a single social class. In other cases, by contrast, musical influence and value have been recurrent or apparently permanent. Yet the composer who seems to be of merely historical importance and the one who endures either in fact or in ideology are not sharply separate. There are numberless intermediate gradations—revitalizations and submergences—in answer to the musical interests and general character of succeeding cultures. The distinction between historical and classical value is one of degree only, for both have the same nature and the same source; classical value is not properly termed absolute.

The ethical value of music and its moral influence on the

character of the individual and of society are easily accounted for in the case of the composite arts and a context of social function. The presence of words and the associated emotional and ideological factors of a given type of social situation imbue the vital forces of the tonal experience with concrete meaning in terms of feeling and action, or conversely, the specific moral attitudes embodied in and taught by the occasion are given through music a hold over our feelings that provides the strongest possible foundation for the attitudes and behavior that are to be sanctioned. It goes without saying also that the specifically musical features of the experience will be intrinsically suitable in their purely sonorous significance and form to the defined ideas and feelings with which they are connected.

But more than this is comprised in the notion of the ethical value of music. For one thing, tone has a peculiar social power that unites us with others precisely because it lacks external objectivity and is so preeminently a mirror of inner experience. This becomes particularly evident in communal song, where the special character of the voice as an expression of subjectivity forms a powerful inner bond that is reinforced by the fusion of sound which occurs both in perception and externally. The efficacy of this bond is further enhanced by the absence of any tangible external source of social unification. The common physical and artistic effort and musical emotion, identical in all, complete our union with our fellows. Music has effaced the confrontation of others, which is an affair of the visual or tactile sense, or of the dominant aspect of speech, and replaced it with its antithesis. Beyond this intrinsically social property of musical experience, however, there is a similarly intrinsic but general connection between aesthetic and ethical value which would also—or still more—account for a moral influence of music without invoking its connection with words or its social context. Is art, practised in isolation and for its own sake, inevitably or even on occasion productive of ethical as well as aesthetic value? It would seem that the answer to this question must be an affirmative one. The complete separation of aesthetic from ethical value is a counterpart of the apportionment of experience among separate human faculties or separate parts of the brain, and even if we take aesthetic to pertain strictly and solely to sensory experience, the fact remains that an organism is a whole even when it has developed the most striking separation and specialization of functions. Formativity and perception are indisputably rational as well as sensory in nature. They not only involve a super-structure of conceptual thought and of deductive and inductive reasoning, but contain as essential ingredients a rationality of their own. Yet rationality is not morality, it does not necessarily involve or comprise action or the decision to act; except insofar as it presupposes the ethical value of reason itself, it does not entail a conception of morality, of good or wise behavior, or of noble sentiments and aims. Whether or not ethical value can be established by reason is not in this connection an issue, but only whether it can be fostered by art, which indeed must take place, if it does, without the intercession of reason, since the rationality involved in art has nothing to do with moral reasoning. If reason as a whole were awakened or furthered by aesthetic experience, we could attribute to art a moral value at least indirectly, but this does not seem very likely, even though Plato, in his concern for the integration of art and reason and of art and life, believed it to be the case. Aesthetics is certainly more than a matter of sense; it encompasses to some extent not only reason but also volition and feeling. The volition, like the ration-ality, may be bound up in and specific to the sensory exper-ience; still more, it may have what we can only term, in view of the detachment of art, a virtual character. Yet it may provide, where reason does not, a path by which aesthetic experience secures ethical import; or the conjunction of the two, activated in aesthetic experience and at the same time separated from life, become a model after which life is fashioned, a play of vital forces free to function without the encumbrances of practical attachments. This free interplay would then become an ideal of life, and in itself constitute an ethical value; life at its highest would be play, and play paradoxically a very serious activity. But this is indeed what we find true of art; it is totally engrossing and intensely pursued; it is free play of the utmost moment, play that is also work and that calls for dedication and discipline. If artistic experience and endeavor do not affect the moral cast of the whole conduct of life—and in pure form such as we find in instrumental music they may not—they are at any rate in themselves ethical pursuits, and a life spent in art a morally commendable one to the extent that it sustains humanistic tradition in the depth and subtlety of its artistic expression.

The humanistic significance of art, however, as opposed to the intrinsic nature and operation of artistic experience in itself, constitutes a further source of ethical value and provides moral enlightenment and benefit as well. Musical styles represent ways of thinking and feeling and perceiving that are cultural and personal; experiencing them or creating them involves an increased or new sensitivity to the potentialities of human being and to humanistic truth, which come to be known in a particularly direct and fundamental form, since their manifestation is purposeless as well as musical; they are expressed for their own sake. The proper understanding of music is accordingly capable—if it is not overridden by other factors—of bringing about a humanistic breadth and refinement of personality. Thus the ethical value of music need not involve a lack of artistic autonomy, an explicit altruism or particular commitment to the betterment of human welfare, a devotion to God or to religious ideals, or any service to external ends such as communal spirit, social ideals, or patriotic action. The alternative to this is found in music itself as well as in its context, but it is not merely sensuous enjoyment or conviviality, for musical value contains a separate ethic and morality of its own, which consists in a purposeless exercise of humanism and vital sensibility, an expansion and deepening of the intelligent sensitivity of life. What is involved, however, is nothing less than a fundamental civilizing force which is capable of supporting whatever value may arise in ethical and religious tradition.

Ontologically the musical work is a conceptual object; it is not an aesthetic object in a literal sense but in the extended sense of its meaning and implications, its associated imagery and sonorous realization. Nevertheless we speak for convenience of hearing a work rather than more accurately of hearing a performance of a work, and we indulge in other related conveniences and substitutions. A closer consideration will reveal, however, that the work is quite distinct from any of its performances and from the totality of them, just as the score of a work is distinct from any copy of the score and from the collection of all of them. But similarly, of course, we often speak of the score when we mean a copy of the score. The work is distinct not only from a performance, but also from any silent realization or partial realization in auditory imagery. In spite of its complexity of constitution as a conceptual object, and the fact that auditory imagery plays a part in its genesis, it can still be distinguished from imagery in principle. Yet although it is immaterial and persisting and public, it is not changeless or eternal or ideal in the Platonic sense, for each era and each new expansion of our musical outlook affects our conception of the past; works of art are clearly individual entities, and they come into existence at a specific time and place and undergo various changes in their characteristics during their life span.

The implications of the distinction between work of art and performance are perhaps most important in connection with temporality; for this distinction seems ultimately to be based on a dualism in the nature of time, the two components of which are separated, one as the ground of the work and the other as the ground of the performance. The separation of the two components and their separate functioning and deployment give a factual although not a conscious recognition to the individual existence of each, and amount to a metaphysical analysis of time in practical terms. The process, especially if its nature is now made explicit, is reminiscent of the analysis of pitch into two components, which we have described as height and tonicity. Temporality seems similarly to be composed of a factor of order, which defines the dimension of before and after and gives a single and unequivocal arrangement to the series of instants, and a factor of flux, which endows temporality with the property of passage and gives experience its transient nowness and its was and will be. The work contains only the order of time, the series that is only potentially a succession, but it is abstracted from temporal motion and flow; it is not embedded in what appears as the material component of time, as the substance that endows it with or comprises its percept-ibility. The performance gives us this material component to-gether with the serial component of order; it represents the matrix of the work imposed on the now and was and will be of the temporal flow, on a now that is unique in its being, that has never before occurred and never will again; the work, on the other hand, can be united during its life span with any number of nows, no matter how close or how distant they may be from one another as measured by a given standard of ordered intervals. The work is in itself a simultaneity of serial patterns, joined in ways that extend from an equivalence of the impor-tance of each pattern and the individual wholeness and inde-pendence of each to the dominance of one of the patterns, a hierarchical arrangement of their relative prominence, and the union of all into an encompassing whole. Thus the work is a layered structure of serial orders, and it is impressed upon a flowing material that is correspondingly capable of supporting several patterns simultaneously and giving experiential life to the full complex of their interrelationships. (In the case of canonic imitation, for example, the positional difference is given actuality in a temporal passage which refers continuously to particular phases of its own past and future.) But apart from the stratified constitution of the work or the performance in itself, the general impositon of order upon flux represents the fundamental temporal superimposition of music; it brings music into our awareness, defines it more closely as a concrete object, and permits it to take up and become united with our consciousness and with its constituting capacities. The composite musical arts may add still other layers of temporality, but they are of secondary ontological importance. During its duration, then, a musical performance will replace the general temporality of life with the special patterned temporality of music; and this replacement or insertion—which represents a repeatable experience—can take place only because musical and everyday temporality are fundamentally of the same nature.

In contrast to the musical work of art, concrete music—as we may call the mode of existence produced and supported by phonorecording—does not separate the order of time from its flux, but preserves the two in their union. Successive replayings, which in the case of composite arts will include videorecords also, do not entail the renewed imposition of order upon flux, but the imposition of the compound of the two upon a later present, and thus of a preserved temporal flux upon a new one. We shape the flow of time not as it passes, but by superimposing upon it the matrix of a preformed flow; the fluid aspect of temporality is such, however, that it conforms perfectly to the preserved compound, fuses with it, and reveals no trace of itself. It is obvious, of course, that in the mode of permanence represented by concrete music, many of the humanistic values created by the musical work of art and by its interpretation in performance will cease to exist.

# CHAPTER 7

# Composites

We have so far considered music as a purely auditory art consisting of structures of sonority that are essentially historical in constitution and meaning. An investigation based on such a conception of music would seem to deal most directly with the specific nature of the art, and thus to provide the shortest and most reliable route for philosophical understanding. Actually a direct approach of this kind is also seriously limited, and we have been able to achieve in each area of inquiry only an incomplete understanding of our object. The reason for this appears clearly if we realize that music as a purely sonorous expression is a relatively rare manifestation; more importantly, it would seem to occur only as a development from more comprehensive artistic genres. Thus both its structures and its meaning, as we in fact often have had occasion to remark, derive in great measure from sources we have necessarily taken little notice of in examining it as an autonomous tonal art. The earlier stages of our study, which have the rationale of their succession in considerations of logic and simplicity, call now for various types of supplementation.

Even as a specifically tonal enterprise, music derives many features of its structure and meaning from its immediate structural and functional context of musical instruments and the human voice; it is intrinsically composite, in a way that cannot be entirely eliminated, but only minimized, by the exclusive use of electronically generated sound. But a compositeness that is intrinsic is little more than a closer characterization of what is generally thought of as pure or absolute music. Composites that are more properly so designated may be divided into musical, functional, and referential categories. The first of these types has its natural ground in the nature of man, and in particular in the temporal character of experience and the capacities of the human body. Thus music most usually occurs as dance and song and opera, so that the tonal experience is part of a larger whole which comprises corporeal motion and language and which has formal and expressive determinants that belong to the totality as well as to each of the components. At the same time, dance and song are closely related to each other, for they are both grounded in the body, and therefore represent the most direct kind of expression we know. Dance-song combines the two, and so does the acting in various kinds of musical drama such as opera or Kabuki drama. Indeed other types of musical performance—conducting, playing an instrument, and singing—remain remarkably similar to acting and dance, and often manifest an elaborate and highly formalized gestural system, as in the case of koto players, jazz drummers, orchestral and choral conductors, or performers on sets of gongs (especially on the Balinese *trompong*).

The properties of the musical composite arts, which will derive variously from the wide range of possibilities provided by bodily motion, language, and gesture together with their diverse kinds of meaning, may subsequently live on as properties of an abstracted art that is purely tonal, but the significance and form of the specifically musical configurations will have their source and explanation in their antecedent and more concrete setting. On the other hand, dance and song and opera are obviously important varieties of music in their own right, and thus legitimate parts of our concern; we may therefore ask not only how they influence instrumental music but also the reverse question: To what extent are dance and song and opera, or even poetry and drama, shaped by the inherent properties of purely sonorous experience? The same question can be asked about literature, poetry, drama, and dance as arts independent of music, for these too may be subject to musical influence in their form and meaning. But this is no longer a problem of composite art, for it involves the relationship of music to other aspects of culture with which it is less directly connected.

It might seem that instrumental music as a whole derives from dance and song, a view which is certainly extreme but which does have the merit of appealing to the natural foundations that exist in kinesthetic and vocal impulses: bodily motions and vocal sounds are always at hand and readily shaped in response to tendencies of play and expression. It seems logical that instruments are subsequent in use, as extensions and accompanying reinforcements of muscular activity or as imitations of the voice. This likelihood is supported by the purely vocal music of societies that have never discovered or adopted the use of instruments, a situation regularly found also in the case of young children. Even opera, in the general sense of sung drama, can easily be included in the argument, for human interaction manifests itself corporeally and vocally, by motion, gesture, and utterance, or musically in dance and song; and here again instrumental music would seem to have a natural source for those properties that resemble features of drama such as conversational intercourse, rising action, conflict, triumphal restatement, denouement, and reconciliation.

Yet instrumental music without question has independent sources and independent properties; nor can we maintain even that it is subsequent to dance and song. On the other hand, it is clear that dance and song serve as a model in many respects, and that many features of instrumental music derive from them spontaneously as well as by imitation and analogy. But even those features that have grown out of dance or song or their combination will not necessarily be conceived or responded to in terms of their antecedents. Instrumental music can develop—whether by analogy or novel invention—into a medium peculiar to its materials, with patterns and expressive qualities only occasionally if at all thought of or experienced as those of dance and song. Even Beethoven's Seventh Symphony, for example, which Wagner took as the prize instance of his theories connecting the origins of the symphony with the dance, may neither have been conceived or heard as dancelike; the almost irresistible impulse it imparts to our kinesthetic sense may yet belong specifically among the legitimate properties of an abstract instrumental art. To be sure, it is tempting to regard the kinesthetic suggestiveness of music as evidence of an inherent connection to dance. Motional implications are invariably present; indeed conducting itself is a kind of dance, and seems merely to make these implications explicit; thus the dance is apparently adumbrated throughout music. But this line of thought does not lead to its intended goal, because musical motion and rhythm—and even the kinesthesis they suggest or compel—are sui generis in nature and thus fundamentally different from the kinesthesis of dance; there is obviously in general no fixed correspondence, either inherent or learned, between particular bodily motions and particular musical progressions: a gestural pattern can provoke or suggest innumerable and widely differing musical counterparts even in the sphere of melody alone, and the same variety is obviously possible when dance patterns are created for an existing musical composition. This theoretical generality disappears, however, after a dance has been formulated, whether as a socially established type or an individual composition; the relation between corporeal movement and music becomes defined, often within close limits, and takes on a character of mutual appropriateness that can not easily be altered.

In dance we are presented with a composite whole; the conception or experience is a unity; the constituents are in general separately distinguished, but they are projected or perceived as set against each other in various degrees of contrast and reinforcement to form a totality. Each is a variety of motion, and although they differ from one another in dimensional structure and only bodily movement belongs essentially to multisensory space, yet music and dance contain suggestive similarities and can thus be convincingly connected

245

in a number of different ways. They possess in common speed, rhythm, intensity, durational pattern, and the possibility of presenting different motions simultaneously; and they both contain qualities such as highness-lowness and volume, the resemblance of which demands the same descriptive or designative term. Not only jagged motion or fluid is found in both, or rest and stationary position, which in music become respectively silence and sustained tones at constant loudness, but also a far and near, a backward and forward, and an upside down. Gesture is an external manifestation, music essentially an immanent one, and perhaps because of this difference, which is grounded in the different natures of vision and hearing and the contrasting mode in which these senses present aesthetic objects to consciousness, the two have a natural tendency to act as complements, to appear as the outer and inner sides of the same event, or the music as the tangible reinforcement of the inner aspects or awareness of gesture. This complementary action may also be fostered by the joint activity of vision and hearing in the normal process of external perception, although the biological cooperation is of course fundamentally different from the aesthetic one. In any event, music defines the quality of a movement; it enables us to feel gestural properties as though we were initiating them, while if they were performed in silence they would leave us relatively unaffected. But music is reciprocally given a definite visual and kinesthetic meaning it otherwise would not possess, and which again—like the musical definition of bodily motion—is internal to the composite art of dance. In general, gesture and music make up a counterpoint of equivalent manifestations or at least of two comparable ones that are perceived as equivalent. But their counterpoint is also an interaction, so that each strengthens the formal, qualitative, and expressive values of the other; the enhancement is mutual, and it is achieved by a functional distinction; there is no dominance or subjugation. The practice of setting dance to music that has been independently composed and experienced as an autonomous art obscures the natural relationship of the two that is evident when they are conceived and formulated or known initially as a composite.

In addition to the distinction in mode of objectivity, dance and music differ in the nature of their temporality. Even to the dancer producing them, gesture and motion in themselves are not adequate an objectification as tone is of the fundamental nature of consciousness. Music will accordingly relate dance to consciousness more directly, as a kind of bridge to its being. But it can do this only because both dance and music are temporal. Thus their difference can become the ground of this new functional complementation only because it contains a degree of similarity.

What inequalities exist between the musical and kinesthetic components of dance are either favorable and intrinsic to their union or unimportant. The differences in mode of objectivity and in temporal concreteness act as an attractive force between them and are responsible for the inevitability or at least the peculiar appropriateness of their combination. Differences in dimensionality and range of possibility, on the other hand, are entirely overshadowed by similarities or rendered irrelevant by the basic requirement that the material of an art must always be defined or limited in some way. Thus it is true that the human body is a more specifically defined entity and its conjunctions with other bodies more limited than the perceivable universe of sound and of combinations of sound. Yet if we add to dance the variety represented by types of clothing and diverse adjunct physical objects as well as by different stage or outdoor settings, and impose upon music the necessary restriction of a specific repertory of sounds or a tonal system, the difference between the two in range of possibilities becomes very much less. The main consideration, however, is that their partnership is not adversely affected by this difference because of the defined ranges of freedom that must be assigned to each component art so that it may be an art. More striking are the similarities and conformities between the two. Music even contains an analogue of gravity and can construct formal counterparts of bilateral symmetry and its configurational expressions in gesture and motion. Polyphony can be coupled with simultaneous gesture possessing corresponding degrees of diversity or with the motions of more than one dancer. A single melody emphasized by unison and octave doublings has its counterpart in choral duplication of gesture and movement; accompanied monody in a single dancer set off by others. Even the external location of performers can be called upon to add to the resemblances. There is indeed no feature of either dance or music that cannot find an analogy in the other medium which is logically and psychologically convincing. But the dance as a work of art does not necessarily seek its unity in analogy or reinforcement. It can also successfully combine music and movement that are diverse, but the diversity will always have its measure and the determination of its character and quality in the unused possibilities of similarity.

In its form and meaning and style, the composite art of dance is subject to the considerations we have already reviewed for music itself. It has a natural basis in everyday patterns of gesture and movement, responsive in great measure to culture, historical period, and social class. Meaning grows from these and from folk dance, but inventiveness in corporeal formulations for the sake of their own expressiveness adds constant novelty to style, including the individuality of personal style, and often entirely without referential meaning outside of dance itself. In choreographer and dancer, composition and performance can find separate embodiments, a condition, along with notation, connected with the work of art as a distinct mode of artistic being. The properties of such a work are again essentially those we have examined. There is a detachment from adjustive and orientational bodily motion, from the purpose and functions of everyday motions and gestures, and finally from social, ritual, and ceremonial dance. The work becomes a durable, conceptual object that provides a definite locus of variation for its successive realizations. The unifying factors of repetition and variation are understandably evident in a temporal art that lacks the structural resource of language; and the wholeness of the work is characterized by recognizable stages in its temporal course, although with genre playing a lesser role in general, the stages tend to lack both the variety and the definition that they have in purely musical works. These features of form and meaning and style provide an inexhaustible extention of the possibilities of joining dance and music into an artistic whole. Starting with varied repetition and running through multimovement works and stylistic mixture or allusion, the resources of this composite art are a double set of those of each component—an essentially infinite reservoir of possible artistic combinations.

Music takes from dance a tendency toward clearly defined rhythms, especially strict repetition of durational and accentual patterns together with symmetrical phrases terminated by weak and strong closes in alternation. The paired phrases are a musical counterpart of a train of movements that is repeated along a general course of motion opposite in direction to the initial one, thus returning the dancer to his starting point and defining and closing a section of the dance. There is asymmetry in dance also, although it makes a smaller contribution to musical form and meaning. More specifically, in abstraction from dance, a continuing series of forms enters instrumental music, patterned rhythmically, melodically, and harmonically in accordance with the gestures and steps of particular dances. This music, however stylized it may become by factors outside dance, continues to bear its original significance with remarkable tenacity; a single characteristic phrase of a Viennese waltz, for example, even sounded in an instrumental tone color that is not typical, is at once identified and tends to summon up vivid visual and kinesthetic images of the corresponding corporeal motions. The qualitative and emotive aspect of the music, not only the structural properties, here derive from the original connection with the dance and its social setting as well as from our tonal response; the force and definiteness which are always given to the meaning of music by associative factors derive in this case from an antecedent composite art and from its non-sonorous component in particular.

If dance gives to music much of its rhythmic definition and kinesthetic qualities, song gives it smoothness and expressivity of melody. Certainly a major factor in the stylization of instrumental music, even in the case of keyboard instruments, is imitation of the prevailing properties of song. Eighteenth-century instrumental melody often looked to vocal style as a model, and the instrumental music of the 19th century makes use of actual song melodies as well as songlike ones. This dependence holds not only for instrumental lyricism but also for the adoption of more speechlike vocal styles including recitative (as in Beethoven's Ninth Symphony and a few of his piano sonatas) and even for the rhythmic and pitch patterns of speech itself (for which Beethoven again provides an example in the last movement of his Quartet opus 135). The instrumental canzona, lamento, aria, canzonetta, romance, ballade, and lied reveal not only melodic vocal influence but also the importation of formal and atmospheric traits, of the whole significance and conception of specific vocal genres. Other more formal patterns are also taken from song by instrumental music, just as they had previously been taken from verse by song, notably the rhythms of poetic meter in both durational and accentual form, and successive phrases which are equal in length (including the identical succession of a litany structure) or which have cadence relationships mirroring those of poetic end-rhyme. Again the question arises, of course, as to how many of these expressive and structural features of music would come into being apart from the influence of poetry and song, or as to whether they invariably point to song whenever they occur. While we cannot insist on the omnipresence of vocal influence and of vocal conception in music, we can at least identify numerous instances where these factors are undoubtedly present. The importance of song and therefore of poetry in the general constitution of music and musical experience cannot be denied.

But there is a reciprocal influence also. Just as dance reaches otherwise unattainable heights of motional imagination and qualitative intensity through the powerful suggestiveness and variety of music, so song exceeds the regularity of simple patterns through the force and precision of tone, as is most strikingly evidenced by the subtlety and complexity of Greek poetry, and by the varied and expressive rhythmical configurations, specific to the genius of each language, of monodic and polyphonic vocal music from the Renaissance to the present. Even simple poetical patterns, however, such as regular verse and end-rhyme, may be due ultimately to tonal influence. Many of the characteristics of dance, poetry, song, and instrumental music cannot with certainty be traced to any given source since these temporal forms generally go back to a composite art that often combined all of them. In the unity of dance-song it is difficult to distinguish the features that are due to a single component alone. Do instrumental refrain forms have their origin in dance or in song? And in which of these lies the origin of metrical patterns or verse structures in general? Language would seem, in the words *foot, verse, movement,* and so on, to point to dance as the fundamental influence; if this is not the case, however, we are at any rate directed to the unity of dance, word, and tone as a source of pattern and meaning for instrumental music.

The composite art of song has certain resemblances to that of dance. For one thing, the restriction of musical resources that the voice itself seems to entail and especially the demand for textual intelligibility no more represent a deficiency than does the range of possibility of corporeal movement; they are again the framework of limitation called for by the nature of art. But dance music seems less called upon to set limits for itself than does vocal music; length of phrase, for example, or extreme loudness, offers no intrinsic obstacle to gesture or motion as it does to the singing voice and the comprehension of words. The rhythm of vocal music also must bear a somewhat closer relationship to verbal rhythm than dance music does to the rhythm of movement, although melodic rhythm can also be quite removed from both the poetic meter and the speech rhythm of the words and even brought into conflict with them.

There is a similarity between song and dance in the historical appearance of literacy, for just as musical notation preceded that of gesture and motion, so, centuries before, verbal notation had preceded that of tone. Thus in both cases there was a long period when these composites were works of art only in part; of Greek and most medieval poetry we have only the words, and of dance from the Renaissance to the 19th century only the

251

music; pictures are of relatively little help for either, and verbal descriptions similarly inadequate in both fields.

The components of song conflict more than those of dance. Not only are they both auditory, but the necessity for conceptual understanding along with musical makes severer demands on the attention than the simultaneity of movement and music. The common auditory nature presents the problem of masking or mutual interference and especially of the perception of the poetical configurations of sonority, the so-called "musical" aspect of poetry, for these are not only subtle but follow entirely different principles of relationship than the principles on which the tonal configurations of music depend. As we have indicated previously, the two diverse modes of organization are contained in the voice itself. Alliteration and assonance and the qualitative resemblances of speech sounds are quite distinct from the successive and simultaneous interconnections of pitch.

But it is the conceptual aspect of language that presents the more fundamental problem. The sonorous configurations of the text with their qualitative emotive properties act as both immanent and external auditory objects just as the significative configurations of tone do; there is thus an artistic counterpoint of sensible objects that can mutually inhibit one another in perception and that constitute in any event a considerable challenge to apprehension. But the referential objects of the words—images and concepts with their relationships and emotive significances—are of an entirely different order; even *auditory* images are quite distinct from actual sounds. Thus song is basically a combination of verbal and tonal auditory objects, both essentially immanent, with the images and conceptions represented by language. This combination of objects again permits a complementary relationship between the component arts of song, but the disparity of the complements is potentially an incompatability; there is no satisfactory way to ensure artistic coherence and unity except by a restriction of the referential complexity of language or a restriction of the configurational and emotive complexity of music. To be sure, dance knows something of this problem also, for it similarly has referential meanings not only in everyday motion and gesture but also in dramatic action and narrative description; but these extrinsic meanings are often dispensed with in favor of the intrinsic and emotive significance of visual and kinesthetic abstraction in itself, while song texts embodying sonority only and dispensing with external reference are relatively rare. Also there is an almost automatic limitation in the referential detail of dramatic or narrative dances; the medium suggests simplicity of action and event by its very nature; but this is not equally true of the texts of vocal music, except for the genre of lyric poetry. Thus song demands attention to the functional relationship of its component arts; great elaboration in either will generally call for simplicity in the other; the conceptual complexity of language in particular makes any considerable deployment of the artistic capacities and values of music difficult to achieve. Beyond this, the complementary nature of the two arts calls for a similarly complementary division of their roles in the economy of the whole. The images and ideas of language add a new sensory and conceptual definition to specifically musical meanings, while music is able to reveal additional aspects of feeling or interconnections of ideas in poetry. To make this take place, however, calls for more compositional skill and insight in combining the arts than in composing either of them separately; or rather, the essence of composing or selecting each lies in an understanding of how the totality is constituted by their interrelationship.

The composite art of opera is another source of the forms and meanings of instrumental music. As a combination of drama and song it is similar partly to song but also partly to dance and dance-song because of the important role that gesture and dance often play. Yet dramatic action, which, set into song, is the essential core of opera, does not necessarily imply external activity and gesture; it can be largely internal or psychological, although corporeal attitude and posture will remain a factor of the representation except in the entirely imagined dramas of oratorio and cantata. Musical drama, however, has tended to incorporate a variety of artistic components, even including instrumental music, so that it is in fact, and to some extent in nature also, the most comprehensive of the musical composites. The theatrical aspect of drama has fostered the inclusion of tableau, dance, procession, and scenic spectacle; a kinetic visual element of virtuosic change of setting and inventive stage occurrence, together with diversified techniques of lighting, are characteristic additions to the fixed spatial design of scenery. And the art of architecture acts as a spatial frame for the whole, even in the case of outdoor theaters, which represent a kind of architecture of nature. The participation of architecture is of course found in music of all types, and even though it has a direct influence on the perceived qualities of a performance, it is not an inherent part of musical works of art or even of music in general, whether absolute or composite, since it merely enters the conception and influences it—even in its visual as well as its acoustic nature—but as a constant condition; it is hardly ever an object or a result of the specific creative process that produces artistic formulations and meanings in temporal media.

There is an analogy of some interest, however, between the place of architecture in the spatial arts and the place of music in the temporal ones. Architecture provides an encompassing setting for sculpture and painting, not just because it houses them in a relatively neutral fashion, as indeed it does also for the temporal arts, but because it is capable of integrating them—as ornamentation or as enhancements of its function—into a comprehensive and unified totality. Music has the same inherent capability with respect to dance, song, opera, melodrama, and film; it does not encompass the components of a temporal composite, for that is not an applicable capacity in this sphere of art, but it furnishes a fundamental and foundational temporal manifestation which can sustain and unite all others. As the most immediate presentation of the temporal nature of experience, it is a measure and a ground upon which the other temporal arts can be projected; they are relatively fluid, less concrete and determined in their temporality; music becomes their fixed standard, something like time itself, or at least like consciousness in itself.

It is because of this fundamental and inescapable temporality that music may be closer to dramatic action than to dance or

poetry, for dramatic action, more than any temporal manifestation except music, or inner life itself, is intrinsically a progress,
a dialectic, a forward or advancing motion. The action is an
external visual object that symbolizes real or imaginary
people and events; in these characteristics it resembles dance,
especially representational dance, but also poetry. The
complementary relationship of action and music, however,
rests largely on the treatment of the conceptual features of the
plot; these can be minimized by the nature of the action, but
when they are present they are usually left in the form of spoken
dialogue or cast into some form of recitative; the music is either
interrupted or severely restricted in its style and resources; the
active ensembles of opera buffa are a rare escape from this
necessity, and they incorporate activity and events more than
conceptual thought and conversation. To be sure, a remarkable
extension in the types of recitative and in diverse styles of
accompaniment permits a considerable integration during the
19th century of the speechlike sections of opera with the lyrical
ones. But in the last analysis the art faces the alternative of a
unity based on a continuous but necessarily very flexible style or
a unity similar to that of a multimovement work, where in
addition to the marked division into acts, the economy of the
work will involve a series of musical sections, and it will depend
in part on the coherence and the interrelated variety of style
they present, on the logic of their succession, and on the effect
with which each intrudes on the appropriately calculated length
of the dialogue that precedes it. It will then be the wholeness of
the action, however, and the functional definition of its stages,
that will be the chief basis of the unity of the work.

There is an interesting resemblance between dramatic ballet
and opera, for they have a common problem in the tendency of
dance and song to intrude upon the course of the drama in order
to develop their independent "lyrical" powers of expression.
This gives rise in both cases to an element of divertissement and
to a problem of integration into the whole. The formalized
dance is not simply comparable to the aria, but more specifially
to the aria that is understood to be such in the drama itself:
romance, ballade, lied, and traditional aria are characteris-

tically used in 19th-century opera not as part of the normal medium of dramatic dialogue, but as explicit insertions that are framed by the surrounding action; the drama will involve a song contest, for example, or a singing lesson, or will call for a drinking song or for the retelling of a legend. But this is the usual manner in which formalized dancing (along with formalized music) enters the dramatic ballet, which is otherwise devoted to representative gesture with a flexible motivic accompaniment—the exact counterpart in dance of the accompanied recitative that comprises the normal dramatic language of the action in contemporaneous opera.

The association of music with drama is as universal as its connection with language and bodily movement, and the dramatic elements in instrumental music have been correspondingly important. Of these, dialogue structure is probably the most obvious formal feature, although instrumental antiphony has other sources in the echo and in the perceptual interest of spatial and tonal alternation. The outstanding expressive influence, on the other hand, is the force of gesture and vocal exclamation, which we can see finding its way into instrumental recitative and sharply rhythmical motifs from the beginnings of opera to the 20th century. There are larger influences too, as well as more pervasive ones. Instrumental music often takes over a charged atmosphere that seems to have its source in dramatic foreboding; the symphonic recapitulation can adumbrate the victorious entry of a dramatic hero; and the conception and feeling of dramatic suspense as well of a joyous or festive outcome often seem to underlie a composer's symphonic imagination.

Another composite musical art that resembles opera in combining dramatic action and music is the melodrama. By employing speech instead of song, the melodrama separates the conceptual component from the melodic one and thus reduces the competition between them; this is true even when the voice makes use of an intoned speech which is intermediate between speech and song, as it often does in 20th-century vocal music; speaking on a pitch or on various pitches remains more speech than melody even when it is rhythmically defined and stylized; tonal configurations do not become prominent enough to usurp the attention, even though the melodrama secures a greater coherence in this way between voice and instrumental accompaniment. Intoned speech also gives the voice more carrying power, but in general, melodrama must make allowance for speech by a reduction of the loudness of the music or the adoption of what is essentially a style of accompanied recitative in which voice and music alternate; both procedures obviously represent a much more stringent and continuous restriction of the prominence and possibilities of music for the sake of the whole than is necessary in opera. Melodrama urges upon music a definite expressive character as well as compactness and pregnancy of emotion. Its momentary operatic use in verismo or expressionism to convey terror or extremities of despair and grief is very much like an intensified version of the insertions of exclamatory accompanied recitative in 18th-century opera to express states of agitation such as jealousy, rage, and vengeance. The coherence and workmanship of melodrama as a work of art are prejudiced by the stylistic disparity between the media that are combined; there is also a limitation on craftsmanship and definition because the coordination of speech and music is not precise enough to permit a fully formulated temporal unity.

With the motion picture, which is to some extent comparable to the melodrama, we leave the realm of musical arts and come upon another type of composite in which music does not play an intrinsic or coordinate part in the whole, but is incidental or functionally determined by an encompassing manifestation of a different and not necessarily artistic character. Besides the sound film, this group includes pantomime, drama, ritual, and ceremony. The sound film adds to music and speech the resources of montage and a moving camera; these are the essential determinants of its nature, and they enable it to exceed even the wide scope of drama and to enter the sphere of changing visual imagery, which is of such intrinsic interest that intrigue and even people become dispensable. The silent film, on the other hand, is a type of dramatic pantomime that employs the special flexibility of the camera. It remains very close to the group of composite musical arts, since it is a combination of silent drama and continuous music, which are accurately coordinated at each performance. Its mode of being, however, is rather complex, and not really that of a work of art. The silent film has no conceptual existence as a whole. The visual and musical components are not equivalent; the music is either improvised at the piano or organ or assembled from a stock of scores at the keyboard or by an orchestra at the time of screening; but the visual component, unlike the graphic notation or film of a ballet, is reminiscent of music preserved only on tape rather than in notation—it allows no room for varying realizations. Nevertheless the silent film is a musical totality, an art if not a work of art, and comparable partly to opera and melodrama and partly to dramatic dance and pantomime in the functional roles of the two components. The scope of musical form and expression is limited only by the practice of adding the music to a film that preexists, but not by the presence of speech or song. The expressive definition of style imprinted by the film on the music was such that the emotional and significative qualities would be read back by association into the instrumental music if this was heard independently, and even could be felt in music of similar style. The strength of associated meaning of this kind was turned to excellent account by Wagner in his development of musical reminiscence and somewhat later, doubtless because of his influence, by the musical scores of innumerable sound films. The mass sale of phonorecords of film music was a subsequent astute application of the same principle.

In the sound film, fluid visual images can become the basis of a narrative art which provides a new possibility for combination with music. Speech can be reduced to a minimum and music employed in the full range of its structural and expressive capacities. The composite is not unlike dance in its character, but although temporal synchronization is technically able to achieve the most perfect precision, as we can see in animated films, in practice the coordination of music and moving image is relatively imprecise, as is the coordination of music and speech in melodrama and melodramatic film.

But the nature of the sound film is probably most fully realized or expressed as an extended variety of drama, in which dramatic or melodramatic action is enhanced by a remarkably flexible visual and scenic technique that substitutes change and motion for the limitations of the stage. Also, of course, what we see and hear are only images of characters and images of scenes which in turn are representations of people and places: the referential symbolism is a double one. But in spite of this and in spite of montage and a moving station point, the effect can approach realism as easily as illusion, very much as the narrative within a narrative becomes more credible than the initial one. To be sure, the flexibility of film, with synthetic scenery, hand-drawn images and designs, overexposure and double exposure, unreal rates of motion and reverse motion, the simultaneous projection of sequences on different screens, and so forth, make fantasy and abstraction readily available, while the effects of large screens and multiple loudspeakers are amenable equally to the creation of environmental immediacy and the play of imagination. The potential influences on instrumental music are correspondingly wide, ranging from concrete atmospheric and dramatic qualities to the strange abstractness of electronically altered noise and electronically generated sound. As in the dance, where drums and percussive instruments and artificial sound play a conspicuous role, the absence or subordination of pitch seems peculiarly appropriate, perhaps because stylistically familiar formulations compete with or contradict the strange or abstract visual and dramatic events. But like incidental music in the drama, film music is often less intimately linked with the dramatic structure, so that we are generally not able to identify detailed properties in instrumental music that can be said to originate in the structural or expressive aspects of the genre. This may become easier to do in the future. There is a panoramic style in Russian symphonic works of the 20th century, for example, that may very well have been inspired or fostered by the landscape music designed for the panoramic and mass scenes of Russian historical films. As a composite art, the sound film is characterized by the looser temporal coordination of music with the whole and by the appropriateness of its incidental rather than continuous use. Thus music is more a contributing functional part than it is an intrinsic fundamental constituent that determines the temporal nature of the totality; the sound film is not strictly a musical whole. It is ontologically unified, however, as a technological work of art that has a conceptual existence and that is grounded not upon a visual notation but upon an artistically formulated and recorded perspective of a single original performance. Although the animated film is produced in an entirely different way, it possesses the same ontological unity; but whether it is representational or abstract, it can easily qualify as a composite musical art.

In pantomime, music is again functional, subservient, and dispensable; unaided gesture can create its own temporal quality. Although music can be allied with gesture to endow it with a new and more concrete character and to reveal its inner nature, pantomime is not inherently musical in its conception, as gesture is in ballet; its expressive form and meaning are more representational than intrinsic.

Dramatic incidental music is also similar to the music of the sound film, but its role is more limited and accessory. The use of pantomime in the drama for long intervals is quite rare, so that the opportunity hardly ever arises for the combination of music with sustained sections of visual imagery, while in the film this combination may become the medium of an entire work. Apart from mimed sections, then, which are in any event generally silent, incidental music will consist typically of an overture, short pieces for linking or introducing acts, inserted songs, choruses, dances, or marches, and possibly one or more melodramas. For the most part these are self-contained musical works; nor to they collectively embody the dramatic action—which is impossible under any cicumstances because they are so few in number—or even its chief moments, as in 18th-century opera or in operetta, but are incidental dramatically as well as functionally (with the exception of melodrama). Thus not only can incidental music be omitted (even songs and choruses can be spoken) without serious detriment to the drama, but also each section of the music is usually artistically satisfactory in itself, as a programmatic overture, intermezzo, or song. It is a consequence of the accessory character of the music, however, that the pieces do not constitute a larger artistic whole as a group; there can be no question of a single or multimovement musical work resulting from their succession, as it often would in the composite musical arts when the visual kinesthetic component is removed from dance, for example, or the text from vocal music. The dramatic whole, on the other hand, remains a work of art also without the incidental music, which is an adornment not significantly integrated, and generally a later addition. But in spite of the accessory function of the music, the composite has exerted a distinct influence on the development of music in general, by giving rise to particular programmatic genres, or referential composites. The independent programmatic overture doubtless has its origin in incidental music rather than opera, and the piano intermezzo of the 19th century seems to be an outgrowth also, with a vague suggestion of some surrounding dramatic whole.

Ritual and ceremony present a somewhat different situation, for the totality is a social institution rather than an art or a work of art, and music is an intrinsic component, although still functionally subservient. Thus it adapts itself in character and form and length to the whole; its structure will not cohere, its meaning will be appreciably changed, if it is abstracted from the occasion, while the music of a composite musical art will not suffer such drastic alterations if it is separately considered or performed. To be sure, individual sections of ritual or ceremonial music may stand on their own as music, but the significance of each will have to be completely constructed in thought and imagination, and at best, only some of the properties of a work of art will be present, such as durability and craftsmanship, while the apparent wholeness and detachment of a section, for example, will be spurious. Still less will a multimovement work result if we assemble all of the music of a given ritual or ceremony; and even in the case of continuous music, the same absence of the encompassing occasion will destroy the musical significance; we must supply the deficiency in imagination, as we do in respect of social context, or by means of a reproduction that is both optical and acoustical (although this still omits the incense, wafer, and wine of the Catholic mass), for in the functional composites we are considering, music is in general too dependent in its form and meaning on the concrete occasion to be performed in part or in whole as though it were functionally autonomous. There are exceptions, of course, although they apply only to parts of the music rather than all of it, and even then a neglect of the whole occasion will involve substantial loss. But just as ceremonial processional music can be performed apart from ceremony, so polyphonic masses from the Renaissance to the present and liturgical Renaissance motets can be performed apart from a religious service; indeed many of them were intended to be performed in this way. Where the two possibilities exist, however, there was necessarily a double conception at work in the compositional process, for aesthetic considerations of wholeness, the unity of multimovement works, detachment, and so forth must have been active along with considerations of liturgical function, so that the music in question would be suited to two ends. A facilitating factor in the appearance of this dual suitability is the nature of the liturgical service, which has always been sectional (if for no other reason than its inclusion of parts specific to the particular occasion and parts used generally). It has always been possible, therefore, to assemble the music fittingly from collections, and the artistic autonomy of the sections is a logical further consequence.

The distinction we have made between musical and functional artistic composites is based most essentially on the status of music as equivalent or subordinate to the other components. In a ritual, for example, or in the film, it is subject to extension or curtailment in accordance with the demands of the totality or of another component—of the course of the ritual, for example, or of the visual or dramatic structure. A true partnership based on equivalence in spite of a functional difference is not in evidence, or only rarely. Although the Catholic mass seems close to religious opera in its nature, and ritual always tends to be close to musical drama, the comparison involves the fundamental distortion of considering both composites from an aesthetic point of view, which in turn causes us to overlook all the differences between the two in respect of the freedom of music and the type of role it plays. Yet there are times, notably in funeral or cremation services but also in various other rites and ceremonies, when an aesthetic point of view is as justified as a functional one; the whole occasion will be dedicated just as much to an artistic purpose as to a social or religious function.

The largest functional composite of all is life, in which music has an astonishing variety of uses. The most rigorous integration it manifests is probably in the life of a monastic order devoted to singing; but in the practice of the cloister in general, the daily and annual round of the divine hours and the mass brings music and life into the most intimate and regular conjunction, with music serving the single function of religious devotion. This music is a repeated and continual activity, artistically formulated and stylistically defined, but with its dominant meaning in its function. It is shaped to ritual, and is not a work of art or a cycle of works, but an art serving the larger art of religious life. There are counterparts of this cyclical use of music in the secular world. Traces of it exist in the uniform function of the cycle of bell patterns that mark the passage of time on shipboard, or in the bells and cuckoo calls and mechanical music of clocks elsewhere. But if we include diversity of function, the role of music in life is seen in its true dimensions. In both nonliterate and advanced cultures, it has a place integrated with the time of day, the season, and the annual cycle of rites and festivities; it accompanies initiation rituals, wooing, marriage, work, hunting, planting, war, victory, the installation of leaders, the healing of disease, relaxation, religious ceremony, and burial or cremation. Modern civilization can add, with the help of electronic reproduction, music to wake up by, music to shop by, to work by, to go to sleep by, and generally to live with; music in automobiles, trains, airplanes, restaurants, elevators, stores, in the streets, and at home throughout the day; even entertainment on radio and television is punctuated by musical advertisements; indeed music is so ubiquitous that it reaches an extreme of subservience in not being attended to at all. At the same time, remnants of an older cyclical attachment to ritual and to the procession of the day and the year remain, often isolated but also with a corollary aesthetic autonomy. The performance of Bach's Passions in concert halls and in radio broadcasts during Easter is such an example, while Wagner's *Parsifal* and his *Ring of the Nibelungen* represent more artificial and synthetic instances. There are traces of cosmic integration also in Bach's *Well-Tempered Clavier* and in other musical works of art that progress through the cycle of keys. In the same way, the song cycles of the 19th century or formal ballets are connected occasionally with the cycle of the seasons or of human life, but more often with cyclical conceptions that are purely aesthetic, or at least not intrinsically temporal, such as the cycle of temperaments, which is already somewhat removed from the seasons.

Although music is used on remarkably numerous and varied occasions, not every aspect of life is suited to act as a functional context; a core of emotional experience or simply of vital feeling must exist which music can naturally complement; otherwise there will be mutual inhibition instead of unification and fusion. Thus states of feeling or revery or even deep emotion are compatible with music, and so is physical work, while concentrated thought directed to other matters will not combine with music and will block it out of consciousness. The use or function of music defines its overall meaning in terms of context, and provides the basis for a social typology. In some cases, such as may be exemplified by ritual, the function combines with the music to form a compound that differs from a composite art only in the social nature of one of the constituents. The external functional meaning is transformed within the art into an aesthetic factor of the whole. In other cases, such as pedagogical music or dinner music, the function will enter very little into the fundamental properties of the music. Convivial

264

music-making, attendance at recitals or operas, and the enjoyment of a phonorecord are not strictly functional contexts at all, since a context must have some existence apart from the music it occasions. Even so, the nature of a particular experience of listening or performance will always be affected in accordance with whether music is regarded as an end in itself, an adjunct of some larger or external purpose, or a means of diversion, and the difference in use will be reflected in the music itself—in its composition or selection. The difference, however, is often one of attitude and conception rather than of objective musical properties.

The varieties of programmatic music make up a referential type of composite art, which differs from the other types we have considered in its proximity to absolute music. If in the functional type music usually has a subordinate place with respect to other components, and in the musical type a place of equal importance, in the referential type it is unmistakably dominant. Thus a criterion of value which has limited applicability to other composite arts—but which logically will come into question in any combination—is now of central importance: is programmatic music able to sustain itself without its program? Does it remain meaningful, even if obviously not in the same way, when it is regarded as absolute music? Perhaps part of the reason we feel it should is that the listener is often insufficiently acquainted with the extramusical reference, and occasionally ignorant of the fact that there is one. But a more basic reason can be found in the belief that the object of reference must also exist as transmuted into a musical object, and that if it is not amenable to such treatment it will lie outside of the range of possible or appropriate objects for this type of music. The requirement is similar to the restriction that has often been placed on the subject matter of opera, notably by Gluck and the German Romantic composers and Wagner, and it is certainly a proper part of the aesthetic considerations of every composer of a composite art, but it must be said that the variety produced by history and culture in opera and song, and in combinations of the arts in general, brings into question any tenets of the intrinsic mutual unsuitability of the components.

The extramusical connection of programmatic music ranges from a fully explicit program, or designated object, which is the variety from which the type takes its name, to a highly distinctive quality or formal property that merely suggests a nonmusical counterpart or conception. In between lie what we may call characteristic musical works with titles of dances, literary genres, categories of feeling and emotion, and ideas, or with verbal indications of these kinds intended primarily for the performer. Each of these diversions is extremely diversified. Program music can be realistic and detailed, taking upon itself the task of vividly depicting scenes, people, and environmental events—a work of visual art, a landscape, or a storm—or of conveying a narrative or drama; sometimes imitation of the acoustic features of the events, as in the case of a storm or a battle or bird calls, will make an appended title or verbal description unnecessary. In contrast, the same objects can be conveyed by a subjective approach, which is based on eliciting analogous musical feelings, although in program music of this kind, titles and descriptions can hardly be omitted and the detail of narratives and dramas must fall away.

In the "characteristic" type of music, verbal indications or markings will frequently refer to a particular dance such as the minuet or the waltz, or to a certain mood such as that of the capriccio or the *Nachtstück*, and the music itself will have a special quality, whether indefinite or specific, which would qualify it—if the verbal inscription was lacking—as an example of the suggestive or associative variety of programmatic music. For the most part, markings tend to be quite general; "dancelike" does not of itself refer to any genre of dance, and *allegro deciso* is hardly different from allegro, which in fact underwent a transformation from an earlier characteristic meaning to a neutral indication in absolute music of tempo rather than mood. The titles of various literary, poetic, and dramatic genres such as "legend" or "ballade" constitute an open invitation to the performer's and listener's imagination which they are at liberty to respond to with specific objects or not. Ideas and categories of feeling such as "heroic" or "tragic," which are related to literary genres, have the same kind of generality. Even the names of musical genres, if they are used to designate stylistic transfer, have a similar kind of generally characteristic meaning—a movement of a piano sonata, for example, that is entitled "Lied." The quotation of a known melody, on the other hand, produces a kind of meaning that is quite specific, but one that is also fundamentally intrinsic to music, even though it may bring with it, as in the case of the *Marseillaise*, a host of emotional and conceptual—that is, programmatic—meanings of its own.

The suggestive variety of programmatic music is essentially coincident with absolute music of a distinctive or individualistic stamp: the individual preludes and fugues of *The Well-Tempered Clavier*, for example, or the sonatas and quartets of Beethoven, possess such a suggestive individuality, while the fugues and sonatas of lesser composers, or even many of the quartets of Haydn, do not. The crucial issue is whether or to what extent the music tends to summon up extramusical feelings or conceptions, which in general will be of such a broad nature that they encompass both the musical work and other areas of non-musical experience as comparable exemplifications: the music acts as a kind of part-for-whole symbol. Very much the same considerations hold for the purely musical meaning of stylistic parody—the reproduction of the Beethovenian manner or of a theme taken from the public domain of high Baroque style. It is obvious, however, that our route has here led to a question we have already examined: the nature of the significance of absolute music, or of instrumental music in itself. And individuality in particular has been included among the properties of the musical work of art.

Programmatic music, which we have considered a composite kind of musical art, can also be thought of as a middle ground between more explicit compounds and instrumental music. In either event it will modify the dual scheme of composite and absolute or at least direct us to the interrelation of meaning between the two. Externally considered, there is an obvious distinction between instrumental music and composite types, but if the meaning of instrumental music is a residue or distillation of more concrete and comprehensive contexts of meaning, the external difference in fact conceals a much more complicated relationship that includes common factors. This is obviously the case in the relationship between purely instrumental music and program music. If there is no prescribed description or narration, or no designation of mood to be connected with an instrumental composition, it by no means follows that the work is free of these constituents and entitled in this sense to be termed absolute music. Much can appear beneath the surface, in the composer's creative process, the performer's experience and the listener's or in the tonal and structural constituents themselves and the associations of the genre. We do not require a caption to inform us that we are listening to a Baroque instrumental lamento or a symphonic scherzo. Do we consider such works to be "absolute music"? And if so, are we not dealing here with a source of meaning in instrumental music similar to what we find in an instrumental minuet or waltz abstracted from its dance? If these considerations hold also for smaller units of structure and meaning, for functional melodic configurations of the various instruments and melodic vocal motifs that adumbrate the occasions of their original use, then musical significance would seem to be at least in some measure derivative. If music in all its manifestations constitutes a continuum rather than a duality of types in respect of meaning, perhaps there is no such thing as "absolute" music. From the opposite direction we have come upon other suggestions that point to the same conclusion; for if individualized works can present a mood that has an extension in human experience beyond music, perhaps the overall quality that attaches to any musical work is not specific to the work or in any event not specific to music. The only distinction to be made would be between works and qualities that resemble each other, which presuppose the prominence of a public idiom, and those that are individually distinctive. In addition to the extramusical meaning descended from composites and original functional contexts and that evoked by music in itself, there are of course often associated extramusical meanings to the composer or performer or listener—visual images, biographical events, general ideas, and so on; but these meanings are clearly extrinsic and fortuitous: they vary with each experience and are certainly not part of the musical work of art.

In spite of the derivative constituents and heteronomous tendencies of musical meaning, we can doubtless insist on a distinction between music that is consciously or explicitly connected in its conception with external events and music that is conceived and therefore correctly performed and heard with no awareness of extramusical meanings. A duality can thus be restored, and although there may be a not fully conscious indeterminate zone containing adumbrations of associated meaning and moods of generalized significance, it is in general clear whether music, as a posited object of perception sharply in the focus of attention, is taken solely on its own terms or in conjunction with outside ideas or feelings. Even in respect of elementary musical structures we find we must leave room for the sensational qualities that are specific to tonal shapes and responses. Nor are the heterosensory and intersensory implications which are often in some way present in music on every level of complexity a valid argument against the autonomous properties of musical experience; they are in fact respectively comparable to associations and generalized moods in their status.

What is true of preexisting elemental configurations that enter into the genesis of style is also true of the elements yielded by an analysis of musical conception and perception such as features of melody, polyphony, harmony, rhythm, tempo, form, and instrumentation: there are innumerable units and aspects of meaning for which only a specifically musical intention and significance can be found to exist. Indeed instrumental music can be regarded not as a distillation of antecedent concrete meanings but as an absorption of such meanings into a purely musical one. The musical composite arts, in which music is essentially continuous, will then correspondingly represent a fusion of external factors with those specific to tone, and all types of music that have generally been regarded as such will be fundamentally and literally musical in their nature. This will imply what is in fact always the case: that the purely tonal component of every musical composite art, and of course of program music also, possesses a specifically musical logic in its own right. A corollary requirement is the subordination of nonmusical components, which music seems so imperiously to demand. Probably because of the strength of the hold of music on consciousness, where extrinsic factors remain unassimilated we feel a duality of artistic conception and effort, or a complexity or lack of unity; in extreme cases we may not see any justification for the existence of the work in musical form. To be sure, such extreme judgments are often due to a narrow construe of the possible nature of purely musical experience in composite works; the incoherence decried initially in Berlioz, Wagner, or Schönberg, for example, eventually yielded to an appreciation of new types of musical logic, and what seemed like a mistaken conception of the role of tonal experience turned out to be a new insight into previously unknown possibilities of meaningful organization.

If the meaning of purely instrumental music is often formed as a kind of deposition or impression of the concrete meaning of composite art, the same process is responsible in turn for a profound effect on the quality and depth of meaning of composite art itself, which thus receives the benefit of what it has earlier bestowed. For the music entering into an opera or a tone poem is not the totally unformed and purely passive medium that Wagner imagined, waiting to receive its shape and significance as imprints of the external events and feelings with which it is combined. It brings with it a wealth of symbolism, a vast potentiality of meaning which can be unlocked only when a key is provided by the extramusical constituents of the composite work to be constructed. It is not only the cross-references of meaning and the subtlety of allusion within a given work which distinguish opera, for example, and can be found in Mozart as well as in Wagner, but the historical and emotional richness of each instance of symbolism in itself. Behind the chromaticism of the crucifixion and of Amfortas's wound in *Parsifal* there are centuries of symbolic significance and an untold number of antecedents, which generate a vast connotation such as a language and its literature create for a highly significant word in the course of time. Indeed the musical reservoir of symbolic meaning is enlarged and deepened by every new composite work of art, by every new popular song and tonal signal, or in a word, by the whole growth of culture and history. Musical meaning is enriched and expanded by a reciprocating process of interaction between sound itself and the artistic and social uses of sound. Thus a natural accretion of musical significance will occur within any continuity of culture, although meanings are not only added or deepened, but also fade and disappear. A study of artistic composites from this point of view will therefore bring us closer to the complex nature of musical meaning, with its fusion of absolute and concrete elements.

But are any musical symbols archetypal? Or do all of them perhaps possess archetypal components? The properties of music strongly suggest that we answer affirmatively—that we are dealing in music with a true cultural invariance of elements and elemental forms. Certainly the connection of tone with consciousness is part of the intrinsic nature of human being, while intervallic consonance and the triad are equally intrinsic manifestations of physical and biological nature and also possess distinctive counterparts in the fundamental qualities of auditory perception. These and other elemental arrangements in the spheres of pitch and rhythm may consequently be described as incorporations in a medium of special potency of the formal possibilities of nature and human nature in general, with their dependence, as we have indicated, upon the dimensional duality of space and time.

Obviously the nature of any external constituent that enters into music will determine its range of possible influence on the artistic form and meaning of the result. From this point of view the most important feature of extramusical components is their own temporal property. If they are not temporal at all—or more correctly, if they have only temporal implications or an essentially unvarying temporal course—their effect will be minimal. The tragic mood (apparently associated with ancient Greek drama) and the Hebrides, to cite two examples, exert an appreciable influence on the temporal qualities of Brahms' *Tragic Overture* and Mendelssohn's *Hebrides Overture* as well as on their expressive nature, but these external references are in no wise so intimately bound up with the structure and detailed meanings of the music as a programmatic narrative or a dance will inevitably be. At the same time, there is a vast difference between the involvement of dance patterns with musical form and expression and that of vocal texts, or between the texts of recitative and those of song, although in every case conformity of the two constituents and an interplay of two independent entities are guiding principles.

But if the composite musical arts contain different kinds of simultaneity in dependence upon the temporal forms of their components, each of these components may in itself also be temporally complex, for the rhythmical polyphony of music has counterparts in other temporal media. What rules and controls such rhythmical and durational complexity, so that the whole simultaneity can tend toward interrelation and comprise an overall perceivable pattern rather than disintegrating into confusion or chaos? The answer will vary with the particular arts that are combined, with the composer and the individual work, and with the syles of different cultures and social groups and historical periods. But in general, because of the tangibility of musical temporality and the directness of its relationship to consciousness, unifying and underlying rhythms will tend to lie in sonority. Music itself, of course, need not manifest a rhythmical figure-and-ground relationship, or even an interlocked connection of equally prominent patterns; there are styles in which it fails almost completely to secure any coordination of simultaneous configurations, just as there are monodic styles that are essentially unorganized rhythmically and vocal music in which voice and instrument go very much their separate ways without regard for one another. Chaos is not the only alternative to precise integration; controlled independence is certainly another. There is in any event no general principle to be applied to the temporal constitution of composite arts except for the intrinsic propensity of music toward dominance; dance, poetry, pantomime, and the moving visual images of the film will be figures on a musical ground, although this is not always true of the prose of recitative and the larger movement of the action in opera, for these things are not always set to rhythmical or temporal formulations in music, as we can see in the secco recitative of an opera buffa and in the fact that some of the dramatic action is not taken up into the arias and ensembles. It is indeed striking, from the opposite point of view, how the action is projected onto the music, or cast against it as well as into it, in the ensembles of opera buffa, or throughout a mature opera of Verdi or Wagner.

The temporal combinations of a composite art can become quite complex. Dance can contain a rhythmical simultaneity of gestures and motion and different dancers, even of moving objects and scenery, with properties of relative prominence and degrees of interrelationship that are in no way less intricate and challenging to creative formativity and perception than the rhythmical configuration and interplay of music. If each medium must be coherent in itself, their combination is subject to the same condition on a higher level, with the interrelation depending on the types and degrees of prominence within each and on the overall formative intention, which can range from coincidence to various degrees and kinds of contrast. In song there are often even in melody alone four superimposed durational patterns or implied patterns: the meter and the speech durations of the poetry, and the meter and explicit durations of the tones. This is responsible, even apart from pitch configurations, accent, and ornamentation, for the infinitude of possible settings of a single poem even in unaccompanied song. Thus the simultaneous singing of different texts and the addition of purely tonal polyphony and harmony can hardly fail to produce in general a combination of several different durational patterns, some of them partly implied, others fully explicit, one or more of them supportive or foundational, others dominant perceptually or in the details of their form and significance.

Other types of temporal complexity are added by representational significance. The dance, for example, or the visual action of an opera, can embody a dramatic action that symbolizes some historical or imagined action. There will then be four durational strata: one of gesture and corporeal motion in themselves that is of complex constitution, a second, equally complex, of tones and sounds, a third of the perceptible representation, and a fourth, existing only in images and conception, of the objects of representation or symbolization. Sung texts are similar, with complex sonorous strata of words and tones, a representation now not sensible but only imagined and conceived, and the similarly imaginary and conceptual object of this representation. In oratorio and cantata and ballade the representation can again be in great part a dramatic action, but now only imagined rather than concretely realized as in opera. Finally, outside of art but capable of entering into a relationship with it, are the temporality of life in general and the historical and astronomical temporality with which life is connected, so that there are potentially three additional levels of temporality in artistic experience. The conception of detachment can be used to characterize the absence of any of these. But the first four are necessarily present in any composite representational art. In literature, exceptionally, even the level of sense perception is not actual, for the sonority of the words itself exists only in conception and imagery.

A consideration of any composite musical work that contains representational significance will reveal something of the complexity of interrelationship between the various levels of durational form. In a ballade, for example, the total duration of the represented imaginary action will be much greater than the duration of the representation, whether we are dealing with a continuous action or with a group of related sections projected in the individual strophes; the same is almost invariably true for an opera and its acts. The pace and fluctuations in the speed of a represented action can often be duplicated in the artistic representation, although here, as in the relationships of overall duration, the artistic conventions of the genre and the style of the time are the governing principles, since they are the defined area of possibilities within which detached formativity and perception occur. Thus an opera will almost always have lyrical sections in which the dramatic action is slowed or suspended to an improbable degree, and a ballet will tend to consist very largely of such sections, much like an opera seria of the 18th century. Even an opera buffa finale will contain sections that are representationally static when the state of the depicted action calls for a dynamic quality; the convention of the genre at such a point seems to demand gesture and bodily motion that are figurative, superadded, repetitious, and semirepresentational rather than a suspension of movement on stage or a realistic depiction of the rapidity of the represented action. Where the lyrical effusion of an aria can coincide with the representation of a state of feeling or reflection and thus with an absence of motion that is conformable actually as well as by convention to the represented drama, the expression of excitement in an opera buffa ensemble cannot be extended musically without some kind of accompanying movements, or there will be a noticeable discord between the representation and its object. Needless to say, the temporal relationships between the musical drama and the represented action are the foundation of operatic dramaturgy. It is obviously impossible to devise a satisfactory dramatic action that will conform inherently and exactly in length, speed, and especially in changes of pace to the conventional artistic needs of any particular genre of musical drama or ballet. The result is a counterpoint of durational forms.

With this the temporal properties of song and music will further contrast or conform. The piano accompaniment in Schubert's *Erlkönig* has a speed and a rhythmical quality that are in obvious accord with the action; even during the dialogues the horseback ride continues and its pace is maintained; at the same time, modifications of and additions to the rhythm correspond to the slower rate of conversation and to more slowly moving objects of description. What is represented in any composite art (unless the only nonmusical component is abstract designs in motion or changing views of natural or architectural objects) is not only a temporal complex of gesture and bodily motion, or an emotional state and a variety of ideas made explicit in song, for the inner experience in each case may have a durational and rhythmic property and even a complex temporal constitution of its own, so that the total represented structure will really be dual in nature.

The temporal aspect of the music, including the speed and

rhythm of the verbal components, can turn to either phase of the represented duality, as Wagner realized in his division of music according to its various intrinsic representational capacities: the voice was assigned to the present and conscious aspects of feeling and ideas, while the orchestra was assigned to description, to gesture, and to the recollective and predictive aspects of inner life as well as general mood. (The memory and expectation and state of feeling conveyed were often those of the audience rather than of the represented figures, so that the role of the orchestra was not entirely different from its role in absolute music.) Even ideas of a temporal kind, such as ceaseless rotation, eternity, recurrence, or succession, can be symbolized by musical properties of duration and rhythm, at times without explicit visual or even textual reference to them. Music itself may then become the representational level of temporality, and the represented level will in any event be enriched by an additional durational form, which may accord or contrast with others.

Generally all the varieties of temporality comprised in a composite art will be detached from those of life and history and astronomy, but the detachment from life and history is only a qualified one. A temporal work of art will ordinarily not be integrated into the general experience of life as music is in a confirmation or wedding or funeral ceremony, or in a primitive initiation ritual. Instead it will be inserted into the temporality of life, when we listen to a phonorecord, for example, or attend a concert or an opera. Insertion differs from integration because it can take place when we wish: it is essentially free of the patterns of temporality in our extraartistic experience; indeed it may often provide a striking contrast of speed and durational pattern and length with the corresponding features of the events of life that surround it; a recording of an Indian *raga* or a performance of a Bruckner symphony is an oasis of remarkable detachment in the rushed and rapid business of modern metropolitan life. To be sure, the detachment and insertion do not apply to the aesthetic occasion in its own right, which is rather an invasion or a taking over of experience that shapes it and controls it entirely, excluding every other influence and purpose.

Implications of historical time will exist even in the original performances of a work of art, but especially in later ones—of its distance from us in history, or from the other music we know, and of the pace of cultural change at the time it was written and since then. These are obviously a result, like the possibility of detachment from life and insertion into it, of preservation and durability. There is the further possibility that the representational content of a work will refer to particular historical people or events, in which case the sense of historical distance and time will be intensified, but usually in a double way, for the style of the work, unless it deals with contemporaneous figures or occasions, will have a different historical situation than the represented object does, even though the style may be deliberately historical or pseudohistorical. Thus there will be a duality within historical temporality itself.

The performance of a work that is historically referential can be comparable to a present reenactment of a religious or mythical event. Partially foregoing detachment, it can take place at the same time of the year (on occasion also in the same place) as the fictive or historical model, as in the performance of *Parsifal* or Bach's *St. John Passion* on Good Friday. Then the astronomical level of temporality will be added to the historical one, along with religious or mythical conceptions of historical time. A similar interconnection with the time of everyday life and of astronomy is suggested every time a clock strikes in an operatic scene, or whenever the season or dawn or nightfall plays a role in the setting or text. The Good Friday performance of the *St. John Passion* will exemplify every possible level of temporal interplay, although the visual representation of gesture and action is present only in imagery. But even the temporal complex of pure instrumental music bears a relationship to the durational features of life in general and of the course of history, and perhaps in addition—through various kinds of analogical symbolism such as the twelve keys in *The Well-Tempered Clavier* or the open fifths and slow gathering and formulation of motion at the beginning of Beethoven's Ninth Symphony—to the durational course of astronomical process.

Indeed the connection of music with recurrence—both its integration into temporal cycles and its internal properties such as repetition and the various ways in which the end of a work returns to the beginning—suggest that the separation of time into transience and serial order may not be an exhaustive analysis, for there would seem to be an intrinsic circular factor as well as linear ones, just as there is in the constitution of theoretical space or of musical pitch. There can be no doubt that what we may think of as the constitution of time is really a function of the temporal aspect of our experience, which is dominated by the course of life and the immediate qualities of awareness. Cyclical patterns are numerous and insistent, however, in astronomy and biology and even in the perceptual tendency of closure and the aesthetic concern with wholeness and unity. Rotation and revolution are as much a part of our experience as motions of translation. It is therefore impossible to overlook the intrinsic properties of recurrence in temporal experience and their frequent manifestation in cyclical artistic forms, even in purely instrumental music, where there is no explicit association with external experience. The temporal distinction between the musical work and its performance may at times cease to be applicable; certainly in the daily and annual round of liturgical chant or perhaps also of recurrent songs of work and play that are as much a part of life as breakfast or sleep, conceptions of the performance of musical works and even of temporal becoming or passage have less relevance than notions of static and endless cyclical repetition.

As far as the general nature of composite art is concerned, the difficulties of securing coherence and unity seem inevitably to be increased. Multiplicity of media is doubtless a special case of diversity of style, and neither is intrinsically lower in value than uniformity. But the constituents of a work of art cannot escape interrelationship of some kind, and it would seem advantageous to the interest of form and the variety of meaning if gradations of interrelationship were available rather than only juxtaposition of differing constituents or their approximate coordination. There are composite arts and works of art, and certainly styles of diverse constitution, which have their own

278

special attractiveness, but always, perhaps, invisible factors making for unity are present—ideological ones, for example, or the convergence of contrasts that is gradually produced by historical distance.

In representational art, which in the case of music includes opera, ballet, programmatic works, film, and in a sense even ritual and ceremonial music of which the occasion has a long tradition, there is an intrinsic potential disparity between the style of what is represented or re-presented and that of the time and culture in which the composition or representation takes place. If the difference between the two cultures is sufficiently great there will be a problem of stylistic unity which would obviously not exist with contemporaneous subject matter. The outcome of the disparity takes many forms, depending upon whether the represented subject is imaginary or historical, upon how much is known about the culture and its form of expression, and upon the aesthetic and stylistic intentions of the composer. The stylistic interplay, the tension, polarity, blending, or contrast of the past and present, or the suppression of the one or the other, constitutes a central constructive factor in representational art, with manifestations as diverse as the duality between the 18th century and the time of composition in *Rosenkavalier* or in Massenet's *Manon* and the more radical transformation and invention of represented style in the historical, legendary, and mythical operas of Wagner. Naturally any further representation within a dramatic action, or any tendency toward formalization, such as the presentation of a self-contained song or the enactment of a ceremony, will heighten the stylistic tension or even increase the number of component styles. In addition, the perception of each of the juxtaposed styles in the art of an older or foreign culture will be colored by its distance from the present.

Conspicuous hindrances to artistic unification are often caused by the use of different media, whether these are deployed simultaneously or successively. The problem is present in film music and incidental music, in the spoken dialogue of comic opera and operetta, in the simultaneity of speech and song in 20th-century works—Schönberg's *Moses and Aron,* for example—and in all mixtures of genre and fusion of media, from the music, speech, and pantomime of Stravinsky's *Renard* and *L'histoire du soldat* to the synesthetic projects of Scriabin's *Prometheus* and 20th-century experimental composites. Electronic technology has intensified the problem because of its technical versatility and its symbiotic tendency; film, television, electronic sound, phonorecordings, and videotapes live a complex and chameleonlike interrelated life that often invades the traditional theater as well as digests everyday life. The result has been more a play with possibilities and individual effects than new forms of art and it seems to comprise a lesson in the difficulties of composite art. Unity is difficult even in the mode of preservation of the components, some of which may be simply remembered, others filmed, others recorded on tape or phonorecords, and still others notated visually or in schematic form. But the very mode of being of art is thereby made indeterminate. And the possibilities of novelty crowd preservation out of existence altogether; no room is left for it in the roster of artistic values.

A simple example of the difficulties that arise in the combination of artistic media can be found in television ballet. There are intrinsic problems at once in the reduction of apparent size and in the unsuitability to television of static settings. The presupposition that more is better, however, leads to the explicit effort to add together the possibilities of the two media so as to obtain an unprecedented variety of expressive forms. Now the deployment of the full resources of montage and a moving camera will inevitably suggest the superposition of images and the use of oblique and changing angles of view. But the utilization of these techniques unfortunately contradicts the fundamental formative force of dance, which is the attraction of gravity and the varying formal value of deviation from the vertical. The result will be confusion or chaos, with the failure of every intended effect and the impossibility of any convincing artistic illusion at all.

What composite art can suffer from primarily is too much freedom. The problem can be seen in its extreme form in the artistic potentiality of life itself, for it is precisely the diversity of life, the difficulty of controlling it as material, that makes it resistant to artistic treatment and formativity, while art shapes only an aspect of life to create, strangely, the deeper life that can be found in a special and detached experience. Artistic material, as we have seen, must be preformed; it cannot exist except in a defined universe of possibilities, and then in further restrictions within that. Typically there is a kind of Chinese-box set of limitations, so that formation takes place in certain perceptual dimensions only. Paradoxically the preformation and limitation give rise to the greatest range and subtlety of significance. Yet alongside of Beethoven's late quartets we do not hesitate to place the *Magic Flute* or *Tristan and Isolde*, in which art has clearly triumphed over the diverse nature of its constituents.

Special value may exist in the universality of complex art, which is more universal only in formulating our experience of the world, but not in respect of either its generality of style or its formulation of our inner emotive experience. Indeed without referential or functional significance, composite art would doubtless have less value than works in a single medium. The combination of instrumental music with nonrepresentational painting or sculpture, or with abstract film, is doubtless more of a loss than a gain. Whether the composite arts tend to involve more participation or more activity in their apprehension is a question related to universality. Actual participation in performance is fostered to a certain extent by artistic composites, notably in religious services, social dancing, and the processions and singing of communal ceremonies. But these are all functional rather than musical compounds, and even the dance-songs of kindergarten, which are distant descendants of the choral dances of Greek antiquity, have at least an external pedagogical purpose. Apart from this, there seems little more impulsion to perform in the *Marriage of Figaro* than there is in a Haydn string quartet. Activity in apprehension, whether empathic or imaginative, as opposed to a detached attitude of contemplation that is confined to the objects of perception, may also on occasion be fostered by composite art. A multisensory aesthetic object can produce a compelling effect on our feelings, the representation or description of human relationships and emotions will readily arouse our sympathy and understanding, and the presence of music can ensure the immediacy and strength of our reaction. It should be noticed, however, that the tendency toward an empathic relationship is due not only to the multisensory nature of composite art, but in great measure to the presence of dramatic action and music; thus music alone will not be markedly inferior in its capacity to produce such a result. At the same time, an emotionally detached attitude is possible not only in drama but in musical drama and of course in absolute music itself. The activity of the imagination is similarly subject to variety in accordance with the nature of the style, the culture, and the listener, but the composite arts with a visual component and purely instrumental music of little individuality would seem to least encourage either visual imagery or emotional imagination. It is difficult to imagine anything of any kind during an opera or a Classical string quartet unless the work of art is more or less ignored or reduced to the status of a background. Individualistic instrumental works, on the other hand, will possess a pronounced overall quality that can become identified with a mood or emotion of general validity and thus summon up images of other concrete occasions that provoked the same state, while programmatic works contain an open invitation to a visual and ideological elaboration of their subject.

Conceptual activity directed specifically to a grasp of artistic form and significance is common to both composite and simple art, but it is more difficult and complicated in composite works and in individualistic instrumental works, and confronted with less of a task in absolute music and in styles that are familiar and accessible. Again historical and cultural factors are important determinants of the nature of style in this respect, for simple styles in an established tonal idiom, with regular rhythm, balanced phrases, monophonic or homophonic texture, a resemblance to folksong and folk dance, and clear relationships in their techniques of extension and consecution will obviously present little difficulty to the comprehension of form and meaning. Yet simple dramatic and narrative structures and simple dance patterns can also provide a clarity of their own that facilitates understanding. It may be said in general, however, that composite arts and programmatic music will discourage activity on the part of the listener, while absolute music has the opposite tendency. An opera or a film addresses and engages our hearing, vision, and intelligence; it can be so explicit as to fill our consciousness and make a passive reception enjoyable and an active one difficult. Abstract instrumental music, on the other hand, encourages and leaves room for imaginative activity, and in particular for the perceptual endeavor to grasp specifically aesthetic relationships of structure and significance. The accessibility or obscurity of the style is not the point at issue here, but simply the relative concreteness of the two types of artistic experience, their biological completeness: whether they can be accepted as suffic- ient—even if not in an exemplary sense—without active supplementation.

Thus there are several respects in which composite temporal arts can be distinguished from absolute music; the values of each are in many ways different, although also in many ways the same. And just as the overall complexion of the culture may be more favorable to one field of expression than another, or to one art rather than another, or to certain properties of an art rather than to others, so it may be more favorable to composite art than to pure, or to particular kinds of composite art. We have only to compare the opera of the last few decades with the ballet and the film to see how powerful this cultural force can be. If all varieties of art are in evidence, as they have been generally in recent centuries of Western civilization, each will still be characteristic in its nature and in its particular virtues and defic- iencies of the time and place in which it originates, although time has become increasingly more important than place.

The question of the significance of art can be answered only in connection with an understanding of its form, and as our discussion has revealed, the study of composite musical arts uncovers new aspects of musical meaning. There can be no doubt of the influence of composite arts on music, but the existence of autonomous musical meaning is as certain as its partially external causation and its capacity to complement other kinds of experience. Thus although absolute music may be in great measure derivative or dependent in its forms and significance, and programmatic and composite genres in great measure specifically musical, the distinction that can be made between the two opposed categories, and the subordinate distinctions that can be made within each, have a basis for their validity in the actual awareness of meaning that characterizes any particular musical experience. It is a matter of historical study to determine the extent that explicitly or ostensibly programmatic forms and experience are also peculiarly musical, or the extent to which phenomenal musical structures and meanings are at the same time partly extrinsic and hetero-sensory, or have been derived from extramusical sources. Our standard in this, however, will be not the antecedents of meaning in a given musical style, nor the adumbrations of secondary significance that can be found in it, nor the possibility of interpreting it according to the attitudes and intentions of our own milieu, but the actual historical context of conception and performance, as this appears to the present.

An examination of composite art finally will cast additional light on purely musical meaning because the presence of an extramusical component and the relationship of meaning between this component and music throws the nature of musical meaning into relief and helps us to grasp it more securely. It has been observed time and again that the same dramatic action or poetic text can be combined in a satisfactory way with innumerable different musical settings. Doubtless this is also true of a given dance or pantomime or film sequence or of any particular programmatic reference. It is obvious that not any music will do, but simply that essentially unlimited variety is possible; and it is also a matter of experience that whichever satisfactory musical setting is selected or created, the resulting composite—although it will be distinctive—will nevertheless take on an aspect of inevitability: it will seem like the single uniquely most appropriate artistic solution, or even the only possible one.

More or less the same thing is true in reverse. With a given piece of music an unlimited number of satisfactory dance and gestural patterns or film sequences or external programmatic references may be combined; with a given melody any number of different poems; but in no case any kinesthetic or visual pattern or any poetic text at all: only a certain group or class with apparently unlimited membership. And again, in spite of the different resulting composite works, whichever of these possible visual or verbal settings is adopted will come to seem peculiarly appropriate or unique. Thus a single melody has often been applied to a variety of poems, the same music realized in dance differently, and the same poetry in different songs. There is a difference, however, for music is more easily made general in style, that is, its differential effect on the overall quality of the different composites can be made relatively small even though at the same time it constitutes a highly appropriate setting for each. It is much more difficult to do this in reverse—when a visual or verbal formulation is provided with a variety of musical accompaniments. Thus a given choreo-graphic composition or a poem combined with different but appropriate musical settings will give rise to works of art total-ly different from one another in character, while a melody combined with different but appropriate poems, or a musical piece combined with different dance figures, will produce a series of closely related works. For this reason strophic songs are an extremely widespread and highly satisfactory variety of composite art. The musical setting will often represent something common to all the stanzas—a river that flows throughout or a constant underlying mood—which the poem may not be able to make explicit or the significance of which it may not be able to express fully. But more fundamentally, the music will establish the same relation to consciousness of all the different thoughts and feelings contained in the poetry—a function that the stanzaic repetition of meter and rhyme scheme only hints at but cannot consummate. The special capacity of music in this regard was doubtless a basic cause of Goethe's preference in the lied for simple strophic settings as well as an important source of his insight into musical meaning. It is also, in fact, very possibly a basic cause of the existence and popularity of strophic poetry.

But what can be deduced about the nature of musical

meaning from the behavior and capacities of music in the formation of artistic compounds? If Goethe saw music as a creative source from which particular images arose and as a general atmosphere which suitably adapted itself to and clothed each, numberless other poets, composers, authors, artists, critics, aestheticians, and philosophers have described it in other terms, although basically similar ones. There are almost as many characterizations as there are people concerned with the problem. In nearly every case, however, music is described or conceived as somehow quite general or abstract in character—even as undefined or unclear in its meaning. Yet music is undeniably very specific, as Mendelssohn so definitely maintained. How can we account for this contradiction? The only possible explanation—suggested even by the variety of associations that are provoked by a given instrumental work but brought to our attention more forcibly by the composite musical arts—is that the specificity and the generality must be different in kind. No matter how general the style of an instrumental work may be, and therefore how much the work will resemble others, there can be no doubt of the unique character of the experience it provides: of the unique course of our experience and its particular overall quality. Its individuality and specificity are beyond question. Yet this specific experience at once takes on a general nature when it is connected with different visual events or texts or programmatic references and images—indeed when it is united even with a single extramusical manifestation. It seems to give us only the dynamic scheme that is common to a diversified family of concrete experiences.

There is the possibility, of course, that the meaning of music may be transformed by contextual associations, but what seems in fact to happen, more accurately, is that two different aspects of music are revealed in the two situations. In itself, music has a specific significance which is constituted by the basic features of consciousness together with an additional development of these features into a formative superstructure that arises from our familiarity with a particular style. But the resultant meaningful configurations of sound are connected with properties of consciousness and feeling that are more fundamental

286

than those facets of awareness which are related to the visual and representational patterns of dance and imagery and poetry; the musical configurations can thus easily be common to many specific visual and verbal ones, and will in fact make up the fundamental vital significance of these specific formulations, increasing the comprehensiveness of the experience they provide and thus bringing depth, intensification, and fulfillment to the peculiar character of each. If a musical setting is changed, then, a new foundational relation to the course of feeling and the flow of awareness is established, and this obviously places the poem or action in a completely different light, concomitantly changing the quality and significance of the whole.

The complementary relation that music so naturally assumes with respect to the visual and spatial and conceptual constituents of the composite arts is thus due to a division of consciousness which has its most conspicuous manifestation in the peculiar emotional urgency of sonorous configurations. But equally significant is the related tendency of music to act as an object immanent to hearing rather than to take its place in the multisensory world, where its equivalent ontological status would result in completely different and more superficial kinds of combination and at times even in conflict rather than union.

# CHAPTER 8

# Context

The contextual aspect of form and meaning in music is not elucidated fully by composite musical genres and social function, for sonorous experience is also affected by more distant forces—by modes of thought and feeling and behavior not connected with music in a tangible way, and by the mere fact that we generally know something of the society and culture in which a musical work arises. Even the forms and meanings we take to be intrinsic to tone may be influenced by an area of experience that is entirely separate from music; the effects are then quite different from the imprint or residue left behind by earlier functional and composite context, and they are produced very differently. The distinction is one between immediate or concrete contextual relationships and those that are more remote or extrinsic. The more distant relationships, with which we are now concerned, may be described as direct, analogical, or synthetic; for music may interact directly with another aspect or area of culture, or it may simply be analogous in structure or expression to some other contemporaneous manifestation even though no direct influence is exerted in either direction, or finally, it may be related to another field of thought or expression only because the two are both parts of the same culture. It is often not simple to determine, however, which of these three types of relationship is represented in a given case, especially because the types tend to be active simultaneously rather than individually.

Certainly a knowledge of the place of music in society and culture is essential to a comprehension of its nature and meaning. It is hardly a matter of indifference whether it is conceived as a species of art, a type of mathematics, an instrument inherently suited to the shaping of emotional or ethical disposition, a division or an adjunct of scholarly or philosophic endeavor, or a special medium of communication with the supernatural or of unification with the fundamental metaphysical forces of the world. And our awareness of its larger context will often entail an additional question: How does music then differ from other branches of mathematics? From other liberal arts? From other creative arts? From language or from other kinds of symbolism and meaning? From other aspects of culture?

As a matter of common sense, we must in principle admit the possibility of interconnection between any two fields of human experience; often there is a conscious transfer of concepts, emotions, and structures from one area to another. That absolute music, which is often supposed to be one of the realms most cut off from the rest of life, if not indeed the most isolated of all, should be susceptible in any degree of such external connections or influences, seems at first sight impossible. That the direction of an interaction would be toward music from the outside rather than away from it is more than likely, but any point of contact or mutual concern seems to contradict the peculiar autonomy of music. But we have already seen that this autonomy and isolation are to a great extent illusory; they are ideals descended from the 19th century and inspired by the development of purely instrumental music and of independent aesthetic thought; they are revealed as false by a more objective and historical view as well as by theoretical examination. Nevertheless tonal experience is palpably different from all other; the perceived entities are essentially immanent, they have no models in nature, and are in no obvious way comparable to naturally occurring sounds let alone to the objects of tactual and visual experience. If the feelings provoked by tonal patterns are not so clearly different from those otherwise known, the sensational qualities of tone are at least in part unmistakably specific to the sensory mode. And the organizational principles and forms of music seem sui generis, and especially mysterious and inexplicable. But the peculiar autonomy of music does not make impossible its interaction with other fields of expression; it only dictates the form of such interaction. In fact, the properties of music that produce its isolation are also those that produce its susceptibility to external influence. Its lack of external objectivity, of natural models, of forms and feelings easily defined in words or readily equated with others, make it lean on more practical and concrete fields of thought and expression. This tendency has been so pronounced, and so particularly directed to the two areas of language and mathematics, that it must be indicative in some way of the intrinsic nature of music; also, partly for that very reason, it will constitute an important basis for a musical typology, different and more fundamental, in its applicability to absolute music, than the typological distinctions based on the immediate context of composite art and function.

Pure instrumental music, then, and compositional thought that is specifically musical even in composite forms of art, make use of connecting paths to the rest of experience; they sustain and define their position in respect of form and significance by means of analogies to language and mathematics. But within the nature of temporal tonal expression itself there are contained inherent properties that underlie the analogies, and that can succeed to independent expression and even to reciprocal influence. Thus we speak of music itself as a language or treat it as a type of mathematics in an original sense, and not only in its dependence on language and mathematics as otherwise known. These analogies exist for composite and functional music also, but they become more significant when closer sources of meaning are absent. In dance music, verbal and mathematical properties are readily masked by the obvious visual and kinesthetic meanings of the composite, and the same is true for music in films. In vocal music, different and conflicting properties can produce a complexity of meaning; the forms and significance of abstract verbal structures in the tonal constitution itself may not be identical with those of the text, or the textual form and meanings may be subordinated, disregarded, or contradicted by mathematical tonal structures, just as they often are by other typical stylistic configurations.

Music is similar to language primarily because it employs sound as a medium, and in particular the human voice, which, as we have seen, often underlies various features of instrumental style also. It has a temporal character, it possesses significance, and it contains meaningful elements that recur in various contexts. These elements—brief melodic, rhythmic, polyphonic, or harmonic configurations—have a relatively constant significance, although they vary in meaning much more than words or linguistic turns of phrase in accordance with the style in which they occur, and are much more dependent upon their musical context within a given style. Also music, unlike language, cannot be wholly analyzed into such units of meaning, and in some styles they are difficult to identify and may be effaced by larger contextual qualities. The meaning itself is different from that of language, since it refers only by exception, rather than consistently and intrinsically, to designated objects; the meaning is internal rather than referential or a compound of the two. And even the similarities to language are really true of melody rather than of polyphonic or athematic styles as such. But music can have strong emotional effects which are reminiscent of those of language, especially of spoken language, and speech secures much of its emotional power precisely by the employment of purely sonorous resources: changes in loudness or unusual levels of loudness, and tone color and rhythm that similarly have a distinctive character or are subjected to artful alterations. Music contains additional resemblances to language in manifesting various styles, the national ones comparable to various languages even to the point of their occurrence in family groups, and the individual ones reflective of personal idiosyncrasy much as speech and writing are. Music also changes in style with time, producing new forms and meaning in response to both internal and cultural forces; and it occurs in a variety of genres, which—again like verbal art—have distinctive forms and qualities. It contains, like language does, styles that are peculiar to locality and social class. It also exists in both improvised and composed forms, and although the visual aspect in comparison with the sonorous does not have the relative importance of literature, it is similarly a later manifestation which grows from a primarily auditory expression and which has far-reaching effects on the art as a whole. The score can be read like a literary work, and it is intimately related to the development of the art of composition and the musical work, as opposed to the more spontaneous activity of improvised music-making. Musical improvisation, finally, can either be a mechanical repetition of a prepared text, or can create itself in the doing, in spite of its utilization of a public idiom and formulated units of meaning, very much like speech that is vital in expression and communication.

That music has therefore turned to language for its structures and meaning can hardly be surprising, even apart from the influence of an art of vocal music that combines the two. Instrumental melody is often articulated into phrases which have various degrees of independence much like clauses and sentences, and the cadences of which have various degrees of finality. A composition will consist of a series of statements which fall into larger groups comparable to paragraphs, a number of these in turn often constituting a section or movement that can be compared to a chapter or other large division of a literary or poetical work. Also music will often take a distinctive initial pattern as a subject, theme, or motif, and structure itself by expansion, elaboration, emphasis, or antithesis of this formulation, a process very much like the verbal development or exposition of a topic or idea; indeed even our descriptive terms—*phrase, period, lyric,* or *refrain,* for example—are to a great extent the same in the two media. Alongside expository structures there are dramatic ones, in particular the dialogue, both as convivial discussion and as conflict or contrast. But tension, denouement, defeat, victory, recognition, and other striking dramatic moments also have their musical counterparts. While the musical flow can seem to become the utterance of an orator or narrator in expository structures, the melodic lines of conversational and dramatic patterns appear to

292

embody various distinct personalities. These are more than purely structural features, of course; often they have a striking expressive aspect that literally merits the designation "rhetorical" or "dramatic." Only repetition, recurrence, and approximate repetition such as sequence are a conspicuous and vital feature of musical form to an extent beyond what we can find in language, even in oratory and poetry; for this the demands of temporal coherence are responsible, since the resources of verbal conception and reference are absent. In language, on the other hand, these resources tend to make any form of repetition unnecessary and boring.

Instrumental music need not look to language for its formal principles; gamelan music does not do so, nor do innumerable keyboard preludes and instrumental dances of the Renaissance and later times. But in general in the West, instrumental music from 1600 to 1900 is strongly reminiscent of verbal forms and expressive motifs, the analogy with language and the adoption of linguistic modes of organization and expression may in fact be regarded as the chief determinants of musical structure and significance, and this remains true in spite of the basically different emphasis beginning about 1750 upon the specifically musical qualities of melody and sonority, which gradually brought lyricism, loudness, tone color, and harmony into prominence as independent factors of expression and form. Music became a special language, now in a figurative sense, instead of a copy or imitation or analogue of language in a proper verbal sense. By contrast, then, it was often, especially at first, regarded as indistinct rather than clear, and the definiteness it possessed in its own right went unnoticed. Occasionally sonority was taken to be a revelation of being, and musical structure of cosmic process. These new conceptions do not displace the established linguistic ones to any great extent, but are simply added to them, sometimes characteristically turning the human drama into a cosmic one, as in Beethoven's Ninth Symphony. But still in the purely musical structures and meanings of a Wagnerian music drama, where the linguistic influence can be seen with especial clarity because of the systematic appeal to language as a source of musical form, just as much as in the Baroque concerto and the Classical sonata, each repetition, sequence, or contrast is informed with the force and rhetorical intent of verbal expression, and the detailed structures are directly comparable to those of language. In the first three centuries of its prominence in the West, then, it is with a peculiar accuracy that we may call absolute music a heightened language; its emotional strength and the greater range and intensity of its rhythms do indeed give it a power and variety that must appear enviable to the orator and the dramatist. Although the two influences are interconnected, this dependence of music upon language is clearly quite different from the dependence of instrumental melody upon vocal, for the latter relationship (like the reverse dependence, of vocal melody upon instrumental) is a stylistic transfer occurring within music itself; language per se is not the model, nor is speech, but rather the singing voice with its specifically musical qualities of tone color and melodic style; that this style is in part the product of linguistic form and meaning does not affect the fundamental nature of the imitative process.

There can be no doubt also of the influence exerted by music upon artistic prose and poetry during this period, especially toward its end and in the 20th century, although the analogues involved were not of the same kind. Apart from the general notion of a "polyphonic" interweaving of strands of narrative and action, which becomes explicit in Aldous Huxley's title *Point Counter Point,* and of the exceptional duplication of an actual overall form, such as the sonata construction of Thomas Mann's *Tonio Kröger,* it is less techniques and generic forms that become models than significative qualities and general formal principles. The patterning and interplay of sonorities takes on an increasing importance and independence in 19th-century poetry and prose, almost detaching itself from verbal meaning completely in French Impressionism and symbolism; literature seems to adopt the principles of thematic development and transformation, of variation, melodic reminiscence, and recapitulation; and stories and novels seek atmospheric effects, vagueness, and ambiguity (Jean Paul is especially fond of ambiguous meaning)—in the belief that these are exemplary musical properties, which is true only when music is thought of in a context of comparison to language and not in its own right. To be sure, these properties of suggestiveness and undefined significance were the very ones that music itself.cultivated so successfully in German Romanticism and French Impressionism (no doubt in answer to general demands of the culture), so that there was some justification for taking music as a model. But that it was intrinsically suited to amorphous significance—or that it can in fact ever divest itself of its own intrinsic precision of meaning—is a view which simply represents a failure to understand the specific nature of absolute music: a relatively new artistic manifestation was beyond the powers of comprehension of a division of philosophic thought that was itself new, and in its autonomy, music was in fact the touchstone of the success of the autonomy of aesthetics, and its most difficult challenge. It is symptomatic of the true state of affairs that the conception of the imprecision of musical meaning, to which there is attached a remarkable variety of conflicting values, was applied in the decades around 1800 both to music of classical formal definition and to music of distinctive emotional character. In any event, the properties of literature and poetry that were derived from music by analogy were quite different in nature from those obvious formal features of poetry such as meter and end rhyme and verse repetition that seem to have their source in an antecedent composite art of song or dance-song.

It was only at the begining of the 20th century, at first somewhat in Impressionism and Expressionist atonality and later more definitely in serialism, that the linguistic model of musical form and expression was to a considerable extent abandoned in favor of principles more intrinsically musical; the discard of melody and of melodic motif and theme was a concomitant and perhaps a fundamental cause of the change. To the extent that the new ways of thought resembled those of other fields, they belonged more to mathematics than to language.

Of all the external connections of music, it is only mathematics that can be compared in importance to language.

Here again the connection is not simply one of external influence, but of inherent properties of music that entitle it in its own right to consideration as a certain kind of mathematics, or more correctly, of applied mathematics. As in the case of language, then, the strength and persistence of external relationship can be explained by the intrinsic properties of music itself. These properties suggest that the influence of mathematics may be more specific to absolute music than that of language, for they reside in part in the physical characteristics of musical instruments, most importantly in relationships of length; and just as vocal music would appear to be the field most susceptible—or at least most directly accessible—to linguistic influence, so instrumental music seems to be especially susceptible to the influence of mathematics. One important modification of this general dichotomy, however, will exist in the case of meter, as a fundamental class of durational relationships, for here mathematics is indissolubly bound up with language, and by that token it is as primary an influence on vocal music as on instrumental. The general similarity of music and mathematics probably has its most basic manifestation in the relatively abstract character of both: of music with respect to sentience and of mathematics with respect to physical reality.

Material amenable to quantitative thought in music exists chiefly in duration and pitch, and the treatment of rhythmical and melodic relationships has correspondingly gone far beyond the spontaneous appeal to sense, guided by patterns and symmetries of an abstract kind. The imposition of short, repeated rhythmical patterns on tenor melodies in their initial and successive appearances, isorhythmic schemes, which similarly structure more than one voice, mensuration canons, displacement syncopation, and proportional alterations of rhythm are characteristic examples of the later Middle Ages and the Renaissance in the field of duration, while the inversion and retrograde transformation of melodies and the alteration of their rhythmical shape by a mechanical displacement of durational pattern are corresponding contemporaneous instances in the field of pitch, and the derivation of tenors from the hexachord or from the vowels of verbal rubrics is certainly speculative if not mathematical. Many of the same procedures are conspicuous again in the 20th century, along with the use of the same intervals of pitch for both chordal and melodic structures, and the freer and somewhat speculative selection of this set of intervals—tendencies that are manifest in Impressionism and in the music of Bartok. The subsequent serialization of pitch, duration, loudness, and tone color continues these tendencies into a generality of organization that turns chordal and melodic configurations into special limiting forms of musical relationship and therefore into merely occasional features of music.

Mathematical conceptions are usually applied not to music but to the musical system and to scales, where the lengths of vibrating segments of air columns and strings, and the rapidity of their vibration, make possible an exact standardization of relative pitches. In this area, musical mathematics does not belong so much to the artistic and practical aspect of music, to composition or precomposition, but to acoustical theory, which for many centuries in antiquity and the Middle Ages, as a member of the quadrivium and the liberal arts, was considered to be a major branch of mathematics in general, significant enough to have a reciprocal influence on thought in medicine, sociology, astronomy, and cosmology. The (approximate) circle of twelve fifths, and the corresponding circle of twelve keys, entered artistic practice as well as musical thought in later times, and of course the mathematical theory of the triad, harmony, harmonic progressions, and harmonic dualism, notably in the works of Zarlino, Rameau, and various 19th-century writers, was intimately bound up with musical composition and perception. But whether in the musical system or in the musical work, the central question about mathematical modes of thought (which has naturally come to attention most in connection with duration and pitch) is their relationship to aesthetic properties. Controversy has always existed about the relative values of proportional theory and audition in the construction of the musical system, and a corresponding problematical atmosphere surrounds the combination of abstract schemes and aesthetic appeal in the musical composition. This often has taken the form—as in the musical treatise of Ptolemy or even the antimathematical one of Aristoxenos—of the relative claims of reason and sense. That number can be combined with sensory quality and aesthetic value in a satisfactory manner is undeniable; indeed it inheres in the very physiology and psychology of sensation; only its precise role and relative importance are what remain to be determined by the spirit of each age and style. It is certain also, of course, that mathematical considerations can easily become irrelevant to tonal perception and musical experience, and that given undue weight they can also work against artistic ends instead of abetting them. But these things are often misjudged through lack of stylistic insight; numerical relationships unperceived in themselves may still have significant aesthetic outcomes; futhermore they may serve an important function in the operation of compositional imagination; while in addition human apprehension can achieve remarkable feats in its ability to combine reason and sense in novel textures of musical conception and enjoyment.

In its very nature, then, music possesses the possibilities of discursive utterance and measurable structure. Although it is properly speaking neither a language nor a moving architecture, it is potentially both linguistic and architectural. Actually it may be not only the one or the other but also both at once, as we may see in many Baroque instrumental works, when realizations of the two potentialities overlap historically, particularly in German music. To these structural models there correspond characteristic musical realms of feeling, the linguistic one more highly charged and expressive, the mathematical cooler and more impersonal, but capable too of arousing the wonderment that attaches to the complex regularities of nature and the ingenuities of human imagination. If music turns to language and mathematics alternately, this is not only a sign of their prominence and ramification in the emotional and intellectual world of man, or again simply an external manifestation of the constitution of music itself, which contains strong linguistic and mathematical propensities, but also the major symptom of the dependence of the art on other spheres of expression, as though music, in becoming autonomous and sacrificing its concrete connections to society and to poetry and dance, had now to secure its independent meaning and form by an appeal to more established modes of thought. But if this conception applies to the rhetorical disposition of instrumental compositions from 1600 to 1900, to their mathematical constitution in 20th-century serialism, and to the structure of the tonal system at all times, we must remember that linguistic and mathematical tendencies exist also in composite and functional music, where they would seem not to be necessary, but where the one is explained by the actual presence of a verbal component and the other—notably in medieval and Renaissance polyphony—by the numerical nature of tonal patterns as such even when they are a component of a more comprehensive mode of expression.

Many of the external relationships of music are in part based on or in some way connected with these fundamental linguistic and mathematical tendencies. This is true of the relationships between music and the other arts, which are an important class of related manifestations, since the linguistic properties of music are partly responsible for its connection with the temporal arts and its mathematical properties for its connection with the purely spatial ones. But the peculiarly close relationships of music to the temporal arts, which we have already discussed, are of course largely due to—and also responsible for—the prevalence of various composite arts in which music is a component. Since dance and poetry are in many cultures inseparable from the art of tone, they continue to have a special connection with abstract instrumental music, which, as we have seen, often derives its form and emotional character from dance and song. But these are really also types of music in its broader sense, and in their employment of tone they partake of the peculiar temporal properties that characterize the art, notably its compelling hold on consciousness, which it is so uniquely able to articulate and objectivize. Like literature in general, poetry and drama have an existence independent of these tonal properties, although not of sound. The specifically verbal arts are related to music in their planned temporal course, but the center of interest and artistic intention has shifted to concrete image and action, or in any event, to the interplay of image with verbal sonority. What is shaped in the arts of language is primarily idea, occurrence, and image; sound is generally subservient to these, but even when it achieves a central position it remains incapable of the structural and temporal complexity that is possessed only by pitch; even in its greatest subtlety, verbal sound—whether in imagery or in actual perception—is unable in itself, unless it is combined with essentially musical structures of rhythm and simultaneity, to support art; for this it must lean on linguistic meaning, or at least on implications of such meaning. Thus the verbal "music" of poetry and literature is quite different from the music of tone; it is not self-sustaining; and although verbal art, by virtue of its temporal constitution, is often able to draw the flow of vital feeling into its illusory world as we experience it, its time does not become our own, even if the work is realized aloud, with any compelling necessity or exactitude; there is no congruence or identity of the two temporal continuities but only an occasional coincidence that is not intrinsic to the artistic medium. As we have seen, the medium in fact contains two temporal streams: the concrete one of the imaged or heard verbal sonorities, and the represented one of the descriptive or narrative or conceptual content; either of these can control the course of consciousness for a time; sometimes both do so at once; but the experience in no case takes on the inherently temporal character of music, where the essential and inevitable meaning of form is the inner process to which it corresponds, and concepts are never primary.

In the compound musical arts, then, tone has the commanding position in respect of the course of vital feeling. The represented temporal events of the text of a song, like the verbal rhythms in themselves, are a secondary content that is entirely swallowed up unless we consciously attend to it, and even then it is more realized than felt. The situation is somewhat similar in dance; the visual motion involves us in its flow by empathy, but with less force than tonal motion; it does not become a subordinate component, however, and dance remains a counterpoint or partnership of unequals. Yet because of the continuity and prominence of sonorous experience, dance is in general a variety of music, even if not in as fundamental a way as song. Pantomime and film, on the other hand, are much less dependent upon sound and tone, in spite of the fact that their combination with music produces a remarkable enhancement of their meaning and effect.

These considerations have a direct bearing on the relationships of music to the various temporal arts, which we have examined in both the present chapter and the preceding one. Instrumental music is particularly close to song, and we find in fact that it is often stylistically related in formal and expressive traits. The chief connecting factor is the dual constitution of the human voice, which spontaneously unites word and tone. The resemblance of instrumental music to dance is also very close, based here on the interrelation of vision and hearing and on the relationship of both to kinesthesis; all three senses are united in organic adaptation and external perception, and the various intersensory or at times even synesthetic relationships make possible a considerable duplication of formal and expressive features. Thus instrumental music—and song as well—often adopts stylistic features from the dance, which reciprocally can mirror those of instrumental music and song.

The purely verbal arts, on the other hand, are in general not so closely connected either with instrumental music or with song. Poetry more than the others can share formal arrangements with music, and thus to some extent with dance also; and the conceptual and emotional meaning of the words is often the same as their meaning in contemporaneous vocal music. There can also be a great resemblance of qualities between poetry and instrumental music—even between prose and instrumental music—based on the similarity of verbal sonorities and rhythm with those of tone and music: dissonant and consonant effects, agitation and repose, are literal properties found in both spheres of art in closely comparable forms. Drama can contain not only many of these resemblances to music, but additional ones, to opera and instrumental music, of dialogue and dramatic action, even of the pace and structure of the action.

301

Narrative prose, however, although it can resemble sung ballades in subject matter, feeling, and action, is generally more removed from music in its structural and emotional features; apart from resemblances based on verbal sonority, its style and form will be comparable to those of music more by analogy than by direct perception. This is also true, as we have seen, of exposition and exhortation.

In the spatial, or rather nontemporal, arts, the situation is simpler and fundamentally different. Inner process is not caught up and structured in the artistic experience; it remains under our control and more separate from the artistic object and from our impressions of it. The eye is the distance sense par excellence, and the visual work of art has an objectivity and externality that joins with its static character to make any identification with our inner state a more conscious and less self-understood occurrence. The connection is also one of mood rather than flow; there may be agitation and motion in a painting or a statue, but as conditions, not as a progress of movement; the dynamism of music is absent. What we see in general is contemplated or inspected; it possesses a permanence that opens it to knowledge. In spite of the possibility of evanescence and indefiniteness in the visual arts, their nature remains one of stability and the presentation of a finished image and feeling, a characteristic that is still distinctive even for sculpture and architecture, where motion within and around and the temporal aspect of apprehension are often part of the artistic conception. For this temporal experience is not the primary field of creation and response, but a means to an end, or at best an accessory field of formativity; the artist works with static form and texture; motion and changing impressions of light are not necessarily involved, but play assisting roles on occasion.

Within this general character architecture occupies a position—as we have previously observed—which is comparable to that of music in the temporal arts; it is the basic spatial framework to which sculpture and painting must accommodate themselves. Unlike abstract instrumental music, however, it is governed by function and symbolic purpose, although its freedom within these determinants in respect of material, form, proportion, and depiction is reminiscent of the freedom of music, which is still more strikingly independent of function and similarly nonrepresentational. The parallel of architecture with music in its broader sense is even closer, for here everything falls readily into place: function, composite nature, and associated arts in the same general field of imagination. Then just as dance and the literary genres can be arranged to show an increasing independence of music and of the intrinsic temporal quality of tone, so sculpture and painting reveal an increasing independence of architecture and of the tridimensionality of space, with factors of representation similarly becoming more important as the material of artistic imagination and experience. On the one hand, verbal conceptions, on the other, concrete visual image, take over the position of the abstract and primary material: tone or spatial form.

The basic division between music and the spatial arts by no means rules out analogy and stylistic resemblance. For one thing, temporality is not really absent from the spatial arts, but implicit. This implicit character takes various forms. Concepts of temporal quality and duration can be evoked either by representational means or by perceptual patterns and their qualitative properties in themselves. Rest can be evoked either by a peaceful scene or by horizontal lines and harmonious colors in themselves, agitation either by the depiction of a stormy sea or by jagged lines and conflicting colors without representational significance. But the temporal course of apprehension is also implicit in a spatial work of art, sometimes as a striking feature, as in large architectural works, landscape architecture, and planned cities; and the temporal course of production is a fourth kind of implicit temporality, with extremes in a rapid sketch and a medieval cathedral, while the range possible even within one type of spatial manifestation—the Salisbury and Winchester cathedrals can be taken as examples—may extend from years to centuries. We perceive in a building more than the simple span of time covered in production, for this is a span that has a temporal structure shaped by successive styles, additions, and changes.

303

Architecture also possesses a counterpart of pictorial representation, as well as the temporally evocative qualities of line and color and form in themselves: not in the temporality of their construction or apprehension but in their function and meaning, the pyramids or Stonehenge suggest the time of astronomical process, or eternity, or also inevitable decay and transience. A final type of implicit temporality in spatial art is the historical distance from the present of the time at which a work was created, or the various dates of its stages of creation or of its constituent styles. There is thus an area of contact between music and spatial art in temporality itself; explicit qualities may differ from implicit ones, but they remain comparable. The spatial and musical arts have still additional connections, however, for all the types of implicit temporality found in spatial art are contained in music as well. Thus the two groups of art may be equated in respect of their time of origin; and the more clearly style reflects its historical period, the greater will be the resemblance between contemporaneous arts. On the other hand, spatial art may even manifest an explicit temporality, for drawing, painting, and modeling can on occasion become arts of performance or improvisation. If the work is apprehended during its production, this initial temporal experience will be quite similar to the perception of a musical performance.

The relationship of music to spatial art will depend also on the connection between the sensory modalities of hearing and vision, or as we may also say, on the connection between their media of formation and expression. There is a considerable variety in relationships of this kind, but of the fact of relationship there can be no doubt. The cooperative action of the senses in biological adjustment and external perception is in part complementary, but it also connects certain visual impressions with corresponding auditory ones—brightness, for example, with certain metallic tone colors and high pitches. There is also a formal connection even between the immanent impressions of the senses: qualities appear in different places in both, for example; curves are related to points somewhat as melodies are to tones; an intermediate hue is unequivocally placed between two others that resemble each other, just as an intermediate pitch can be placed between two given tones; and the differences in sensations with respect to any property in either modality depend on relative rather than absolute differences in the corresponding dimension of the physical substratum. If this formal relationship can be a basis for conscious analogy, it can also be one of the bases for the spontaneous connection that is found in synesthesia, which may rest in addition on inter-sensory cooperation, on customary or especially vivid association, or on still other factors that cannot be identified and that may derive from the intrinsic nature of perception as such or from antecedent generalized modes of sensitivity in evolutionary history.

A consideration of the physical media of vision and hearing is also instructive, since it will suggest a similarity of visual color to auditory tone color and pitch, or perhaps more accurately, to tone color and tonicity, the qualitative component of pitch. Color does appear psychologically to resemble tone color and pitch, and in the form although not the nature of its physical substratum, it also resembles them, since a color is generally correlated with a band of light frequencies or a spaced pattern, and a tone, especially if vibrato is included in its constitution, has a similar correlate, although in mechanical rather than electromagnetic vibrations; a stimulus of a single frequency is an exceptional technological product in both fields, and the perceptions correspondingly attenuated in quality. Peripherally the senses of vision and hearing are not closely comparable, since one is chemical and the other mechanical; but retinal spatial patterns do have a counterpart in the spatial patterns found in the cochlea, and this appears to provide a basis for the resemblance between external visual location and the "height" component of pitch. The peripheral spatial comparison can be pursued in neurological terms, and a similar spatial comparison, both in the sense organs and in their nervous pathways and projection areas would seem to uncover part of the basis for the resemblance between visual and auditory volume. Neural discharge rate must also be taken into account, of course, and it plays an important role again in sensible intensity, which is interrelated with spatial properties, and in other intersensory qualities such as brightness. A physiological spatial comparison can also be made between binocular vision and binaural hearing, where a similar basis for localization and depth perception in both senses will be found; the relationship this supports between spatial art and music is exceptionally close; it concerns not the central immanent structures of music, however, but the antiphonal properties deriving from the external location and arrangement of performers and instruments.

This factor is on occasion of considerable importance; it is a basis not only of the immanent structural parallelism of phrases (and even of functional harmonic relationships), but of the special kinship of music and architecture. For if music and architecture have analogous positions in the temporal and spatial arts respectively, if they share, in spite of the symbolic and functional significance of architecture, a certain abstract, nonrepresentational, formal, and mathematical character, and if they possess comparable temporal and durational properties whether explicit or implicit, there are still additional connections because of the fact that music is performed largely indoors. Architecture is thus often specifically joined to music: in music rooms, concert and recital halls, opera houses, and churches. This is essentially a functional relationship: the architectural interior serves the purpose of providing a setting for the music, and the music consummates the purpose of the room or building. The reciprocal internal function can subserve an external one, ritual or ceremonial, but will exist in any event, even in convivial or purely aesthetic experience. To some extent the music becomes part of the architecture: it reveals the acoustic nature and the musical signifiance of the interior through reverberation and resonance, the placement of performers or organ pipes, and the motion of singers or processions. But in these very same relationships the architecture becomes part of the music; indeed we can say that the two interpenetrate and form an artistic compound that can become the basis for a conjunction of all the arts, spatial and temporal, since architecture and music respectively are foundational in the two divisions. We are no longer dealing here with analogies between separate arts, however, but with a peculiar kind of composite art and the stylistic features it produces in each component.

Just as the spatial arts are temporal, then, so music is spatial. It comprises not only an intrinsic type of spatiality, but also, like properly spatial art, a literally spatial or environmental aspect. There is still another fundamental connection between the two divisions of art in their common temporal foundation, which is obscured on the one hand by the objectively perceived temporality of music and on the other by the conspicuous spatiality of the static visual arts. For art is concerned with the enhancement of perception and perceptual values; and taking the temporality of consciousness and of the physiological processes of all sensory perception as a basis, it thus tends by its nature to prolongation. Just as composers and performers dwell on the aesthetic values of sonorities and textures, and music often extends itself indefinitely or creates the impression of doing so, the spectator similarly prolongs his visual experience of a painting or statue or building, even apart from the time he may take for various and changing views. Time is thus a fundament, as well as a condition, of all the arts, although this is doubtless true, in different ways, of space also. The distinctions lie in the various kinds of role each of the two factors plays in each of the arts, and it is obviously this variety that supports the division of the arts into spatial and temporal. Much of the general quality and effect of works of art is due to length and size—in the resistance to aesthetic prolongation or magnitude, for example, or the conflict with it, that we find in small pictures, in paintings of brief instants of action or fleeting conditions of light, or in very short or very rapid musical works. But there is also a factor here of human scale, of the comfort and sense of well being we are afforded by small objects that can be easily controlled or mastered or readily surveyed—objects that reduce what they represent or that exceed the normal rapidity of human processes and activities. In contrast, vast buildings or mural paintings or extremely slow or loud or lengthy musical works tend to emphasize sensory values and to achieve sublimity, if not in fact to overwhelm or exceed our perceptual powers.

There is a final general basis for the relationship of music to spatial art in the modes of being manifested by the musical work of art and phonorecord, for the property of permanence along with a visual or tangible instrument of formativity enable music to duplicate the characteristics of spatial works of art. Not only the relationship that consists in this duplication comes into existence—an equivalence of definition, durability, historical style, detachment, craftsmanship, individuality, and value—but more specific relationships within these characteristics, in the particular manner and degree in which each manifests itself. The general equivalence in artistic status and mode of being thus becomes the condition for the existence and the prominence of detailed analogical relationships.

The connection between the arts includes resemblances in addition to those we have discussed, for there are stylistic and qualitative similarities among contemporaneous arts which go beyond the traces and influences remaining form artistic compounds or the structural and expressive resemblances due to related temporal, spatial, mathematical, physical, and sensory constitution. The more comprehensive similarities with which we shall now be concerned are in part those of the overall aesthetic quality of works of art—an individuality grounded in historical and cultural style—but they are also partly those that extend beyond the province of art and works of art and in some form or degree affect all the manifestations of a given culture.

How music is related to other expressions of human intelligence and what properties it may share with culture as a whole are questions of great interest in themselves and of obvious relevance to our understanding of experience and culture in general. They remain important also, however, in a study of music itself, for even if music were so unique in nature that it possessed nothing in common with any other product of thought or creativity, it would still be more profitably examined and better known in context than in isolation. The place of music in culture has been different at different times, changing in accordance with the prevailing conceptions of art and knowledge and with their social functions. How we envisage and explain any activity is to some extent a determinant as well as a result of its nature. This does not mean, however, that there are no intrinsic connections between music and any other area of expression, but merely that such connections are potential ones, which may or may not be realized, or may be realized only partially, in any given historical configuration of culture. The complexity of the general problem has already been forecast in our consideration of the compound musical arts, of the functional roles of music, of the dependence` of music on language and mathematics, and the analogical relationships of music to the other arts. The types of relationship that can exist will clearly be very varied.

In any event, the interrelationship of the arts is really part of the coherence of culture in general; the conditions and even the existence of the smaller problem are dependent upon the larger one in which it is embedded; the very notion of the arts as a group of related activities, for example, presupposes the recognition of a common principle in man's formative endowment and the appeal to sense; and the thesis of mutual influence among the arts if not of common properties is no more than an instance of the conception of the unity of culture or the interconnection of its various aspects. In the decades around 1700, the arts were all subjected to the standard of rationalism; music was elaborated from a single thematic formulation and followed rigorous logical principles of sequential and tonal progression; harmonic theory found a similar deductive form with Rameau. In the mid-18th century ideas of natural simplicity and clarity were evident in every department of culture and thought; the arts took up a time-honored common principle in imitation, which was really more proper to epistemology than to aesthetics, and instrumental music looked to language and song for its explanatory basis, although each art remained distinctive in its goals and character, as these were dictated by its particular medium of expression. In the 19th century, the unity of culture became a center of interest and speculation, and the arts were correspondingly conceived as essentially the same, their sensible form a relatively secondary circumstance through which the same universal feelings and metaphysical creativity came to expression; thus they combined and fused and borrowed from each other freely, seeking common artistic purposes and qualities.

It is indeed only apparently difficult to understand how instrumental music may be connected with other manifestations of culture. Music formulates and articulates the flow of emotional and vital consciousness in a particular sonorous mode to which this consciousness is peculiarly accessible. It is able to devote itself solely to this function, even dispensing with conceptual and representational subject matter and with visual and objective associations and concomitants. The other temporal arts are akin to it, for the properties of inner experience are to a greater or lesser extent their concern also, but only as these properties become connected with or constituents of more particular ideas and representations which are the central concern. Thus the problem of how abstract instrumental music can be grasped as a part of culture has at least one available if partial answer in the fact that its subject matter is not unique, but is related to other subject matter dealing more concretely with human experience. Naturally if we maintain that instrumental music is sui generis, that it is conceived and apprehended by a totally separate department of the soul, the mind, or the nervous system, it will as a corollary be difficult or impossible to find it connected or related to any other art or expression of culture. But this problem disappears if we determine that what music deals with is an aspect of our experience ingredient also in extramusical affairs; that its content is the progress of volitional and emotional consciousness abstracted from the particularities of incident and circumstance but mirrored in the form of tone. That the qualities of such experience can be sensitive to culture rather than invariant, indeed that they must be responsive in this way to the extent that human experience is culturally rather than biologically determined, we have already considered. But the cultural setting is reflected in the formal aspect of music as well as in its meaning, for the patterns we construct in tone are again by no means so peculiar in nature as to be unrelated to visible structures and those made of physical material. Here the connection exists via the organic unity and interrelation of the senses and in the consequent general aesthetic validity of a given mode of thought. If balance in visual form has a hetero-sensory counterpart in auditory recurrence, or visual high and low a counterpart in pitch, the same characteristics and techniques of organization can manifest themselves in the different departments of art and indeed throughout all the fields of human endeavor and expression.

It is thus both in its content and in its form that music is generally related to other departments of culture: in its meaning and its structure. This relation, however, does not imply that music, or any single cultural expression, merely repeats or echoes all the others. For coherence and unity, whether in a culture, an organism, or an artistic totality, can be constituted by parts very different among themselves, as different as an ear is from an eye, Schönberg from Einstein, or the first movement of a symphony from the second. Correspondingly, the question we can ask about the relation of music to other manifestations of culture is whether it is similar to these or complementary; or with respect to culture as a whole, whether music mirrors its qualities or is an essentially distinctive constituent of them. Both answers can be given together, for music can be partly similar and partly complementary to painting, for example, in making up the overall cultural configuration; and it can be both similar to the cultural whole and also distinctive in its qualities. It only seems unlikely, although it is not logically impossible, for it to be neither similar nor distinctively constitutive, but simply unrelated. As a matter of fact, such a situation would imply not only the dissimilarity of music to other areas of human experience, but the lack of coherence of culture as a whole. Now there are at least some ways, and not entirely sophistical ones, in which this cannot be the case. For the culture is the milieu of the individual who makes the evaluation we are considering, or if he is outside it socially or historically his observation of it will be prerequisite to statements about it. Thus different cultural expressions will have a minimal relationship in coexisting experiences of a single person, and here, apart from any other similarities they may possess, they will take on at least an associative relationship to each other and to the whole which is

311

a consequence of the unity of an individual personality or of the unity of mentality. To the historian the distance of a culture in time lends a distinctive stamp of style to the whole and to each of its manifestations, so that the disparities that were glaring originally are gradually modified and brought together into a resemblance and a unity. Needless to say, of course, innumerable factors seem inevitably to lead to more intimate resemblances and unity, and the coherence of culture—or its style—is generally striking. This is particularly true of groups of manifestations that are united in their conceptions and nature by the special outlook of the culture; we have taken the arts to be potentially such a group. At the same time, we must realize that there is no general principle which enables us to assert the inevitable correspondence between all or even any two departments of culture or between the specialized histories of the various fields. Indeed it is really more by exception and even by coincidence that contemporaneous manifestations are related, and the whole notion of a general history of culture—like those of world history and universal history, which encompass the entire spatial and temporal existence of man—rests at least in part on a uniform application of a mathematical scheme of chronology that is in no way responsive to knowable human affairs.

Music often has resemblances to natural science and to philosophic thought, to the first because of its mathematical and structural properties, and to the second because of its concern with the nature of consciousness. The arithmetic, harmonic, and geometric proportions of consonant intervals and scales, and the mathematical relationships of scales among themselves and with respect to the whole tonal system, have produced a recurrent tendency to equate music with the natural world. The circle of fifths, the recurrence of the scalar qualities of tonicity at each octave, and in musical rather than tonal terms, the repetition of a melodic phrase literally and especially sequentially, or progressive harmonic modulation through successive fifths, all tend to suggest astronomical and geographical and physical counterparts. The result has been a series of correlations with planetary distances and speeds, with the seasons and months and hours, with the symmetries of plants and animals and with the body and soul of man (in this context we omit architecture and sculpture and painting), with the structure of crystals and atoms, and with various kinds of physical rotation and revolution. These correlations extend from ancient China and Greece to the 20th century. Sometimes even the materials of which musical instruments are made enter the comparisons. In general, the resemblance of music to nature has two implications: music may be conceived as nature, which acts through the creative genius of man to produce art, a higher nature; and nature—both physical and biological—may be conceived as music, a notion that is supported in part by an intersensory or even synesthetic factor. The emotional potency of music is also part of the correlation, and it has its counterpart in astrological influence on human actions and character. Fundamentally this is an analogical method of organizing the diversity of experience, but the analogies or equivalencies can be established only because there is in fact some kind of parallelism or correspondence, whether structural or material, between the phenomena that are to be connected. A striking example of the "discovery" and development of such a parallelism and concomitant analogy is the history of the quadrival sciences in the West, which extends from Greek antiquity to the 17th century. In the beginnings of the quadrivium in Pythagorean thought, arithmetic, geometry, music, and astronomy shared common elementary principles and deductive elaboration, their theoretical structure was uniform, and they thus accounted for perceptible phenomena in a uniform way. Even the Renaissance theory of visual art, both harmonic and perspectivic, descends from this conceptual framework.

Perhaps more importantly, however, parallelisms within a culture exist even when no explicit connection is made. Looking back at a culture or standing outside one, the historian or the anthropologist will see many similarities that are not visible to those who are members of the society. Paradoxically, the context of music will therefore be different and in general broader when a culture is viewed from an external station point. Thus there is a resemblance between the corporeal and concrete

313

nature of the ancient Greek conception of number and the quadrivial sciences, and the nature of their composite musical art of dance, poetry, and tone; or a resemblance, as Spengler felt, between the development of calculus and functional mathematics, and the contemporaneous development of instrumental music; or a resemblance, in the 20th century, between the crisis in physical theory and the crisis in tonality, or between the new theories and discoveries in physics and astronomy, or even in space technology, and new theories and practices in serialism and nontonal music. And just as there is a striking difference between the proportional mathematics of antiquity and modern topology or the theory of groups, so there is a corresponding difference between Greek scalar construction and recent serial construction. Or again, the exploration of the earth contrasts with the exploration of the solar system much as the cyclical and gravitational properties of tonality contrast with the more extended relationships of serialism or the bewildering freedom of nontonal sound. Also the musical and scientific and mathematical developments of the first half of the 20th century have given us a comparably new vantage point in all three fields, so that we can look back in much the same way on the nature of tonality or Newtonian physics or the structure of deductive science and see them whole, with their inherited presuppositions and their historical career and limitations. In every case the differences between historical periods or cultures serve to point up the similarities within each. But the similarities are in general difficult to uncover and difficult to specify. As convincing as the feeling of the stylistic unity of a culture may be, or of its distinctive outlook, the complexity of each of its manifestations and the complex of possible relationships each may sustain with any of the others make the connections between them elusive and the search for resemblance often inconclusive as well as fascinating. Analogies explicitly made at the time are the most reliable guide, superficial or apparently logical similarities are the most treacherous, but unfortunately much easier to find. Connections are more often below the surface than exposed to view; and they lie more often in basic and pervasive modes of thought and ways of feeling than in formulations specific to any given two areas of comparison. There is thus no substitute for a knowledge of the culture in question that is both comprehensive and profound.

Conceptions of evolution and progress became powerful models of thought starting in about the middle of the 18th century. The influence of ideas of this kind—and also of metamorphosis and the cycle of life—reveals that biology can be as important as physical science in determining the general outlook of a culture. Theories of the origin and development of language, impressively formulated by Rousseau and Herder, contained a strong negative implication for the historical course of music and language. Decline replaces progress in Wagner's view of this historical course, and his criticism of the poor state of opera and drama (which was by no means without a foundation in fact) leads logically to his radical and comprehensive revision of musical drama. The general applicability of evolutionary thought is astonishing; the biological conception of Darwin was extended to philosophy by Spencer and to geology by Lyell and has continued as a powerful constituent of science up to present-day theories of the cosmic evolution of forms of matter and of the periodic series of the elements. It is understandable, then, not only that notions of evolution and progress were applied to musical history and that the pattern of birth, growth, maturity, decay, and death was taken as a model for the developmental course of a style or a genre, but also that the intrinsic forms of musical continuity and organization came to consist more and more in the common derivation of a variety of thematic forms from a single underlying abstract nucleus, as in Schumann, and in the progressive transmutation or transformation of initial or archetypal themes—even in the genesis of a theme from an initial amorphous state, as in the opening of Beethoven's Ninth Symphony or of a symphony of Bruckner.

It is doubtless because of the importance of fundamental ways of thought and feeling, of basic conceptions of reality and basic formulations of temporal and spatial experience, that a kinship of music and philosophic thought can become conspicuous. As music is related to mathematics because they both

315

are concerned with the underlying properties of experience, with the possibilities and properties of feeling and thought respectively in their own right, apart from their connection with or application to external concrete matters, so it is related to philosophy in much the same way and for much the same reasons. Thus Plato's harmonic conception of the cosmos and society and the soul was exemplified by and intimately bound up with music; there was even a mutual influence and interaction. The same kinds of connection are found in ancient Chinese thought. And in more recent times there are examples in the resemblance of rationalism to tonality, of an autonomous discipline of aesthetics to an autonomous instrumental music, of dialectical and evolutional historical processes to developmental and transformational thematic techniques respectively, and of voluntaristic philosophy to musical subjectivity. There is even an explicit identification of music with philosophy that reaches from German idealism and Schopenhauer to Bergson and French existentialism. This may very well be a consequence in part of the propaedeutic function of the quadrivial sciences which is established and exemplified so·brilliantly by Plato and is still clearly followed by Descartes.

The relationships of music to society and to the individual personality represent still other complex and problematical instances of the external connections of music; in these areas, conceptions of influence have been more widespread than notions of analogy or resemblance, although support can be found for both types of view. In the composite musical arts the textual and visual components are the bases of explicit relationships to social institutions and ideas and structures. The *Marriage of Figaro* is a clear depiction of 18th-century social classes and their interrelationship; *Die Meistersinger* of the guild traditions of Nuremburg; the medieval *sirventes* and the modern patriotic songs and political ballads an explicit embodiment of contemporaneous events and attitudes. Still more directly, music is of course literally and intrinsically social in constitution; its structure, in term of both participants and audience, may serve to define or display the relationship of the various groups that compose society. There are ceremonial occasions, especially in nonliterate societies, that enlist the participation of a social hierarchy in its entirety. But this kind of connection between music and society is no longer solely a contextual relationship. Even though the structure of society exists apart from its ceremonial exemplification, it also becomes an intrinsically musical structure without change, for the music is a formulation in environmental space, and it is an activity rather than an object; even an audience will become a group of participants as well as observers. But even a modern audience at a concert or opera has a stratified composition that reflects economic and social distinctions; it also has a role to play in the performance, as we can discover whenever the attendance at a musical event is very small or exceptionally large, or whenever strong enthusiasm or disapproval is expressed.

In general, however, the connection of music and society is not a direct one: it neither consists of explicit depiction or description, nor is it confined to a literal embodiment of social relationships in musical structure. Except for the various types of political song or of comic opera, the action projected by most composite genres of art will be simply analogous to the social situation of the time, or still more indirectly, song, opera, and dramatic ballet will convey ideas, scenes, stories, or dramatic action that represent characteristic interests of the culture, although certainly for reasons that are in some sense basically social. In these categories, for example, we can place the Classical subject matter of Baroque opera, the heroic tradition of opera in general, especially with its changing types of protagonist in the 19th and 20th centuries, the revolutionary political ardor conveyed by several of Verdi's operas, the element of the demonic and supernatural in German Romantic opera, or the feeling for nature in the Romantic lied. Musical subject matter will necessarily represent the outlook of the time even if it is historical, legendary, mythological, fanciful, or of such a universal type as the contemplation of nature, the youthful spirit of adventure or combat, the joys and sorrows of love or lust, or the quiet resignation of later life. For if any subject matter achieves an impressive or definitive expression, or becomes widespread, it will necessarily reveal something of the state of society in which it occurs and will in fact assume a specificity of form and matter and meaning that raises it from the level of a general or universal category to a particular cultural representation. Intentional analogy of subject matter, however, as of a Classical hero with the personal virtues of a noble patron, or of French rescue plots with the actualities and concerns of the period, or of operatic parody with political institutions and with the interests and behavior of the higher social classes, is inevitably allied to moral objectives, whether of exhortation, inspiration, or ridicule.

But the ethical value of art is evidenced, although in different ways, by all varieties of music. It belongs to the direct depiction of society as well as to the presentation of characteristic interests and of conscious analogies. It is in fact the corollary of the social constitution of music, and the two oppositely directed influences together make up the relationship of music and society. In a functional context, composite forms of music manifest their most intimate and obvious social relationship; they become integrated with behavior and purposes that have an extra-artistic definition; thus their significance and structure are intrinsically social and their impact on personality, emotion, and action achieves its greatest force. The ceremonial and ritual manifestations of music, from primitive fertility and war dances and ancient Greek civic and ritual choral dance to medieval religious rites and the public patriotic and memorial ceremonies and communal song of recent centuries, give music its strongest social stamp both in visual and textural meaning and in its form, and endow it at the same time with its strongest power in respect of social cohesion, effectiveness, and unity of feeling. To be sure, this moral force in its turn subject to moral judgment; it ranges from nobility to propaganda, manipulation, and depravity; but of its strength—which resides both in the psychology of group behavior and in the nature of musical perception—there can be no doubt. For music in a functional context, and to a lesser extent simply in its varieties as a composite art, the negative aspect of the relationship to society can become as conspicuous as the positive one. The meretricious and synthetic quality of ceremonial music in present-day manipulated mass society, the immorality of song texts and of dramatic action in the motion picture, the license of social dancing, the combination, in commercial music, of stereotyped form with a superficial variety and a rapid change of fashion, and the extreme level of loudness and artificial qualities of tone in popular music, together with the extremities of feeling deployed, from tawdry and blatant sentimentality to dizziness and erotic intoxication, are not only a faithful expression of the disintegration of society and tradition and humanistic values, but a further potent force making for this disintegration.

In the case of absolute instrumental music, or even of the specifically musical component of a composite art or a functional occasion, the connections to society have no tangible bases, and would seem possible only as analogies that rest on deep common factors of human experience and formativity. Even in pure instrumental music, however, music is in itself a social form of activity to a degree and in a variety that makes it unique among the arts. Is it then for this reason also a microcosm of society at large? Or is it in any event analogous to society chiefly or solely by virtue of its own social constitution? And is its social influence also grounded in this property? A decisive factor here is certainly the degree of integration or autonomy of the social form of the music. A military platoon singing a marching song represents a high degree of the functional integration of music and society; the formal relationship between the two approaches an identity, and the social influence of the music a correspondingly maximal force. The same is true of the congregational singing of a Protestant hymn. And in both cases there is an external power, the one essentially social and the other in a certain sense divine, that prescribes the music and its form and directs its communal meaning and strength to a higher purpose. In these functions music and society converge; but the forms and relationships of society in general may be very different and conform to different principles and purposes. This is still more the case, of course, with nonfunctional music and abstract instrumental music, especially in forms that have been preserved from older times or imported from other cultures. .

The complex interplay between the members of a string quartet group, for example—the controlled contrast, mutual support and enhancement, precisely timed coordination, and subordination of indivduality in favor of the group result—represent an island of the leisured and courteous cooperation of distinctive personalities which is set in a chaotic sea of a faceless commercial society that is frantically competitive and immoral. Some ethical benefits may accrue to the four performers, but even a kindergarten relying on the social values of music would be ineffectual in a society governed otherwise by the belief in material progress and the practice of unprincipled self-advancement. It is quite common, as a matter of fact, for quartet performers to confine their sensitivity and responsiveness to one another to recitals; conflict is frequent in extramusical matters and it also invades performances as well as rehearsals in the contest of interpretative opinions. It is a rare chamber music group that does not know dissension and the dominance of one of the members, not always because of his acknowledged superiority in artistic judgment. Yet members of performing groups seem to feel more of a kinship and community than those of most other cooperative undertakings; this is certainly true of small vocal groups such as madrigal singers, but even of orchestras and choruses and large community groups.

The chief distinction that can be made in the social constitution of music is that between performers and audience. In music that is exclusively or essentially for performers, when listeners are at most incidental, the social structure and meaning are defined solely by the cooperation and functional roles of the participants. The roles can be equivalent, as in an imitative motet of the 16th century, or they can be distinctively different, as in the instrumental performance of a slow-moving cantus in a tenor mass of the century before. They can be individual, or performed by a group rather than a soloist, a distinction which occurs not only in polyphony, but also in the contrast between monophonic and monodic music. At the other extreme there is the predominance of one or more soloists or of a leader, who may not himself perform or sing but have only a specialized conducting function. All of these relationships are

320

social ones peculiar to music, and they may duplicate, resemble, or contradict those of extramusical society, with the additional possibility of both a qualitative and a formal influence being exerted in the one direction or the other. An audience makes the social relationships more numerous and complex. It is connected also with soloists and conductors, who consequently take on a double relationship—to the performing group and to the audience. The solo singer or instrumentalist often seems to symbolize possession by a spirit, which enables him to exercise a kind of shamanistic spell over his audience; this is abetted by abstract gestural configurations related partly to the motions of performance, and partly—as in dance—to the visual and kinesthetic interpretation of musical form and significance. In the case of a singer, of course, gesture is often adapted largely to the histrionic demands of the role that is implied in a song or embodied in an opera. The other performers and even the conductor become helpers, disciples, fellow devotees, and the virtuoso seems to parallel the skillful orator or the demagogue in his effect on the listeners. The conductor is somewhat similar, except that his relationship to the chorus or orchestra resembles his relationship to the audience, for he controls and dominates both.

These various inherent social structures of musical performance and therefore of musical conception are certainly the primary basis of relationship between music and society in general. It is difficult to overlook the significance of the tradition of reflective solo performance of the Chinese scholar on his zither, which seems to find an echo in Schopenhauer's flute playing. Solitary people have always had an inclination to express themselves and their companionship with themselves in individual performance. Apart from the electronically reproduced music of the 20th century, this has obviously been literally solo music and usually monodic. Its forms extend from the piping of the shepherd and the singing of the American cowboy, through introspective performance on various individual instruments, to everyday whistling and humming and singing. And that such personal music-making is so conformable to aloneness can be seen at once by the effect of another person, who will generally feel that he is either intruding or being overlooked, with corresponding feelings on the part of the performer; there will be a mismatch between the form of the music and the social form with which it is connected. Similarly the small ensemble of Indian music, the orchestra of Indonesia, the madrigal group of the Renaissance, the operatic castrato of the Baroque, the instrumental virtuoso and conductor of the 19th and 20th centuries, especially in their changing significance: each tells us in terms of the internal social structure of music itself something about the structure and attitudes and classes in the society of its cultural context.

But there are factors more intrinsic to music, factors themselves not social in nature, that also seem analogous to the patterns and forces of the society in which they exist, and that again may influence or reflect society in some way. Thus the domination of a single formalized thematic subject in Baroque music, together with the comprehensive organization of a composition controlled by a single central tonality, seem to constitute a musical reflection of political absolutism and at the same time an artistic regime adapted to reinforce the regulation and ordered formality of society. In a similar way, the growth of melodic spontaneity and harmonic freedom during the 19th century seems to mirror the expansion and contradictions of bourgeois society and the destruction of the old aristocratic order. Lavish and virtuosic instrumentation provides a musical counterpart for the arrogance and ostentation of imperialism and for the triumph of technology and materialism, while the emotional turmoil and atonality of early 20th-century music seems to reflect a pervasive intellectual ferment and social disruption. Neoclassicism sought stability in the past and serialism in principles of form, but they were both manifestations of the estrangement of art from society. At the same time, commercialism manifested itself in all the areas of tonal music, which was done up in various kinds of packaging and which increasingly flooded the mass market. The introduction of factors of chance, improvisation, participation, and combined media represents a reaction against the formalism and social isolation of intellectual music. Apart from the impulse toward experimentation, play, and exploration, which was supported by electronic technology, there was a desire to extend the defined boundaries of the arts—to efface the divisions between them, however these might be grounded in tradition or nature, and to integrate them with life and the world at large. The very nature and existence of art was brought into question, as part of a generalized social and moral revolt, now added to the radicalism of science, engineering, and philosophic thought. The analogies of music to the social order are indeed as various and complex, but also as speculative and difficult of demonstration, as its analogies to the world order of science and philosophy; the one is a relationship to forms of human behavior and the other to forms of thought.

The relationship of music to the individual personality is equally complex, and because of the social constitution of personality and the dependence of society on the individual, it is of course bound up with the social import of music. Where individuality is not a prominent feature or value of society or a given class of society, general rather than personal styles will be a logical concomitant; examples can be found in the ritual music of primitive societies, the anonymity of Gregorian chant, the entertainment music of 18th-century courts, bourgeois piano pieces for home use in the 19th century, and 20th-century commercial genres of music. At the same time, however, songs in nonliterate societies can be the special property of individuals, and there is often remarkable personal variety in performances of traditional and folk music. The solo performer or conductor even of musical works of art has almost always infused properties into his performance which reflect his personality, whether in its emotional disposition, its historical objectivity, or the analytic cast of mind that seeks to clarify structural relationships. Similar connections seem to exist also between the personal traits of the composer and the characteristics of his music; we feel the kinship of the man and his music very strongly in the case of individual composers such as Beethoven, Chopin, or Wagner, not only in the choice of genre and subject matter, but in every detail of workmanship, style and expression. As in the case of society, however, the correspondences are extremely difficult to define closely. This is due in both cases to the complex constitution of musical form and meaning on the one hand and of personality and society on the other; and it is also due to the fact that music deploys particular modes of formativity and significance which are to some degree specific to the art and simply do not have counterparts in outside experience. As far as personality is concerned, we cannot without further evidence identify emotional disposition—and certainly not moods or individual events—with established ways of conceiving and working out music, for these are not automatically and often not at all influenced by external matters—even by matters of the greatest personal or social import. Naturally this is less true of musical improvisation and of occasional and autobiographical types of composition. The connection between personality and music depends upon the particular composer and in turn upon the kind of music fostered by a given culture; it is well to seek it and to take account of it in the case of 19th-century composers, but only a careful consideration of the specific circumstances and facts is a reliable guide; generalities are never dependable. This is more especially the case because subconscious factors are involved in artistic creation; what we can learn of a composer may often be insufficient to reveal any analogies with his music, since the relationships may rest on forces that have little or no discernible surface manifestation, particularly if we are restricted to what can be determined after his death. With these various factors in view, it is obviously naive to wonder how the characteristics and qualities of a musical work can ever be so completely removed from or even contradictory to what we may know of the composer's external circumstances, emotional state moral character, or intellectual pursuits. Yet relationships of music to society and personality can be assumed to exist; the intellectual and emotional and social nature of music is a guarantee of this, and its alternative would be for music to have no hold over us and no meaning.

The interaction and conflict between individual freedom and the social order is a relationship which has been reflected increasingly in music in the basic interrelationship of personal and public style. Is it also reflected by the very employment of a theme or subject, with its distinctive formal and expressive character and its characteristic musical treatment. The nature of the theme, its prominence and its degree of formulation and individuality from Josquin to the 20th century, would then represent a corresponding type of subjectivity, even as already shaped by social forces, while the integration of the theme into the work as a whole, its repetition, recurrence, variation, extension, dissection, development, and transmutation would represent its mode of accommodation to society, or in musical terms, to the established norms of harmonic and structural order. In this context of thought, each aspect of the theme and of its role in the musical complex, each variety of polyphonic texture, of athematism, or of formal incoherence would represent some attitude or position of either the individual or society or some ideal in this respect to which man might aspire. Although the development of this idea in detail, as we find it in the writings of Adorno, must proceed without any satisfactory kind of evidence and therefore belongs to the realm of imagination, there can be little doubt that we feel the presence or assertion of individual volition in many musical themes, particularly in Beethoven. In the elaboration of a given melody type, or indeed in improvisation and performance in general, the individuality of the music is obviously a reflection of the individuality of the performer and of his relation to social prescription, at least in a musical sense. And choral song is factually an expression of group feeling or intention, and therefore a natural medium of social expression for external as well as musical sentiments and ideas. The social subject matter of French grand opera, for example, led to a new importance of the chorus as a representative of group forces in the drama. But what is true either literally or by intuition of the fundamental connections of music to society and the individual is doubtless no longer true of the details of artistic feeling and form, where forces and concerns intrinsic to art will inevitably join with or cover over the underlying interrelationship of music and society.

The complex and varied relationships of music to society and culture represent one extreme of a range of possibilities open to art; the opposite extreme is suggested by the notion of "art for the sake of art." On the one hand music would present us with experience as it is generally known in life, changed at most in being shaped and intensified; it would exist in an inescapable context of cultural relationships and social function, in its composite forms, and with traces of the adjustive, orientational, and biological values of sound it has for the most part discarded. On the other hand music would represent an experience isolated from all other; it would contain peculiar values neither found elsewhere nor comparable to others, and take the form of a purely tonal and instrumental work of art, purely aesthetic in nature, removed from multisensory space, from religious, ethical, and social value, complete in itself, autonomous, and freed from history and even from time by preservation in notation and phonorecording. Here questions of the nature of this special experience, of its meaning and value, are obviously entailed, and they are solved in part—although only in part—by a modification of the original assumptions of isolation and idiosyncrasy, for these can only be approached rather than realized; they are impossible to fulfill even by the mere fact of the interrelation of the senses and of the unity of the human organism. Implications of biological and social function, of visual and tactual and kinesthetic experience, of composite types of art, will always remain in music; suggestions, grounded in resemblance, of other temporal experience, of other structures, can never be eliminated. But even beyond this, the specific core of musical experience activates vital forces and functions that are intrinsic to all experience. Thus music cannot escape its connection with other departments of life and thought. It is unique and distinct but also variously interrelated with other human activities. Its historical character will accordingly have two aspects: integration into culture, and social and personal specificity. Of the specificity of style there can be no doubt; but it then becomes extremely unlikely that music is unrelated to other contemporaneous fields of expression and to culture as a whole.

# CHAPTER 9

# Conception

In the comprehension and apprehension of music we are aware of tonal patterns and feelings, of dance motions or a dramatic action, or of a sung text with the conceptions it articulates. In the background of this awareness are adumbrations of biological significance and practical experience that underlie perceptual values in spite of their aesthetic detachment, giving music deeper and more comprehensive dimensions of meaning. But the nature of preception and perceptually directed formulation encompasses a higher ingredient as well as a lower one, an element of conceptual thought as well as one of everyday life. Both the lower and the higher constituents of meaning are double, for just as practical activity—or let us say, social and economic behavior—grows out of environmental adjustment, so conceptual thought would seem to evolve from imagery.

Thus human experience necessarily contains an order of images, recollections, concepts, or ideas bearing upon its primary materials, upon what they are or what they should be. Every human activity gives rise to and incorporates some aspect or superstructure of reflective thought by which in turn it is shaped and guided; its own inherent forces and tendencies are not blind determinants, but include abstractive features of form and meaning, and of the meaning that resides in form. Thus a factor of formulation, an element of mediacy and distance, enters experience and behavior. Memory and imagery are the prerequisites of the abstraction that is intrinsic to perception, but they rest on a synthetic action of consciousness that constitutes a perceptual object from a temporal succession of elements, from their relationship to the perceiver, and often from their simultaneity as well. We perceive sounds, melodic phrases, and melodies; we perceive them as objects that are auditory; and we perceive them in conjunction with an auditory background or with other similar objects—all by virtue of processes that are themselves automatic and not easily objectified. But we perceive them only because we have previously perceived them or other objects like them, and only because there have been intervening times when we have not perceived them. The apprehension is based on recollection, on the recognition of a perceptual object after it has been absent. But the ability to recognize a previously experienced object can further produce the ability to imagine it to be present, which brings the trace in memory under our control and makes it explicit. This new capacity in turn can lead to a synoptic, condensed, or summarized image which compresses the temporally extended one into a more simultaneous and instantaneous presence. If the image is now replaced by a conceptualization, perhaps by a visual image of the functional occasion in which the melody has its place, or in a final transformation, by a visual or auditory linguistic symbol that represents the musical object, or simply by the thought of such a symbol, we have arrived at a concept of the music that will be a normal constituent of the succeeding auditory experience of this object.

The process we are considering is one of the development of musical apprehension as founded in the synthetic operation of consciousness, its automatic projection of a sphere or type of objectivity, and its powers of retention and imagery and conceptualization. These factors do not act successively, but in constant conjunction and reciprocal effect, so that normal perceptual activity in a given style grows up over a certain period of time and with more or less explicit and specific cultivation and instruction. The resultant capability to project or perform or apprehend music will vary considerably, as we

328

know, in response to the conceptual education and resources of the individual; musical meaning is clearly bound up with concepts and conceptions, and does not reside in automatic intentional processes and reactions that occur on a supposedly pure sensory-emotional level. Even a single sound or tone or chord, or an elementary melodic pattern, takes on an astonishing variety of meanings in dependence on what is brought to it conceptually; each is different even by the fundamental fact that it has been heard before or that it resembles something heard before; but other equally important aspects of meaning accrue to it for those who know it as conforming to a systematic musical context of materials or scales, or as belonging to a familiar function and style; or for those who have seen it performed or performed it themselves; or for those who have seen it or visualize it in a written notation, or who know that it is a C-major triad or the subject of a fugue by Bach. Conceptual factors need not be objectivized as such or brought into conscious attention; they may be simply ingredient in the perceptual experience without becoming explicit or being singled out; but they must be present in some manner and in some form in every purposeful or perceptual activity, or we cannot with justification speak of meaning or of apprehended object or of conscious experience but only of animalistic reaction, uncomprehended stimuli, lack of awareness, or pure sensation.

The very existence of a public musical idiom is bound up with conceptual formulation. As soon as there are identifiable elements or units of structure in music, whether these are functionally specific or interchangeable, there will be meanings that involve at least an initial or implicit form of conceptualization. But units of some kind—chords, melodic turns of phrase, and so forth—are really a precondition of style; they become especially conspicuous when music is a centonization or a mosaic structure; and it is clear that in this respect music will possess a counterpart of the individual words and formulated phrases of language, with at least the incipient conceptualization that is entailed by the mere existence of structural units. Thought contains not only a hierarchy of concepts, then, but also gradations of abstraction.

We cannot in fact perceive anything, we may say rather para-doxically, unless we already know in some sense what we are perceiving. To be sure, there are elements of every experi-ence—from time to time and also throughout its duration—which are not fully conscious; these are indeed of vital import-ance in artistic creation and apprehension, and responsible for qualities and implications of significance which are a major factor in the value and nature of the resultant experience, but without a nucleus or core of sensitive and intelligent attention this experience will not fall within the domain of art or humanism.

Yet it is well to keep in mind the whole nature of experience—even perhaps of the experience of childhood, sleep, derange-ment, and states of crisis—if any part or aspect of it is to be fully appreciated and understood. Certainly we may focus our atten-tion upon various areas at will, but these will always be limited in extent both spatially and temporally; outside of the sharply defined immediate object of perception consciousness will fall off or fade out in characteristic gradations, and we will no longer be able to speak of object or perception, or finally even of consciousness. There are indeed also aspects of experience—generalized and indefinable dispositional states, for example—that by their very nature can never be brought into full consciousness and objectified or perceived or analyzed. Beyond this, the very act of directing attention upon any aspect of experience that would not ordinarily or at that time be posited as an object gives it a special character peculiar to the special circumstances of observation, and transforms the nature it possesses as an ingredient of normal experience. Thus the thoroughgoing rationalization of experience is impossible, but also undesirable, and we must describe it as it is, with both its clarity and its shadows, its precise figures and its ineffable vagueness, its conscious logic and its automatic machinery.

Musical perception is of a highly complex nature, bringing into focus different aspects of the music in turn, and producing the finished object of perception through an automatic fusion of sensational material and conceptual categories. Into the perceptual process enter concepts of tones, intervals, chords, and rhythms; of instruments and performers; of motif, theme, melody, and genre; even of music itself, and the nature of art. Visual imagery can obviously play an important role. Notation itself is an embodiment of a whole system of concepts and in turn a constantly active cause—even when it is not literally present—of the participation of conceptual thought in every type of musical activity. But in addition to the unconscious involvement of the intrinsic machinery of thought, we may also on occasion consciously entertain musical conceptions and bring them to bear on our primary activity. Thus we may make explicit what we feel to be a characteristic symphonic theme and consider how a specific instance conforms or fails to conform to this conception. In songs such an explicit comparison of auditory object and conception is much more the rule than the execption; setting a text rarely neglects the factor of appropriateness to words and rarely proceeds unconsciously. And in program music, conformity of music and conception is indeed inevitable, and again can hardly escape a degree of conscious comparison. The influence of conceptual elements will even make it possible for us to perceive random everyday sounds as music, if they are transferred to a phonorecord or brought into a concert hall. In their conscious application to music, however, concepts and conceptions can also become not an abetment of perception but an interference. Instead of joining, concept and percept may compete for attention, and conceptual thought and musical experience may produce mutual inhibition instead of reinforcement, for each is to a considerable extent the alternative and substitute of the other.

The conceptual activity bearing on the primary objects of aesthetic experience often succeeds also to an independent existence in its own right, so that it is elaborated apart from any involvement with actual musical experience. It will then have its own historical course, although one generally parallel to that of music itself. The relationships between the music and the ideas are nevertheless not constant, but comprise various and varying tendencies, particularly because different types of music as well as different types of musical thought may coexist. If there is a type of reflection that grows out of musical practice and that seeks to understand and analyze this practice decades or even centuries after its appearance, there is also a type of speculation that leads musical style, projecting technical structure, aesthetic properties, or ethical effect as new ideals to be realized in the immediate or distant future. We must really think of two related but independent activities, the reflective in general directed to the perceptual, but now following and explaining, now leading and envisaging; at one time the ideas of composers or critics or technical theorists in close contact with musical activity, at another the more general views of philosophers, aestheticians, or poets with a more distant view of the nature and goals of music, which are typically seen in some larger context—metaphysical, moral, or aesthetic. The conceptual thought connected with music ranges from technical to philosophical (which can include a concern with history, culture, and society), but whatever its kind, and whatever its degree of independence or ingredience may be, the nature of music will not be fully or correctly comprehended if concepts and conceptions are left out of account in the consideration of musical experience. Indeed it is theory in a general sense, or reflective thought, that is responsible for musical change and history, and in this way also for the additional manifestation of conceptual thought that exists in historiography. For tonal systems and scales, notation, and codified principles of musical construction represent a vantage point from which we can examine and consider musical experience instead of only being immersed in it; they foster rational properties in music, produce or at least make possible a demand for change or novelty, and provide means of preserving records of this change so that the change itself may be examined in the future.

The role of conceptual thought in music is obviously very varied; there are many types and degrees of conceptual formulation and these are connected with music in many different ways. In general, however, we will understand their function correctly only if we take into account a creative element in their production of meaning. For it is we who create the essence of music by what we bring to it, and this is true not only of our comprehension of its meaning in general, but also of our understanding of a single musical work or our experience of an individual musical performance. Even the composition of a work involves an infinitude of possibilities for the creation of meaning; in shaping his music, the composer also shapes the meaning of that music for himself. Thus the meaning that resides in the style of a work can arise not only from a simple familiarity with the constituent elements of the style and their interrelationships but also from more explicit awareness of the environment of other works surrounding the one in question, of the temporal and social location and range of its style and its relationships to those preceding and following it. But this is all phenomenally present both in our conceptual grasp of the work and in our aesthetic experience of a performance; it is not, or not only, an accompanying and extrinsic knowledge about our perception, but ingredient in it as part of the perceived properties. The meaning of the work is thus something that we constitute and formulate through the total resources of our previous knowledge and experience, and these include the personal and cultural and social contexts in which the work exists or originally existed. However extrinsic the functional relationships of a work may seem to its perception, however irrelevant to a performance its position among other contemporaneous manifestations of culture may appear, these contextual features may also be not only accompaniments of a primarily aesthetic experience but may become phenomenal ingredients of the experience itself. A musical performance is not only sounding sources, external sounds, and immanent patterns of sound with adumbrations of orientational and adjustive meaning; it is not only a web of familiar configurations belonging to some given style of personal and cultural origin; it is also a work of a certain kind, a certain genre, with a resemblance to rhetoric or a certain kinship with painting. Contexts become conceptions, and this is the route by which they enter aesthetic experience. Music as a liberal art is heard differently from music as a fine art, and the difference—which is arrived at imperceptibly through a gradual shift of the whole orientation of culture and is effective for the most part as a kind of presupposition and without explicit awareness of its presence—is a vital and even overriding determinant of musical meaning. It is important not only what a composition is—a Baroque oratorio, say, or a Classical piano sonata—but also what music is.

The same factors will equally be operative in our understanding of music as a whole; and this understanding, as will now be apparent, will in turn enter into the experience of an individual work. Our present inquiry, for example, undertakes to define the essence of music first as a specifically tonal and stylistic expression varying with time and place and often united to other temporal forms of expression, and then as a manifestation that stands in various contextual relationships within culture as a whole and that has various conceptual concomitants. This is not always what music has meant, or if it has, certainly not in the particular values and interrelationship of constituent factors that are part of our description now.

In the area of more technical conceptions, the notion of genre seems to be central and to govern a host of other ideas. We cannot intelligently conceive or respond to a musical work without thinking of it as a specimen or a variant of some established type. Indeed if we are unaware of any relevant or applicable genre we lack a fundamental standard for devising themes or form, or for comprehending or evaluating what we hear. Musical creation, performance, and listening will thus always take place within some framework, whether made explicit or not, that allows the work to assume a meaning and form by its relationship to established generic configurations. A theme obtains its distinctive properties only by reference to the expectation attached in a given genre to themes of that specific position and function; given the genre in question, the theme becomes unusual in various respects, or similar, for example, to certain traditions of thematic construction belonging to the genre, or perhaps merely a routine or trite formulation that correspondingly will be judged of little value. But no such judgments can be made except with some frame of reference, a frame which can extend as far as the very conception of music itself, but which will be defined internally by genre, for what is routine as the theme of a Classical symphony, for example, would be remarkable as the subject of a fugue.

The same considerations extend to all the formal features of a work, and to the feelingful aspects of structure as well. Around 1800, for example, trombones, which had been a traditional feature of the church music and opera seria of the preceding era, were of extraordinary effect in the symphony. Especially impressive instances of the relationship between musical meaning and the conception of genre can be found in Beethoven's Ninth Symphony, particularly in the introduction of the work and in the last movement, where the novelty is due less to stylistic transfer than to personal imagination which effects a transformation of traditional features as part of the achievement of the artistic individuality of the Symphony. In a similar way, every constituent of a musical work has a significance that is necessarily relative to some genre and its associated conceptions. Innovation can be appreciated in general only if it bears some relationship to familiar experience and a conceptual framework; for this reason innovations in the sonorous material of music, in its intervallic structure, in its scalar and chordal and systematic foundations, are particularly difficult to grasp experientially or to define conceptually; it was not so much the powerful expressive forces around 1600 or 1900 that provoked controversy, but the expansion and transmutation and disappearance of genre, and still more the advent of new tonal patterns and systems and to some extent of new types of rhythm.

Thus genre carries with it not only a group of subordinate conceptions—theme, medium, harmonic idiom, form, emotional character, and so on—but also a group of more general ones, which are essentially comprised by the notion of style. What is meant in this connection is not the idea of style as subordinate to the genre, as the style appropriate or peculiar to it, but rather those larger aspects of style that are common to all the works of a composer, to all the music of a given locality or of a historical era. Along with the adoption of the concept of a genre, as the genre of a particular time and place that is now to be exemplified, the composer also implicitly accepts the commitment to think and create within a style of the times, and often also within a local, national, and personal idiom; the genre becomes the focal point of these more general styles, the nucleus around which they crystallize, just as it is also the larger conception which subsumes numerous others. Alone, however, the more general styles remain abstractions; we cannot simply compose, nor can we listen to music, except in a way that lacks definition and reserves final judgment, without the concrete focus that genre provides.

The more philosophical rather than technical notions that surround and accompany musical activities are those concerning the nature of music, its effects on man and on the natural and supernatural world, its place in the realm of intellect, feeling, and history at large, its relation to other areas of expression and experience, and its role in human life and society. In this sphere of thought, there were two types of conception that were characteristic of ancient civilizations. The first of these was that music, or more specifically, tonal relationships, were found throughout nature, so that the constitution of society and of man mirrored that of the cosmos, and audible music was no more than the sensible counterpart or aspect of larger structures that eluded auditory perception. Secondly, and in part as a result of this cosmic connection, audible music was seen as possessing remarkable influence over the natural world, the stability of society, and the character and behavior of man; it was a ceremonial and educative force of the utmost potency. These ancient notions appear to be rationalizations of earlier ones; they seem to have descended from prehistoric beliefs that regarded music and tone first as the source and vital core of being, and then, partly as a corollary, as a magical and curative power, capable of bringing about desired results of the most various kind both in nature and in human affairs. The connections of music with the natural and supernatural and social orders, and with the constitution and behavior of man, were to some extent an outcome of intersensory relationships and at times even of synesthesia, but they were still more a manifestation of a scientific mode of thought grounded in correspondence and analogical order; the emotional force and expressive immediacy of music and its obvious involvement with bodily activity, natural materials, and society provide the remainder of the explanation. Prehistoric beliefs of these kinds are taken up into the literary works of the earliest high cultures where they furnish a background and basis for more specifically philosophic thought. They also have been found in nonliterate cultures of recent times, where they are directly bound up with ritual practices that are conceptualized in associated myths. Music in nonliterate societies seems to serve memorial and ethical purposes also, in the intoned recital of legends and lineages, and it is used for the secular ends of pleasure and entertainment; but practical and aesthetic values have little if any place in conceptual thought.

This is to a great extent true in ancient civilizations also, although treatises devoted specifically to art are concerned with aesthetic questions as well as technical ones. Aristotle's *Poetics* is the most famous example, and the musical treatises of Aristoxenus and Ptolemy, even though they are devoted to the elements of their subject rather than to composition, reveal what was evidently a characteristic concern with an aspect of our present problem: the relative roles and functions of sense and reason in musical perception, or more specifically, in the discrimination and judgment of intervals. Reason was understood in ancient philosophy to be somehow constitutive in sense perception, but it was also given its own role and regarded as cooperative. Aesthetic considerations are in general of fundamental importance in the writings of Aristotle's disciples Aristoxenus and Theophrastus, where music is not treated either as an ethical force or as a metaphysical and mathematical manifestation, but phenomenologically in terms of its own tendencies of form, which are constituted by an intrinsic capacity of perception. This shift from a mathematical to an aesthetic viewpoint obviously had a foundation in musical experience, and it is connected significantly with an appeal to the singing voice rather than to musical instruments. Yet extended considerations of the overall aesthetic properties of musical works have not come down to us; we have discussions of drama and poetry, but more specifically musical values are essentially confined to intervallic and smaller configurational structures. This seems to be in part an accident of preservation, but it undoubtedly also reflects the fact that tonal form was known largely as a component of composite art in which it often had an elementary and accessory character. The context of compound art is partly responsible in addition for an emphasis on the ethical influence of music, whether as a force for good or for ill. Musical ethos or character, grounded in the epistemological conception of art as imitation, was the property that gave it its potency in the cultivation of personality and the preservation of social order; and even when this power was seen to reside in specifically tonal formulations, it was still the ethical influence of music that remained paramount; the ethical aspect of aesthetic features was their most noteworthy one, not their independent value. In recent centuries, although the social influence and pedagogical use of music have remained in evidence, explicit attention has been given primarily to its aesthetic values.

Just as the fundamentally cosmic and ethical views of antiquity have predecessors in prehistory as well as counterparts in nonliterate cultures, so the later conceptions of music as a variety of mathematics and as a type of language of the emotions can similarly be regarded as descendants of ancient views. The mathematical conception of music in fact continued to treat it as one of the four sciences that dealt with the quantitative nature of being; while the view that music was expressive of feelings saw the art in terms of the persuasive techniques and capabilities of oratory, and by this means was able to preserve the moral effects of music in a changing society, although it necessarily transformed these more profound and lasting effects into transient emotional ones. At the same time, however, the ancient belief in the specifically ritual efficacy of music was continued in the Christian view that music was a divine gift intended as an instrument of praise and thanks to God and possessing the power to elevate the soul and turn it to piety.

In general, it can readily be seen that philosophic conceptions of music fall into two major classes that correspond to the two major external relationships of music: mathematics and language. These give us a basic typology for musical conceptions as well as for music. They have an equivalent expression in terms of art in the categories of architecture and literature (or poetry or oratory); in music itself they can appear

338

as instrumental and vocal; and in characteristic aesthetic concerns they are manifest as formalism and expressionism, or with historical implication, as classicism and romanticism. Just as it is obvious, however, that music unites structure and meaning, so it is apparent that these aesthetic conceptions have in various ways coexisted, interacted, and combined. One important reason for this can be found in the fact that duration is amenable to numerical measure, especially in the form of quantitative meter. Thus in the essentially Neoplatonic outlook of Augustine, language is a logical part of a basically cosmic and mathematical view of beauty, and the aesthetic values of poetry are transformed altogether into those of number; even the symbolic meaning of language is taken from the words as such and carried by number to its highest essential significance. Religious conceptions, like aesthetic ones, are able to absorb both formal and expressive philosophies, both those of mathematics and those of feeling, with equal facility. Formal properties are taken as evidence of metaphysical and divine order, while expressive ones are applied to human feeling, and thus serve to evoke piety and reverence. Language itself spans both fields; it is not only allied to feeling and expression, but is equally a manifestation of reason. This is true not only of its durational form, as we have mentioned, but also of its logical propensity. The structures of discourse are those of reason as well as those of expression, and language is viewed in myth and philosophy as the characteristic manifestation of human rationality and therefore of the divine in man; it is a gift of inspired invention or of a god. Thus as far as music is concerned, religious, aesthetic, and even linguistic conceptions encompass mathematics and reason as well as feeling and expression. At the same time, however, feeling and expression are not necessarily viewed as irrational. The formulated, analyzed, and classified feelings of Baroque intervals and themes turned the realm of emotions into conceptualized form under the banner of reason and built the melodic figures that codified these emotions into musical structures in the fashion of rhetoric.

During the 17th century, when music turned increasingly to feeling for its proper content and to language for its structural and expressive models, the conception of music similarly came to center less around mathematics and more around the affections and rhetorical figures. Yet religious conceptions as well as mathematical ones did not disappear, but were less prominent in thought, and remained subordinate from then on in spite of the Romantic belief in the cosmic connection of music. Leibniz's notion of music as an unconscious numerical activity of the soul seeks to fuse the mathematical and emotional properties of music, very much as did Plato's theories of the soul; and mathematical explanations of the emotive and sensational qualities of music were to remain an important feature of more technical writings from Rameau to 19th- and 20th-century theories of the perceptual nature of major and minor and of consonance. From the 17th century on, however, such theories had a physical and physiological foundation, not a strictly mathematical one, and this undoubtedly enhanced their relevance to feeling and facilitated the combination of the two types of musical concern.

The views of Schopenhauer, Hegel, Wagner, and Nietzsche remain in the predominant volitional-emotional orbit, but the tendency to connect music with language, especially from an evolutionary viewpoint, also persists strongly throughout the 19th century as a compatible parallel current of thought. Even the formalist aesthetics that has its foundation in Kant is less a mathematical outlook than one supporting a conception of a sui generis play of sensations and feelings. From the point of view of significance, music becomes a language of feelings; from the structural point of view, a language of tone, this formulation possessing the advantage, for a world impressed with the recent development of autonomous instrumental music, of avoiding the problematical inner aspect of meaning or content, and thus not permitting the confusion of musical experience with feelings and significance of other kinds. Both conceptions, however, do not necessarily deal with the relationship of music to linguistic structure, which remained central in fact although it had the ideological disadvantage of emphasizing clarity and reason, which were in disrepute. Almost inevitable in vocal music, the adoption of linguistic forms by instrumental music was assured simply because of the transfer of style and of actual compositions from one medium to the other. It was increasingly evident in instrumental music from 1600 to 1900, alongside of and then largely displacing the influence of the dance. Organization by phrases that have various types of interconnection and internal repetition will doubtless always be the most obvious basis for a musical logic, the most convincing way in which abstract music can "make sense."

The distinct but interpenetrating spheres of mathematics and language are connected with the textures of polyphony and homophony respectively. Homophonic and of course monophonic music, even if it is not vocal, is obviously able to adopt without difficulty linguistic structures and expressivity, while melodic simultaneity and continuous and complex styles cannot easily employ language as a model. Thus contrapuntal works such as Renaissance mensuration canons or Baroque fugues, where there is melodic overlap and a lack of structural articulation into phrases, have a greater kinship with mathematics than with rhetoric or poetry or narrative. The two tendencies are often active at the same time, however, sometimes with a certain amount of evident conflict, as in the isorhythmic motet. Bach achieves the highest imaginable realization of both, whether in alternation or in combination.

From the time of the late Renaissance, feeling gradually becomes the dominant theme of musical aesthetics, appearing in the most various guises and conceptions. Music was thought of first as a heightening of speech and as a formulation of expressive patterns derived from and coordinated with language. The new importance of the audience had a great deal to do with the emphatic musical realization of these ideas. The expressive figures were formalized but also direct in emotional impact, although by the 18th century the formalization had become their most conspicuous aspect. In this linguistic conception of feeling, which was derived from the ideas of Greek antiquity, imitation logically provided the underlying philosophic principle, and the imitation of speech and thus of the feelings that were expressed in language remained a standard for music, both instrumental and vocal, for most of the 18th century. During the latter part of that century, however, the feelings connected with music began to be regarded differently: as peculiar to music, as virtual or fictional rather than realistic copies, and as dynamic and changing in their temporal course. Music itself reflected these conceptual tendencies in its own way: by its melodic inventiveness, its interest in sonority, its graduated dynamics, and its variety of expression. At the end of the century the separate and special status of musical feelings was seen in their indefinable character, in their supernatural existence, and in their metaphysical significance; they were removed almost altogether from the realm of human feeling, or at least extended far beyond it, and escaped identification with feelings as otherwise known. The possibility of excluding feeling from the essential nature of music completely was a corollary that was worked out by Hanslick. What remained to instrumental music was thus a special kind of significance that called for closer definition; physiological impact was only part of the answer, no more satisfactory than the play of sensational feeling described by formalism; these were both deficient in meaning in respect of their relationship to the nature of consciousness and to history and personality. Eighteenth-century notions of taste and judgment had at best conceived a conformity of perceived qualities with cultivated discrimination and with the intrinsic properties of understanding.

In the 20th century, feeling was brought into the orbit of the symbolic nature of art; Langer views music as a formulation of vital experience, symbolic in the presentation of this experience but not in any further referential meaning, and distinct from the reality of nonartistic experience in having an existence in its sensuous appearance only. A fundamental confusion remains, however, between the work of art and the aesthetic object, and between the significance of the musical object as a whole, and the significance of any part of it or of its temporal course, while style and history are left unaccounted for. The revision necessary in the musical conception of feeling involves a change from feeling to a way of feeling, which is a matter of history and culture and personality, and from an identification with extra-artistic feelings to a definition of the distinction from and the relationship to other experience, which depends on the specificity of musical feeling to sonorous form and on the instruction to be gained from the place of music in compound arts and in its larger functional and cultural contexts. In spite of its presentation of a particular historical, cultural, and personal way of feeling, and of its specificity to sound and tone, music remains universal, for man cannot be freed from culture, and must necessarily exist in a particular form, which is therefore not justly termed "accidental." It is important in addition that music possesses, to a degree greater than any other manifestation of culture, a direct relationship to the universal features of experience and consciousness; it is especially adapted to reveal the universality in human particularity.

It is only with the serialism of the 20th century that musical conceptions, in step with music itself, abandon language for mathematics, and while musical thought looks to numerical structural principles, music produces impressions and emotional effects reminiscent at times of those aroused by nocturnal patterns of stars and planets. The serial music evolved during the first half of the century has no longer any connection with the discursiveness and persuasive structures of oratory, but only with the inherent mathematical properties of the system of tones that is employed and with the perceptual properties of their interrelationship. It is true, of course, that the mathematical properties have the phenomenal clothing of sounds distributed in space and time, but time is now essentially an equivalent of space rather than the vital shaped substance of discourse, a change that appears at once in the suppression of traditional melodic forms and in the striking use of silence and of tones of short duration. A reaction against this mathematical conception appeared with the reassertion of spontaneity and expressivity; ideas of chance and improvisation comprised the inevitable antithesis to serial constructivism. But there were established and more impressive alternatives to mathematics in the humanism of history, which uncovered a storehouse of past musical styles as a foundation for new creation, and in the humanism of ethnology, which furnished a wealth of traditional rhythms and melodies. The art of music could turn to nature in vital forms as well as to nature as reason.

And the philosophy of music can similarly turn to history and

ethnology—fields of thought that become increasingly prominent in the 20th century— where the humanistic conception of
music preserves its importance alongside mathematical tendencies. Historical conceptions expand the modern symbolic
theory of art, established by Ernst Cassirer, which in a very
broad sense is a type of linguistic theory, and make it possible
for a humanistic outlook to subsume and absorb a mathematical
one. Here the central notion of style reveals the perennial kinship of music with language, and in spite of the mathematical
nature of much of the analytical theory that is applied to older
music, the historical view regards music as a cultural variable
rather than a fixed numerical structure, for it is connected with
man rather than with nature. This historical interest has for the
first time made all the music of the world copresent today, a
situation that permits an unprecedented historical sensitivity,
eclecticism, and diversity to the composer, performer, and
listener, while at the same time, in the field of musical theory,
philosophy, and aesthetics, making possible the utmost generality and breadth of view in the formulation of new conceptions.

Changing conceptions of the nature of music necessarily
produced corresponding differences in the position assigned to
music within the whole spectrum of culture and human concerns, and this relative location—apart from the interest it
arouses in its own right—created a type of context that had a
powerful influence on the way music was created and performed and perceived. Thus in antiquity musical practice was
conceived as a basic force in education and in sustaining civic
pride; it was a member of the circle of the preparatory liberal arts
of the aristocracy, a partner and counterpart of gymnastics that
was devoted to the cultivation of the mind. But this use laid the
groundwork for a subsequent theoretical study of music, which
had a higher philosophical position as a division of the
mathematical sciences that led directly to philosophy. In expert
instrumental performance alone, since this was a manual
activity, did music descend to the lower status of visual art. But
the two realms of art were connected only by the notion of
imitation, which may have been attached originally to dance
rather than painting, and their separation has persisted through

344

numerous ideological changes. Visual art became liberalized when it was connected with mathematics, with geometry and music, in the Renaissance, while musical practice was similarly dignified at the same time with the permanence of musical works in which tone was no longer merely an adjunct of language. The equivalence of the two fields was additionally grounded by the sciences of anatomy and counterpoint respectively.

But even with the explicit recognition of a kinship of the arts a considerable amount of attention was given to their differences as well, and music in particular has resisted full membership in the newly conceived group of fine arts from the 18th century to the present. Yet its prominence as an art rather than a liberal art has profoundly affected our attitude toward it. More for this reason than because of its mathematical and cosmological heritage, it took on extraordinary importance in the 19th and 20th centuries; our expectations of it were altered and it was often consciously assimilated to the other arts; stylistic influences were exerted in both directions. This situation, too, is a particular historical manifestation, valid more, perhaps, for a middle class or mass audience than for connoisseurs or composers. Yet it has durable conceptual concomitants that bear on the general understanding of art, which has turned successively, motivated in part by the influence of instrumental music, to imitation, beauty and the aesthetic categories, expression, play, symbolism, and communication in search of a central criterion. There is some validity in all of these, but art now appears to be characterized best as intrinsically meaningful form, where the meaning is a product of the creator and his culture rather than a manifestation of changeless principles. The designation of an artistic achievement as a "work" conveys the predominating importance of the activity of formulation.

The emotional aspect of music is an excellent illustration of how endlessly varied the experience of music is as a manifestation of the creativity of culture, particularly as this is revealed in its network of fundamental concepts. For musical expression has been variously identified with the feelings of the composer, the performer, or the listener. It has also been regarded as a property or quality of music itself. And it has been conceived as literally the same as extramusical feeling, but also as peculiar to music. But then what is "feeling" thought to be? Is it a consequence of the physical motion of bodily fluids or the violent mechanical agitation of the nerves? Is it sustained in its temporal course or susceptible of variation or of rapid change in character? Does it have an existence independent of attendant circumstances or can it be defined only by concrete events that precipitate it, follow from it, or accompany it? Is it in fact clearly definable at all? And are we to regard musical feeling as actual or as virtual? If we are dealing with actual feeling, how can we account for our ability to experience such rapid changes and diverse juxtapositions as we find in music? Or for our enjoyment of sadness and tragedy? Or for our ability to experience time and again, in compositions with which we are thoroughly familiar, the same impact of surprise and suspense? Certainly repeated reading of literary works soon becomes uninteresting, although where actual sensory values are the artistic material and sometimes even actual performance comes into question, as in poetry or drama particularly, our tolerance and enjoyment of repetitions of the same work are not too different from our experiences with music. But perhaps the alternative of actual or virtual is not applicable to musical feeling. If it is some third kind of feeling, can we maintain that it has a wholly secular nature? Or does it rather reveal man's participation in universal or spiritual forces that are beyond his power to specify? Is it homogeneous in each of its instances, or can we not really separate feeling from auditory sensational quality, and one or both of these from a generalized aesthetic pleasure or an aesthetic attitude and from the moral or ethical force of music? If instrumental music is taken as a guide and standard for musical significance, then music will seem either to be a meaningless play of sensations (or a dazzling—but otherwise again meaningless—display of muscular dexterity) or to possess a peculiar significance of its own. The question then arises of the relationship of this special significance to feelings known outside of music and to moral and social behavior, a matter which can be relegated to an examination of the composite arts. In a world of vocal

346

music, on the other hand, meaning will seem to derive from the text, from its concepts and feelings. But then the specifically musical constituents—or instrumental music itself—will appear to derive their meaning from a vocabulary of tonal patterns borrowed from vocal expression, or to be relatively inarticulate or undefined, or to be an inconsequential matter of auditory pleasure or kinesthetic suggestiveness rather than of feeling and morality, or else to be altogether without significance of any kind. But even style, of course, could not come into existence if it could not build on some meaningful basis in auditory perception.

Now the solutions to problems of this kind are obviously a matter of considerable importance in musical experience. The conceptual apparatus with which we approach music, even if it is not made explicit but remains in the form of unrecognized presupposition, will clearly determine the fundamental features of our experience—how in fact we hear or perform or compose and what it is we come to know or create.

But a further consideration will reveal the creative nature of personal experience, which is added to the creativity of culture. For in what we bring to bear in confronting a musical work of the past or of another culture, in our resources of knowledge concerning the theory and meaning of music, the function and significance of the work, its genre and history and its entire social and cultural setting, will be contained numberless possibilities of experience and understanding. Our varying selection of contextual features, whether unattended to or carefully considered, can ensure the endless novelty of each occasion of listening or performance, just as a lack of knowledge—especially in the case of an unfamiliar style—can reduce musical experience to a condition of inauthenticity and falsification. We can find a simple demonstration of this point if we listen to a narrative symphonic poem without any knowledge of its program and then subsequently make ourselves familiar with the narrative and connect it in detail, during a second performance, with the course of the music. The remarkable transformation of the composition will be as astonishing as is the now evident inadequacy of our earlier uninformed experience. The same effect will occur if we have heard dance music without ever having seen the dance that belongs to it and then have the opportunity of experiencing the composite as a whole. The music will again be remarkably transformed and its true meaning will seem suddenly revealed to us.

In all its forms, then, conceptual thought is intimately bound up with the nature of music. Musical perception is formed in part by conceptual ingredients, which act together with the innate formative tendencies of sensory activity. Ideas of the function and effect and nature of music accompany musical experience and determine its quality. Speculation about technical and aesthetic innovation provokes actual change and novelty; indeed even an analysis of the technical and aesthetic features of older music or contemporary music acts as a force for an extension or change of present musical forms and significance. Historical and ethnological knowledge is no exception, for it is endlessly suggestive of possible modes of musical organization and expression. Our familiarity with a wide range of music and conceptions of music has a significant influence on contemporary musical experience by way of conceptual thought as well as directly through new perceptual capacities; but it is equally true that this broad historical and cultural knowledge affects the course of musical history itself. Like all conceptual thought in music, historical ideas sustain notions of stability and change, and provoke and guide experimentation and novelty. Thus humanistic thought is closely connected with the phenomenon of artistic progress and advancement and with the value of individuality. At the same time, of course, the sheer mass of preserved music, especially since auditory and visual recording have been added to graphic notation, constitutes a continuously increasing challenge to human assimilative powers, and equally importantly, a competitive body of music that obstructs the acceptance of new compositional efforts by leaving less and less place and time for them in the whole spectrum of available musical experience. Musical history and ethnology are thus both positive and negative in their effects; along with other varieties of experience and conceptual thought, they expand our horizons and stimulate artistic exploration, but they can also paralyze and obstruct creativity.

Art remains, however, the freest and most typical aspect of humanity. As a manifestation of sensitivity and imagination for their own sake, less subject to considerations of utility than other areas of culture, it is most readily able to exemplify and suggest new types of organization and order, and new significance based on varied relationships with tradition. It provides a model for social and cultural change, or also a celebration of it and a distillation of its essence; for society as well as music faces the alternative forces of the weight of history and the demand of self-realization which is inescapably related to the past in some way. In the interaction of music and culture—their mutual support, nourishment, stimulation, or antagonism—conceptual thought plays a dominant role. It may envisage music as an instrument of stability and the preservation of tradition, of the enforcement and maintenance of power, of revolutionary change, or of the flexible expression of individuality based on sensitivity to the heritage of culture. Yet the enlightened use of music, and the values of human freedom it is best able to realize, are not indestructible, but themselves subject to larger historical trends. Among the possible products of historical change is a lack of interest in the past, which in turn reacts upon the nature of change in the future, making it less considered and controlled, and deficient in meaning. Today in the civilization brought about largely by the Western world, musical values are being destroyed by a number of powerful forces. One of these is electronic reproduction, which makes music too readily and widely available in total disregard of its context and treats the products of the avant-garde and of specially cultivated social circles of the past as though they were fit consumables for a mass society. Here music is involved in the problem of large integrative social organization, of the intrinsic conflict between the individual and the tendencies of technological progress.

Another destructive force is musical commercialism, which, in alliance with electronic technology, manipulates the musical consumer and subjects the marketing of popular varieties of music solely to business interests. This promulgates ways of listening which are inimical to the aesthetic possibilities of music, and it does not leave music as an art unaffected, since it draws all types of music into its machinery and sharply limits the audience available for artistically directed musical activity. It is obvious that conceptual thought plays a role of decisive importance in this area, for it is the publicity and propaganda about particular singers and pieces which are the major determinant of the qualities of the musical experience. Articles and advertisements and broadcast comments create public opinion even before the music in question is introduced. What is then heard is what the mass audience is told it will hear; it has no means of combating the implanted conceptions. Thus the alliance of commercialism and electronics has produced startling changes in the character and significance of music and in the nature of listening, which has now been divorced entirely for the average consumer from performance as well as composition. All of the individual features of music are erased along with any trace of artistic apprehension. Music is simply identified as such; it becomes an external fact, part of the accepted social order, and stripped of any humanistic meaning. This is the condition that presents itself as the antithesis to the isolation of art, overwhelming the music which was once a last haven of individuality, but which increasingly lost its vital connection to society and its public intelligibility.

A third force destructive of musical values, which is again connected with electronic technology, is the multiplication of aesthetic materials and means: of artistic composites, of scales of pitch, and of types of sound in which pitch is unimportant or absent, such as bands of frequency and nontonal sound. Here two conditions of artistic value are being set aside; one is the essential restriction that turns matter into material and provides a framework of limitation; the other—which is connected with the relative artificiality of the new material—is the essential relation to the past that gives significance to the present and the future. If these two conditions are not met we will seek in vain to constitute meaningful configurations in what we hear; we may bring artistic contexts and concepts to bear on what is presented, but the other side of what is called for

350

to produce a musical experience will simply not exist, and successive hearings will furnish only the apparent substitute of a synthetic "history" based on the personal recollection of previous occasions of hearing the same assemblage of sounds.

Part of the artistic failing of the multiplication of materials will obviously consist in the nature of the conceptions brought to bear on musical experience, for these will be essentially restricted to doctrinal and programmatic statements about the composer's intentions and beliefs; the rich and varied hierarchy of technical, aesthetic, and cultural conceptions that enter into properly artistic experience will necessarily be absent.

Thus scientific and technological progress, together with industrial methods of production and distribution, give rise to an eclectic and comprehensive world of music in which historical and cultural values tend to merge and disappear. Historical and ethnological research paradoxically serves the same end. Within music itself, the ideal of progress is coupled with mathmatical, speculative, and mechanical methods of composition. The composer begins to lose his dominant position. We are reminded of the Middle Ages, as individuality and historical perspective become less and less evident.

In a number of ways, then, the humanistic values of music are being destroyed or submerged by pervasive and deep-seated changes in society and culture that appear to be extremely difficult and perhaps impossible to control or stop or reverse. But it is only when humanism has begun to disappear that it can be seen and described as a whole. And just as initially our recognition of the historical character of aesthetics was tied to the envisagement of a broader philosophical study of music, so finally we must acknowledge the historical character of humanism also, with implications for the nature and knowledge of music in the future that extend beyond the field of our inquiry.

# Index

Rameau, 297, 309, 340
Relationship: of aesthetics and philosophy, 30, 38–41; of aesthetic experience and philosophy, 15; of history and aesthetics, 24–30; of sciences ad humanities, 12–14; of voice and instrument, 109–110, 114–115; of music and architecture, music and culture, music and personality, music and philosophy, music and science, music and society, music and the other arts: *see* Music. *See also* Duality of musical form
Relevant disciplines, 7–12
*Ring of the Nibelungen, The,* 134, 219, 221
Ritual, 261–263, 318
Rousseau, 315

*Schein,* 35
Schiller, 35
Schönberg, 96, 171, 190, 270, 311; *Moses and Aron,* 279–280; String Quartet opus 10, 190
Schopenhauer, 18, 316, 321, 340; the Will, 18
Schubert, 179; *Erlkönig,* 275
Schumann, 123, 170, 180, 190, 207, 315; *Humoreske,* 158
Scriabin, 280
Serialism, 53, 77, 92, 105, 166, 193, 194, 299, 343
Song, 249–253
Sonority: conceptions of, 75–78; ideal of, 74–75; overall, 73–74
Sound, nontonal, 136–137
Sound sources: types and meanings of, 137–147

Spatiality, 56–57. 86–87, 91. *See also* Pitch; Volume
Spencer, 315
Spengler, 314
Stradivarius, 45
Strauss, Richard, 190; *Rosenkavalier,* 279
*Stravinsky, 7, 36, 61, 168, 171, 190;* L'histoire du soldat, 280; Renard, 280; Symphony of Psalms, 190
Stylistic change; *see* Types
Stylistic coherence, 194–195
Stylistic interplay in representational art, 279
Stylistic mixture, 180–182, 189–191
Stylistic novelty, 193–194
Symbolism, 26, 271–271

Television ballet, 280
Temporal patterns, 84–86, 90–92
Temporality, 55, 88–91; circular factor in, 278; dual nature of, 239–241; in composite musical arts, 272–277
Theophrastus, 76, 337
Tonal attributes, 94–101; meanings of, 136. *See also* Duration; Heterosensory and intersensory qualities; Loudness; Pitch; Quality; Volume
Tone, 127–132
Tone color; *see* Quality
*Tonio Kröger* (Thomas Mann), 294
Types: of humanistic study. 31; of musical philosophy, 40; of stylistic change, 172–175: *See also* Language; Objectivity; Sound sources